RECASTING EAST GERMANY

Recasting East Germany: Social Transformation after the GDR

Edited by

CHRIS FLOCKTON

and

EVA KOLINSKY

FRANK CASS
LONDON • PORTLAND, OR

First published in 1999 in Great Britain by
FRANK CASS AND COMPANY LIMITED
Newbury House, 900 Eastern Avenue, London IG2 7HH, England

and in the United States of America by
FRANK CASS
c/o ISBS
5804 N.E. Hassalo Street, Portland, Oregon 97213-3644

Website: http://www.frankcass.com

British Library Cataloguing in Publication Data

Recasting East Germany: social transformation after the GDR
  1. Post-communism – Germany (East) 2. Germany (East) –
  Economic conditions. 3. Germany (East) – Social conditions
  I. Flockton, Christopher   II. Kolinsky, Eva
  330.9'431'0879

ISBN 0 7146 4936 8 (hbk)
ISBN 0 7146 4496 X (pbk)

Library of Congress Cataloging-in-Publication Data

Recasting East Germany: social transformation after the GDR /
edited by Chris Flockton and Eva Kolinsky.
    p.   cm.
'First appeared in a special issue of German Politics, Vol.7, No.3,
December 1998' – T.p. verso.
    Includes index.
    ISBN 0-7146-4936-8 (h/back). – ISBN 0-7146-4496-X (p/back).
    I. Germany (East) – Social conditions. 2. Germany (East) –
Economic conditions. I. Flockton, Christopher. II. Kolinsky, Eva.
HN460.5.A8R43   1999
306'.0943–dc21   98-44192
                                                            CIP

This group of studies first appeared in a Special Issue of *Germany Politics*,
Vol.7, No.3 (December 1998), ISSN 0964-4008
[Recasting East Germany: Social Transformation after the GDR].

Printed in the UK by
Antony Rowe Ltd., Chippenham, Wilts.

Contents

Acknowledgements

The contributions assembled in this volume arose from an ESRC-funded seminar on Social Transformation and the Family at the University of Potsdam, and from meetings of the Social Transformation Study Group of the Association for the Study of German Politics (ASGP). Special thanks for helpful comments on draft papers and in discussion are due to Rainer Dobbelstein, Charley Jeffery, Hildegard Maria Nickel, Ilona Ostner and Willie Paterson.

Recasting East Germany: An Introduction

CHRIS FLOCKTON and EVA KOLINSKY

When the eastern German Länder opted to join the Bundesrepublik on 3 October 1990, they entered the uncharted waters of recasting a political system, an economic order and a society that had been shaped by 40 years of socialist control. The brief interlude of parliamentary government in the closing months of the GDR had already ended one-party dominance but did not set an agenda for the future. Prior to the elections on 18 March 1990, the last unelected Minister President of the GDR, Hans Modrow, tried to shield existing structures, elites and institutions from change, although the Round Table, the main innovative force at the time, prepared a constitution to replace the discredited socialist model with a better one. Since its authors shared the basic political assumptions of the regime they purported to recast, their efforts had no lasting impact.[1] Following the March elections, the CDU-led government of Lothar de Maizière did what it had been mandated to do: passing the legislation and authorising the procedures required to facilitate unification. A first benchmark, the Treaty on Economic, Monetary and Social Union, was reached in 1 July 1990. It unified currencies by introducing the Deutschmark in the GDR and directing its economy and financial institutions to reorganise along market principles. Ratified by the parliaments of the two German states, the Treaty of German Unity finally detailed the system transfer from west to east and turned the Basic Law into the constitution for the whole of Germany.

Compared with the processes of post-communist transformation elsewhere in eastern Europe, east Germany occupied a special and privileged position.[2] The Basic Law had provided an effective framework for parliamentary democracy and stable government and gained popular recognition among west Germans as a guardian of civic and individual liberties. While other post-communist polities had to start from scratch and draft new, untested constitutions, east Germany adopted a ready-made, reliable product. Moreover, the unification treaty held out a promise of constitutional reform to accommodate new and possibly east German ideas on democratic governance. The constitutional debate, however, ended without agreeing substantial change.[3] For east Germany, therefore, the constitutional order was little more than a cast provided by its senior partner

Chris Flockton, University of Surrey; Eva Kolinsky, Keele University.

in unification, an outer shell that needed to be filled. The same applied to the social market economy, the administrative structures and organisational processes that were transferred from west to east: each of them challenged east Germany into closing gaps, meeting expectations, learning established rules. The region and its people encountered and ventured changes in their way of life that amounted to a transformation.[4] Recasting east Germany has unleashed a social transformation that bears hallmarks from both German cultures. Reinvented after unification,[5] this east Germany is neither a replica of the FRG nor a continuation of the former GDR, but has an emerging, albeit problem-laden and unsettled, identity of its own.

In exploring this fractured identity, *Recasting East Germany* presents detailed case studies of key areas of economic and social organisation and explores how they have been transformed since unification. On the one hand, the volume takes stock of structural transformation and shows what has happened in east Germany during the last decade. On the other hand, *Recasting East Germany* considers the complex issue of whether social transformation was inevitable in the direction it has taken and whether it has been successful. Measuring success is, of course, as varied as transformation itself and will not render one answer that could apply to all areas. While focusing on specific aspects of economic and social development since unification, the chapters in this volume will ask common questions with regard to the transformation process and its impact: Has it achieved what it set out do? Were aims defined at the outset and backed by the individuals who would be involved and affected by it? Has the actual transformation that followed the system transfer from the west built confidence in post-unification developments and created opportunities of social participation or has it generated new mechanisms of exclusion and new patterns of inequality?

PHASES OF TRANSFORMATION

During the first years after unification, recasting the system dominated the agenda of transformation. This first phase lasted until 1994 when the Treuhand, the agency designed to administer the privatisation of state-owned enterprises in the former GDR, declared its task accomplished, when interim financial support that had been provided by the German government to cushion the negative effects of transformation on the labour market, on incomes and on the cost of living generally came to an end. This first phase of transformation also included the 1994 elections in the new Länder and at federal level, which broadly confirmed the two main parties, CDU and SPD, as the preferred parties of government in east Germany, albeit with reduced margins and amidst reduced electoral participation, in particular among young east Germans.[6]

The first phase of transformation defined its parameters. In the second phase, the recast system consolidated its impact on all aspects of economic and social life. If unification had gone to plan, this phase would have replicated the economic miracle of the early 1950s and marked the onset of a *Wohlstandsgesellschaft Ost*, an affluent society in east Germany with no less bright a future than its western counterpart. Unification did not go to plan. As will be shown in this volume, east Germany remains dogged by an under-performing economy and ravaged by unemployment. The second phase of transformation constitutes a 'problematic normalisation'.[7] 'Normalisation' indicates that the political and social order and its institutions are in place and are unlikely to change drastically in the near future. People can get used to their recast system, function effectively in it and draw on it for support. This is only half the story. The system transformation shattered GDR immobilism and recast the fault-lines of east German society. Geissler has shown how ideological precepts had obstructed social mobility and differentiation, income development and even administered access to higher education and elite positions.[8] Despite its ossified character, however, it created an essentially predictable social environment for east Germans, allocating them to education, training, employment, housing with little scope for choice and equally little exposure to uncertainties. In the recast east Germany, uncertainties and the dismemberment of state-administered life-courses go hand in hand. Had unification gone to plan, the 'elevator effect' (Ulrich Beck) might have replicated conditions during the economic miracle when living standards rose across the board and (west) Germans developed a sense that their socio-economic future was secure.

Given that east Germany was recast 40 years after the post-war boom transformed and stabilised west Germany, could the 'problematic normalisation', with its fickle economic performance, its persistent labour market insecurities and its mood of uncertainty and disorientation, have been avoided? The system moulds, of course, had hardly changed between the foundation of the West German state and German unification: the Basic Law and the social market economy had been amended, adapted, modified but had not been recast. This continuity did not pertain at the more complex level of society, its fabric and its processes. On the eve of unification, the landmarks of social stratification in west German society had become more individual and more volatile. Stefan Hradil documented that social status no longer matched background or occupation but increasingly reflected personal attributes such as education, income, life-style choices or beliefs.[9] Increasingly based on individual attainment and circumstances, social positions themselves have become less permanent and less predictable. The individualisation of life chances boosted opportunities of advancement and participation but also intensified risks of social demotion and exclusion. By 1990, west German society had become a 'risk society'.[10] Employment biographies had become *Bastelbiographien*, many interspersed with periods of unemployment and most incorporating retraining, upgrading and a high degree of flexibility and adaptability. Beck estimated that one in three west Germans were 'losers of modernisation', unable to benefit from the affluence and favourable living standards attainable for those who succeeded in the new risk environment. Studies of poverty in west Germany have argued that one in ten suffer social exclusion through income poverty – often caused by unemployment – while one in five west Germans were affected by unemployment and income poverty within the last five years.[11]

This Germany bore little resemblance to the consumers' paradise east Germans had constructed in their imaginations from occasional visits to the west, their resentment of the persistent shortages in their everyday lives and, above all, the images of western lifestyles beamed into their living rooms by west German television advertising. The west German risk society also bore no resemblance to the 'employment society' that prevailed in the east: average incomes were low (one-third of west German levels), social stratification was frozen with over 80 per cent of society 'working class', and employment was virtually compulsory for women and men above the age of 16.[12] Overmanning, erratic supply of raw materials and other inefficiencies of the planned economy meant that many working hours were not actually spent working, a daily experience which filled east German blue-collar workers in particular with scepticism about the viability of the system and their personal prospects in it. As a system, however, the GDR *Arbeitsgesellschaft* knew none of the uncertainties of a risk society and had no need for the personal strategies of risk management that had become commonplace in west Germany.

With the two societies so different when unification brought them together and the system transfer purported to set a common direction of development, transformation developed no workable formula of economic or social 'normalisation' other than the hidden assumption that system change would suffice to have all else fall into place. In east Germany, a transformation of economic structure and social order which would normally take decades to emerge was compressed into a few years; structure change became structure break. The hiatus between 'employment society' and 'risk society' exacerbated the dislocating impact of restructuring and system transfer, forcing east Germans to find their own strategies of adaptation and post-unification survival. This individualisation is essentially crisis management. As such it lacks the liberating effect of enhanced opportunities and scope for personal development but betrays its defensive purposes: much of it harks back to the former GDR and its presumably superior ways; much of it conjures up a new collectivity of east Germans as second-class, disadvantaged citizens. Not unimportantly, the 'problematic normalisation' during the second phase of transformation clouded the agenda for democracy that had contributed to the collapse of the GDR and inspired the unification process. The two historical precedents in German history of recasting a polity on the basis of a democratic constitution, the Weimar Republic and the Federal Republic, suggest that economic stabilisation and perceptions of socio-economic security are paramount in generating acceptance for democratic governance and a democratic civic culture.[13] In the recast east Germany, social transformation remains too turbulent and too fraught with uncertainties to generate the working relation of security, confidence and representation between citizenry and state on which democracies are built.[14] This third phase of transformation has yet to commence in east Germany.

THE SCALE OF ECONOMIC AND SOCIAL TRANSFORMATION

It is instructive to recall the very depth and scale of the upheavals which have taken place in the east since economic and monetary union, and since unification itself (although the decay of the eastern economy and its demography commenced significantly earlier than July 1990). Partly through emigration from late 1989, and partly as a result of the collapse in activity, the population in east Germany fell from 16.666 million in 1988 to 15.54 million in 1996.[15] The birth rate itself fell sharply, with the number of live births in 1993 reaching only 40 per cent of the 1989 level. The numbers of marriages likewise plummeted to 38 per cent of their pre-unification level.[16] Divorce also became a very minority pursuit in the early 1990s, before climbing towards its pre-unification level once more. This 'birth shock' and collapse in marriage rates was clearly a direct response to the depth of the economic slump, the ensuing personal insecurity and loss of familiar organisational support. By the end of 1991, output in the manufacturing and energy sectors stood at only 60 per cent of its pre-unification level and recovery from this deep depression began only at the end of 1992. The total numbers employed fell from 9.7 million before unification to 6.6 million in 1994. In industry itself, the numbers employed fell by four-fifths – from 3.3 million to 660,000 in 1998. In the case of the farm sector, 750,000 jobs, or two-thirds of the total, had been lost within two years of unification. Overall for all sectors, by 1994, only one in four of those in employment still worked at their original enterprise.[17] Open and disguised unemployment in the early 1990s approximated 30 per cent of the labour force, with the low official unemployment statistic veiled by the eventual 750,000 who had taken advantage of a favourable early retirement programme, and by the short-time working provisions, lasting two years, which covered 1.6 million workers by 1991.[18]

The German Unity Fund was established with a DM 115 billion fund to pump-prime the pension, health and unemployment insurance systems, to conduct widespread infrastructure renewal, and to support local authorities in their new tasks and renovation projects. The Bundesbahn and Bundespost were faced with infrastructure renewal bills of hundreds of millions of Deutschmarks. The Unification Treaty, which brought unification on 3 October 1990, admitted the new Länder under art. 23 of the constitution, but of greatest interest, from the present viewpoint, is that this treaty confirmed the priority given to the Treuhandanstalt of speedy privatisation, it established the right of restitution of property to expropriated owners (rather than financial compensation), and it provided for the transition to the west German housing system, specifying that a rise in rents would have to parallel a rise generally in incomes in the east. Financially, the federal government expected unification largely to pay for itself, primarily through asset sales, but it foresaw initial federal deficits of DM 45 billion arising annually as a result of supporting restructuring in the east.[19] In practice, of course, the gross federal transfers alone have continued at DM 140 billion annually, and even in the late 1990s will continue at DM 95 billion. Total gross transfers from public authorities and insurance funds have topped DM 200 billion annually and, in aggregate, more than DM 1 trillion was spent there by authorities in the west to the end of 1997. The federal deficits and the deficits of the health and social security funds, which have generated so much discussion of a crisis in the welfare state, have arisen in the 1990s primarily as a result of support for the east.[20]

The recovery in the east began from early 1993 and led to rapid regional GDP growth of eight per cent or nine per cent annually, with growth rates of 18 per cent per annum in productive industry (construction and manufacturing). In practice, much of the early growth was supported by a boom in the construction sector, fed by public infrastructure and buildings contracts, as well as by extremely favourable tax reliefs for investors in real estate construction projects in the east. By the mid-1990s, manufacturing growth had reached double figures, reflecting both the commissioning of large, prestige industrial projects in semi-conductors and automobiles, as well as the output of a raft of locally owned medium-sized firms. However, the structure of the productive economy has been extremely distorted, with an outsize construction sector and a manufacturing sector growing from a small base: in 1996, construction accounted for 16 per cent of output, while manufacturing accounted for only 14.6 per cent. This compares with five per cent and 26 per cent respectively in the west German structure of output. It hardly surprises then that, following the expiry of the very favourable tax reliefs for construction investment at the end of 1996, a construction slump ensued, dragging the eastern economy almost into stagnation.[21] In 1997, eastern GDP growth reached only 1.6 per cent, compared with 2.2 per cent in the west, and so the phase of catch-up with the old Länder has paused temporarily. If east Germany is to catch up with the west within a generation, then it needs annual growth rates of five per cent. In the meantime, alongside the highest unemployment levels in all Germany since 1933, east Germany has had to endure unemployment rates of 19 per cent (over 22 per cent for females). This very heavy dependence of the eastern economy on construction activity and on demand from west Germany displays key weaknesses in its manufacturing sector. Outside a few large plants with state of the art technology, belonging to west German concerns, the manufacturing sector in the east is typified by medium-size or smaller companies which continue to suffer from a small capital base, insufficient marketing, and poor export penetration: east Germany only accounts for three per cent of total German goods exports.[22] Financially, the profitability level of east German firms is weak, suffering as they do from high unit labour costs. The fact that productivity in eastern manufacturing is still considerably below that of the west, but wages have topped 85 per cent of the western rate, means that the labour cost per unit produced is still substantially above that in the west. Productivity outside manufacturing is even worse, such that in 1997 the average productivity level per hour in the east was only 58 per cent of that in the west.[23] Hence, if private services are to contribute more to growth, when their current productivity level is only 42 per cent of the western, a shake-out of labour will also be needed there.[24]

EASTERN ECONOMIC DEPENDENCE AND REGULATORY DIFFICULTIES

It is therefore very difficult to assert that the transformation of the east German economy is largely complete, and that a phase of normalisation is now in progress, when the regional economy is so dependent on western demand and transfers, its structure suffers from certain major distortions, and there continues a high level of intervention and regulation in the economy. As we have seen, the recent downturn and quasi-stagnation in the east has revealed the full extent to which it is dependent on western demand and transfers to sustain it. The structural distortions arising from an outsized construction sector and a relatively small manufacturing sector leave the economy very exposed to downturn in manufacturing demand, or policy change affecting construction. The private services sector, which grew at above average rates before 1995, has since been growing more slowly, due to weak consumer spending and low business services demand. The situation for public services is worse: here, after a cutback of 30 per cent in employment in territorial authorities, 1991–97, tens of thousands of jobs remain at risk, since there is still considerable overstaffing. Ratios of employees per thousand inhabitants show that there are still 25 per cent more staff in relation to the population than in the west.[25] It is, therefore, scarcely surprising that the federal government plans to continue federal support at a gross DM 95 billion annually to the east until the year 2004. At this date, the recently renewed regional development assistance programme for the eastern Länder will come to an end, and the *Länderfinanzausgleich* (States Revenue Equalisation Fund) will require renegotiation. Therefore, in spite of many calls by right-wing and market liberal politicians for a scaling back of assistance to the east (on the basis that 'transformation' is completed) and appeals to the Constitutional Court by southern Länder for a renegotiation of the *Finanzausgleich*, financial support for the east will continue at the high levels seen throughout the 1990s.[26]

There remains a range of characteristics of the east German economy which set it apart from the west, and which generate concern among economic liberals that the social market is being seriously distorted in the east: intervention is too great and certain features lead to a distortion of regulation. In terms of direct intervention, it is in the labour market and the inherited issues arising from Treuhandanstalt (TH) privatisation that most concern is expressed. As the chapter by Flockton on the labour market makes clear, the federal government continues to sustain a high level of subsidised job creation schemes, training and wage subsidies, as a way of moderating the impact of mass unemployment. Since 1997, job creation schemes have been extended for recipients of social assistance. Other than the extent of this intervention, worries have been expressed about the anti-market effects of the provisions. The most vociferous criticism has been directed against the so-called 'employment enterprises', founded by many eastern local authorities on the basis of work promotion law provisions as a means to absorb local unemployment. The enterprises have paid 100 per cent of the previous wage, at the expense of the Federal Labour Office, and have provided heavily subsidised competition to the small, commercial firms competing for business. The second area of intervention, which has been criticised as counter to the spirit of the social market, is to be found in direct subsidies to ex-TH enterprises, designed as liquidity credits to keep them afloat, and as investment subsidies. The BVS, the successor to the TH, still manages huge areas of eastern farm, forest and commercial property (including 500,000 hectares of forest, 1.01 million hectares of arable land and 56,000 built items of real estate). It also has 3,200 previous TH privatisation contracts which remain problematic. In terms of restitution, there remains 20 per cent of the original 2.12 million claims for return of property to expropriated owners still to be resolved.[27] However, assistance in several celebrated cases (Volkswagen in Saxony, the SKET engineering company, Magdeburg, assistance to the Leuna chemical works) has led to direct clashes between the Brussels competition authorities and the federal government, and in other cases (Bremer Vulkan in Rostock and Schwerin, the Werkstoff Union chemical works in Saxony) there have been cases of misappropriation of government aid. The EU's Sixth Report on State Aid of July 1998 shows that over the period 1991–96, the Federal Republic was the second largest subsidiser in the EU, after Italy. In 1996 alone, Bonn gave a total of ecu 13.5 billion in manufacturing subsidies to the east, or 8,216 ecu per employee in east Germany.[28] In celebrated cases, such as the clean-up of the chemicals triangle of Buna–Leuna–Bitterfeld, DM 30 billion has been paid to maintain a workforce of perhaps 2,500.

In the matter of distortions to regulatory regimes, it is the structure of operations and provision in east Germany which creates differences of treatment and outcome, compared with the west. Three examples help to give a sense of the extent to which the east remains 'different'. In its agricultural structure, the eastern farm sector retains many of the characteristics of the earlier dominant, and very large, state and co-operative farm structures, with one-quarter of its farms greater than 100 hectares, and nine per cent more than 1,000 hectares.[29] This structure sits very uncomfortably with a common agricultural policy (CAP) regime and Bonn structural policy, which seek the maintenance of small farm incomes and grant windfall gains to larger farmers. Secondly, the eastern electricity sector is dominated by a *de facto* monopoly of the four large western power suppliers, a monopoly agreed by Bonn in exchange for assurances concerning the future of eastern brown coal. This keeps power prices far too high in the east and is a major impediment to the electricity supply liberalisation which is in progress in the west.[30] Lastly, the housing market in the east displays a range of very distinctive features, and these are discussed in detail in the chapter by Flockton. The structure of ownership is dominated by housing organisations with close links to the local authorities and the rate of home-owner occupation, at 27 per cent, is far lower than in the west. These structural features fit uncomfortably with policy in the west since the later 1980s.[31]

STRUCTURE, THEMES AND CONCLUSIONS OF RECASTING EAST GERMANY

Recasting East Germany seeks to elucidate how the system transfer was accomplished in the years after 1990 and to explore the 'problematic normalisation' that followed. Under east German conditions, the transfer has met with considerable difficulties and there is no certainty that system process and practice will fall into line with the west. The contributions in this volume discuss eastern distinctiveness and whether it can be expected to persist. They are case studies on their respective themes. Between them, they contribute to an understanding of how civic society in east Germany has been transformed and where this transformed society is placed in the socio-economic environment and political culture of unified Germany

The first part of *Recasting East Germany* examines the impact of transformation on market principles and western institutional models in key areas of the economy. Wendy Carlin argues that the system transfer produced an institutional mismatch. The adaptation to western wage levels has not been supported by the high levels of productivity and innovation that have characterised the west German economy. Moreover, despite restructuring, record investment compared with other European countries and a significant programme of modernisation, the east German economy continues to under-perform and lack export potential. Chris Flockton also identifies rapid wage rises and relatively high income levels as a factor inhibiting economic performance in east Germany. He argues that welfare support programmes in the labour market and in housing cushioned the full impact of economic transformation and curtailed social exclusion through poverty while further increasing the dependency of the region on massive injections of public funding from the federal government. With regard to industrial relations, Karl Koch shows that an initial phase of institutional transfer from west to east established the social partnership model of trade unions and employers' associations. However, its core of collective wage bargaining was soon undermined as smaller firms, and also east German works councils, opted for local agreements and micro-corporatism at plant level. In the housing sector, a different east–west divergence developed. Analysing the transformation of the sector in line with market economic principles, Chris Flockton documents ownership patterns, the adjustment of rental charges and public policy to alleviate hardship. He shows that housing in east Germany remains distinctive through a high proportion of publicly or collectively owned property, the slow emergence of a market especially for *Plattenbau* properties and a generally lower standard of housing quality.

The second part of *Recasting East Germany* looks at the transformation of personal living environments and opportunity structures. Mike Dennis examines adjustment to family structure and function since the *Wende* and finds a heightened instability of the family as a social institution, although east Germans continue to value the family in their personal lives. High divorce rates, low marriage rates and a steep drop in the birth rate are landmarks of family transformation. With special reference to women, Eva

Kolinsky argues that unemployment has hit women with children particularly hard, forcing east German women to develop personal strategies of avoiding labour market exclusion. One such strategy has been to postpone childbirth. In general, east German women have retained strong employment motivation and displayed considerable resourcefulness in combating labour market exclusion.

The transformation of the educational system, the theme of Rosalind Pritchard's chapter, has broadened access to advanced secondary and higher education. Migration losses and the low birth-rate, however, make the tiered school system untenable, in particular at its lowest level. A shortage of apprenticeships has exacerbated the risk of social exclusion for the least able of east Germany's young people. Hans Oswald and Christine Schmid present the results of empirical investigation into the political participation of young people. Focusing on grammar school students as potential members of future elites, they evaluate the influences of home, school and social environment and show that young east Germans are more likely to endorse conventional forms of participation as they grow older. The study also produced evidence of gender differences: with regard to policy issues, the young women in the survey preferred social and ecological themes, the young men governmental and international affairs. Electoral participation was lower among young women than among young men.

The concluding chapters of *Recasting East Germany* probe into specific aspects of the GDR legacy and their significance in east German civil society. Anthony Glees reveals the extent of human rights abuses in the GDR. Tolerated by most east Germans, they were virtually ignored by western GDR research eager to project the other Germany as a modern, even a model, state. Remaining silent about the Stasi and the established practices of imprisonment, torture and unlawful killings amounts to a failure to expose the GDR as an *Unrechtsstaat* and to help set an agenda for creating a democratic civil society in east Germany. Finally, Eva Kolinsky argues that the exclusion of contract workers and other foreigners from GDR society left east Germans ill prepared to receive asylum seekers, as stipulated in the unification treaty. Since 1990, negative experiences of social transformation have intensified existing xenophobic tendencies and resulted in a sharp increase in xenophobic violence. In east German society, multiculturalism and the acceptance of newcomers from other countries and cultures on which it is based have yet to emerge.

12 RECASTING EAST GERMANY

NOTES

1. M. Thompson, 'Reluctant Revolutionaries', *German Politics*, Vol.8, No.1 (forthcoming April 1999). Also U. Thaysen, *Der Runde Tisch* (Opladen: Westdeutscher Verlag, 1990); C. Joppke, *East German Dissidents and the Revolution of 1989* (London: Macmillan, 1995), also the chapter by M. Dennis in S. Padgett (ed.), *Parties and Party Systems in the New Germany* (Aldershot: Dartmouth, 1993).
2. H. Wiesenthal (ed.), *Einheit als Privileg. Vergleichende Perspektiven auf die Transformation Ostdeutschlands* (Frankfurt/Main: Campus, 1996), especially the chapter by R. Rose and C. Härper, 'The Impact of a Ready-Made State. Die privilegierte Position Ostdeutschlands in der postkommunistischen Transformation'.
3. For details see K.H. Goetz and P.J. Cullen (eds.), *Constitutional Policy in Unified Germany* (London and Portland, OR: Frank Cass, 1994).
4. For a comprehensive survey of economic, social and political transformation see Kommission für die Erforschung des sozialen und politischen Wandels in den neuen Bundesländern (ed.), *Berichte zum sozialen und politischen Wandel in Ostdeutschland*, 6 vols. (Opladen: Leske & Budrich, 1996). See also E. Kolinsky (ed.), *Between Hope and Fear. Everyday Life in Post-Unification East Germany* (Edinburgh: Edinburgh University Press, 1995); and E. Kolinsky (ed.), *Social Transformation and the Family in Post-Communist Germany* (London: Macmillan, 1998).
5. For the concept of 'reinventing Germany' see A. Glees, *Reinventing Germany* (Oxford: Berg, 1996).
6. R.J. Dalton (ed.), *Germans Divided. The 1994 Bundestag Elections and the Evolution of the German Party System* (Oxford: Berg, 1996); and G.K. Roberts, *Superwahljahr: The German Elections in 1994* (London and Portland, OR: Frank Cass, 1995).
7. A. Segert and I. Zierke, *Sozialstruktur und Milieuerfahrungen. Aspekte des alltagskulturellen Wandels in Ostdeutschland* (Opladen: Westdeutscher Verlag, 1997), p.48.
8. R. Geissler, *Die Sozialstruktur Deutschlands. Ein Studienbuch zur Entwicklung im geteilten und vereinten Deutschland* (Opladen: Westdeutscher Verlag, 1992), pp.205–11. Also M. Vester, M. Hoffmann and I. Zierke (eds.), *Soziale Milieus in Ostdeutschland. Gesellschaftliche Strukturen zwischen Zerfall und Neubildung* (Cologne: Bund Verlag, 1995).
9. S. Hradil, *Sozialstrukturanalyse in einer fortgeschrittenen Gesellschaft* (Opladen: Leske & Budrich, 1987), pp.13–58.
10. U. Beck, *Risikogesellschaft. Auf dem Weg in eine andere Moderne* (Frankfurt/Main: Suhrkamp, 1986).
11. W. Hanesch, *Armut in Deutschland* (Reinbek: Rowohlt, 1994), p.173; also M.M. Zwick, (ed.), *Einmal arm, immer arm? Neue Befunde zur Armut in Deutschland* (Frankfurt/Main: Campus, 1994), especially P.A. Berger,' Individualisierung der Armut', pp.21 ff.
12. M. Kohli, 'Die DDR als Arbeitsgesellschaft? Arbeit, Lebenslauf und soziale Differenzierung', in H. Kaelble, J. Kocka and H. Zwahr (eds.), *Sozialgeschichte der DDR* (Stuttgart: Klett-Cotta, 1994).
13. G. Almond and S. Verba, *Civic Culture. Political Attitudes and Democracy in Five Nations* (Boston and Toronto: Little, Brown and Co., 1963); D. Conradt, 'Changing German Political Culture', in G. Almond and S. Verba (eds.), *The Civic Culture Revisited* (Boston and Toronto: Little, Brown & Co., 1980); E. Kolinsky, 'Socio-Economic Change and Political Culture in West Germany', in J. Gaffney and E. Kolinsky (eds.), *Political Culture in France and Germany* (London: Routledge, 1991).
14. O.W. Gabriel (eds.), *Politische Orientierungen und Verhaltensweisen im vereinigten Deutschland* (Opladen: Leske & Budrich, 1997), especially the chapter by D. Fuchs, 'Welche Demokratie wollen die Deutschen?'; see also W.P. Bürklin, 'Die politische Kultur in Ost- und Westdeutschland: eine Zwischenbilanz', in G. Lehmbruch (ed.), *Einigung und Zerfall. Deutschland und Europa nach dem Ende des Ost-West Konflikts* (Opladen: Leske & Budrich, 1995).
15. Statistisches Bundesamt, *Statistisches Jahrbuch 1997 für die Bundesrepublik Deutschland* (Stuttgart: Metzler Poeschel, 1997).

16. *Wirtschaft und Statistik*, 1 (1997), p.21; 12 (1995), p.887.
17. C.H. Flockton, 'The Federal German Economy in the Early 1990s', *German Politics*, Vol.2, No.2 (1993).
18. Deutsche Bundesbank, Monthly Report, various; also C.H. Flockton, 'Economic Transformation and Income Change', in E. Kolinsky (ed.) *Social Transformation and the Family in Post-communist Germany* (London: Macmillan, 1998).
19. C.H. Flockton, 'The German Economy since 1989/90: Problems and Prospects', in K. Larres (ed.), *Germany since Unification: The Domestic and External Consequences* (London: Macmillan, 1997).
20. C.H. Flockton, 'Germany's Long-Running Fiscal Crisis: Unification Costs or Unsustainability of Welfare State Arrangements?, *Debatte*, Vol.6, No.1 (1998).
21. 'Zur wirtschaftlichen Lage in den neuen Ländern und in Berlin-Ost', *Wirtschaft und Statistik*, No.3 (1998).
22. 'Zur Wirtschaftslage in Ostdeutschland', in Deutsche Bundesbank *Monatsbericht*, April 1998.
23. 'Zur wirtschaftlichen Lage in den neuen Ländern und in Berlin-Ost'.
24. Deutsches Institut für Wirtschaftsforschung (DIW), 'Öffentlicher Dienst: Starker Personalabbau trotz moderater Tarifanhebungen', *Wochenbericht*, 5 (1998).
25. 'Zur wirtschaftlichen Lage in den neuen Ländern und in Berlin-Ost'.
26. *Handelsblatt*, various; DIW, 'Die Lage der Weltwirtschaft und der deutschen Wirtschaft im Frühjahr 1998', *Wochenbericht*, 20–21 (1998).
27. *Handelsblatt*, various; L. Blume, 'Sollte die BVS über das Jahr 1998 hinaus fortbestehen?', *Wirtschaftsdienst*, IX (1997).
28. European Commission, *Sixth Report on State Aids in Manufacturing*, Brussels, July 1998.
29. 'Zur wirtschaftlichen Lage in den neuen Ländern und in Berlin-Ost'.
30. N. Eickhof and D. Kreikenbaum, 'Liberalisierung des Energiewirtschaftsrechts und Befürchtungen der Kommunen', *Wirtschaftsdienst* V (1997).
31. G. Hallett, *Housing Needs in West and East Germany* (Anglo-German Foundation, 1994).

The New East German Economy: Problems of Transition, Unification and Institutional Mismatch

WENDY CARLIN

This paper identifies three different problems faced by the east German economy in the wake of reunification. The first is the problem of transition in which an effective state has to be established, and credible macroeconomic conditions, powerful market forces, a functioning banking system and effective corporate governance of enterprises introduced. It is argued that this set of problems was largely solved via unification. Yet unification brought with it a serious regional problem. Government policy has sought to deal with the regional problem by a programme of subsidising investment, but the costs imposed on the east by the transfer of the wage bargaining and social security systems remain. The heart of the east German economic problem lies with the successful transfer of some but not all west German institutions. The resulting institutional mismatch is likely to be difficult to resolve, with the consequence that a slow process of convergence of the east German economy to the level of output per capita of the west can be expected.

The economic strategy implicit in the west German government's approach to the new Länder was one of replication. The argument of this paper is that whilst replication was effective in solving the problems of transition, it brought with it a severe regional problem. Government policy has sought to deal with the regional problem by a programme of subsidising investment, but the costs imposed on the east by the transfer of the wage bargaining and social security systems remain. The west German economy is able to bear its very high direct and indirect labour costs because its institutions are well adapted to produce high quality goods and to promote through innovation the continuous improvement of goods and production processes essential for success in international competition. The heart of the east German economic problem lies with the successful transfer of some but not all west German institutions. The resulting institutional mismatch is likely to be difficult to resolve, with the consequence that a very slow process of convergence of the east German economy to the level of output per capita

Wendy Carlin, University College London.

of the west can be expected.

The extension of west German macroeconomic policy, the removal of all internal barriers to trade and factor mobility and a resolute privatisation policy centred on the acquisition of east German enterprises by west German companies were expected to solve the key problems of transition. There would be an effective state, credible macroeconomic conditions, powerful market forces, a functioning banking system and effective corporate governance of enterprises. Yet solving the transition problems through incorporation into the Federal Republic has not solved the problems of the east German economy. East Germany is now a market economy but it is heavily dependent on the rest of the Federal Republic. Problems of transition have been supplanted by problems of the incorporation of a poor region into a rich country. As the experience of the Italian Mezzogiorno testifies, convergence of levels of prosperity between regions within a nation does not occur automatically.

Proximate determinants of regional convergence appear to be relative investment levels and levels of cost competitiveness. Unification policy in Germany has promoted high levels of investment in the new Länder, which would tend to boost convergence but has led to poor cost competitiveness, which hinders convergence. The weakness in cost competitiveness of east German business reflects the specific characteristics of the economy into which the new Länder have been drawn. Labour cost competitiveness comprises two elements: the cost of wages and social security contributions per employee in east as compared with west Germany and relative productivity levels of the two regions. The much more rapid convergence of relative labour costs as compared to relative productivity levels created a competitive disadvantage for east German business. The instant transfer of the west German wage setting and social security systems was responsible for the former; the protracted difficulties in transferring the training system, the inter-firm networks and technology transfer systems are responsible for the persistence of the latter.

The first section addresses the issue of economic development in the new Länder from the perspective of the economics of transition. The second section examines the regional problem created by the terms of unification and the third focuses on the issue of institutional mismatch. Section four presents empirical data on the economic performance of east Germany and the article concludes with an evaluation of the prospects of the new Länder.

EAST GERMAN DEVELOPMENT AS A PROBLEM OF TRANSITION

The key problems for post-communist economic development identified early in the new field of transition economics were the establishment of (i) macroeconomic stability and credibility, (ii) liberalised prices and competition in goods and factor markets and (iii) effective corporate governance for financial institutions and non-financial business under largely private ownership. More recently, the importance of a functioning state able to create a credible environment in the form of predictable, non-arbitrary rules for private business to operate in has been stressed.[1]

The first two problems were solved immediately by unification, as was the problem of the creation of a credible government with non-arbitrary taxation rules and legal enforcement of property rights and contracts. The solution of the third problem of restructuring, privatising and creating effective governance of the financial and non-financial enterprise sectors was twofold. The banking system was reformed before the enterprise sector was restructured.[2] Even before the economic and monetary union of July 1990, the Bundesbank had in practice taken control of the east German state banking system. The Deutsche Kreditbank, the arm of the former state bank of the GDR comprising the branch network and virtually all enterprise accounts, came under the control of west German commercial banks (Deutsche Bank and Dresdner Bank) immediately after monetary union. The stock of 'old loans' accrued under the GDR state banking system was isolated in the balance sheet of the Kreditbank, so that Deutsche Bank and Dresdner Bank acquired a branch network and ongoing banking relationships with corporate customers, but no potentially bad enterprise debt.

Second, the privatisation agency, the Treuhandanstalt, took effective control of the state enterprise sector including all non-financial enterprises. These two steps enabled east Germany to avoid the 'bad loans' problem characteristic of transition economies in which state-owned banks burdened with bad debt continued to lend to indebted enterprises on the assumption that the state would bail them out. The greater the overhang of bad debt, the more likely would be a bail-out and hence the lower the incentive for banks effectively to monitor their new loans to enterprises.

The east German solution was the complete carve-out of enterprises from the banking system and the centralisation of enterprise restructuring in the privatisation agency. This can be contrasted to an alternative approach – taken, for example, in Poland – in which enterprise restructuring was delegated to the banks, which received subsidies to undertake monitoring.[3] The German approach meant that the privatised banks could concentrate on rapidly modernising the technical operation of the payments system, building up their personal sector business and establishing a client base in the new private and newly privatised enterprises. Taking as given the rapid increase in product wages in east Germany and the consequent unprofitability of the great majority of enterprises, full carve-out may have been efficient. Such an argument depends on the depth of the profitability crisis in the enterprise sector and hence on the burden on bank resources that bank-led restructuring would have entailed, on the possible complementarities and economies of scale available to a state agency and on the existence of an effective budget constraint for the state agency.[4]

The following stylised facts characterise the process of enterprise restructuring and privatisation in the transition economies of eastern Europe. There has been a very wide variety of methods and speeds of privatisation and yet patterns of enterprise behaviour have been rather similar. Whilst there is some evidence of improved efficiency and profit orientation of privatised firms as compared with those remaining in state ownership (once possible selection effects have been taken into account) the only clear evidence of deep restructuring involving major investment and strategic decision making has been observed in cases of foreign ownership. This is normally interpreted as reflecting the weakness of the corporate governance structures of firms and the underdevelopment of the financial institutions characteristic of a well functioning market economy.[5]

By contrast, privatisation in east Germany took place rapidly and resulted in a pattern of ownership in which there were typically clear outside owners with the incentive to maximise profits and with the resources in terms of finance and management expertise to carry out the required restructuring.[6] This outcome raises the question of how such rapid privatisation entailing the transfer of control to outsiders was achieved, what role was played by complementary policies and whether the speed of restructuring was too fast. Enterprise restructuring refers to the changes to state-owned enterprises that were required in order that they could survive in the market environment. Such changes included labour shedding, changes in internal organisation, the spinning off of non-core activities including social assets, the closure of non-viable units, capital investment and equipment modernisation.

The Treuhand presided over the major restructuring of the economic landscape of the former GDR during its four years of operation. It played a substantial role in the breaking up of enterprises and the reduction of employment in them.[7] For example, in 1991 the ratio of multi-plant to all enterprises was approximately 50 per cent higher in east than in west Germany – two years later, east Germany had just half as many multi-plant firms.[8] When it began, there were over four million people employed in Treuhand enterprises – by the time it closed in 1994, there were less than one-quarter of this number in ex-Treuhand firms. By the end of the intense privatisation phase, the east German economy was characterised by a population of firms with an average size well below that of west Germany or the UK.

The Treuhand sought buyers for the core businesses of its enterprises. In general both extensive pre-privatisation restructuring and a subsidy on the purchase price were required to attract a buyer. Many enterprises were sold at negative prices. Although in theory auctions are more efficient than sale through negotiation with a small number of potential buyers, the Treuhand was not in the position of selling valuable well-defined products in a market with a large number of prospective buyers.[9] A more accurate picture of the Treuhand's task is to think of it seeking to buy restructuring plans for its portfolio of enterprises. Seen from this perspective, it is clear why the Treuhand had to take a detailed interest in the identity of the purchaser. This was operationalised in the Treuhand's procedures through the use of contractual guarantees that privatised firms undertake specific levels of investment and employment. A successful bidder had to guarantee to carry out sufficient investment per head to make the enterprise competitive at west German wages in three to five years and was granted a subsidy in the form of a discount on the current asset value according to the number of jobs guaranteed.

For enterprises judged by the Treuhand as non-viable, it organised its own liquidation procedure along the lines of the United States debtor-oriented chapter 11 model in preference to the standard German creditor-oriented bankruptcy law. This allowed the Treuhand to keep firms out of the official bankruptcy process and to take account of the broader social costs of closure.

The rapidity with which enterprises were broken up and employment reduced in east Germany can be explained by the imposition of a hard budget constraint on enterprises by the Treuhand. Most enterprises were loss-makers and they required liquidity to survive. The Treuhand controlled access to liquidity through fairly effectively controlled guaranteed loans and because of the prior privatisation of the banking system firms had no access to soft loans. This reduced the scope for managerial resistance to restructuring. Their incentive to engage in restructuring was heightened by the opportunities for managers to signal their quality on the external labour market because of the Treuhand audits of managers, the external evaluation of managers by potential investors and the presence of West German managers on the supervisory boards of large east German enterprises prior to privatisation. The third aspect promoting pre-privatisation restructuring in east Germany that was not present elsewhere in transition economies was the availability of compensation to the losers from the restructuring process. Initially this took the form of payment for short-time working – even in the case when zero hours were worked – and was then replaced by special labour market measures of retraining and job subsidies along with generous unemployment and early retirement benefits. Finally, the implementation of the German welfare state provided east Germans with access to health care, education, and so on, outside the enterprise, thereby lowering the costs to employees of labour shedding.

But was restructuring too rapid in east Germany? As will be discussed below, the privatisation policy was not the primary cause of the massive loss of industrial jobs in east Germany. Responsibility for that lay with the terms of unification. The application of employment subsidies in the sales and liquidation processes by Treuhand provided some offset to the excessive cost of labour. However, the absence of a general employment subsidy meant that the Treuhand had the incentive to cut employment by more than would have been optimal in the enterprises for which it was seeking buyers. Its employment policy was dictated by the requirement to control its own deficit. The cost of those unemployed was transferred to the budget of other government authorities. Had an employment subsidy applying to all jobs in east Germany been in place, then labour shedding in the pre-privatisation phase would have been less extensive. It is possible that the Treuhand's rather successful policy of management buy-outs could have had a broader base, leaving an economy less dominated by the subsidiaries of west German (and to a lesser extent foreign) companies.[10]

The need to find profit-oriented owners for former state-owned enterprises is a major problem for transition economies. The privatisation method adopted by the Treuhand solved this problem for many east German enterprises. The result of the privatisation process was to produce an economy with a very highly concentrated ownership structure. Ownership was dominated by companies (usually west German) and by families (usually from west Germany). Two-thirds of all ownership stakes of west German companies or families were for 100 per cent of the east German firm. Ownership by west Germans was more prevalent in larger than in smaller east German firms. It seems that about three-quarters of employment in privatised east German enterprises was in those owned by west Germans and foreigners.

The extent of concentration of ownership by outside companies and families in east Germany suggests the potential for effective control over management by profit-oriented owners. This impression is reinforced by information on the structure of the boards of privatised firms. Comparison of the board structure of east with west German subsidiaries found that the post-privatisation phase in east Germany was characterised by tighter management control by the parent firm than was normally the case for west German subsidiaries. The east German case resembled the high levels of control over management by the parent observed when west German subsidiaries were undergoing reorganisation, restructuring or rationalisation.[11] One rationale for the strategy of the Treuhand that produced this outcome is that control by a western owner was necessary in order for east German firms to gain access to finance, markets and management.

In common with any case of foreign investment, there was a trade-off between these benefits and the danger that owners could use their control to strip the assets (including the markets) of the east German firms. Whilst many cases of exploitation of east German assets have been documented, the broad picture emerging from the privatisation process is a high level of investment in the east German firms and high levels of management transfer.[12]

EAST GERMAN DEVELOPMENT AS A REGIONAL PROBLEM[13]

The major economic implication of German economic and monetary union was that east Germany could run a current account deficit with the rest of the country that would be financed by transfers from the west. Unification meant that convergence of per capita income and consumption, and hence that of living standards, could precede the convergence of per capita output (that is, GDP). Unlike a country, a region can run a current account deficit indefinitely – or, more precisely, for as long as political support remains for the continued transfer of resources from the rich to the poor region. The transfer of resources from a rich to a poor region or from one with lower to one with higher unemployment occurs automatically in a political union: a unified tax and transfer system along with common scales for the payment of central/federal government employees (such as teachers, police officers, civil servants) are all that are required to produce this result. The greater the productivity and unemployment differences, the greater the level of 'automatic' transfer. The extent of transfer will further increase with additional deliberate measures of regional support.

The recent literature on regional convergence suggests that convergence of state output per capita in the United States occurred over the 100 years from the 1880s and in Japan between the prefectures in the post-war period. The successful convergence of the regions of central Italy to those of the north fits this pattern but the failure of the southern regions to converge does not. The Italian Mezzogiorno had a per capita income level of 70 per cent that of the centre-north when unification occurred in 1862. The gap widened to 55 per cent by the late 1940s and further in the early 1950s. The only period of convergence occurred in the 1960s (by about ten percentage points) followed by divergence in the 1970s and 1980s. The Italian experience underlines the fact that a process of regional convergence is not automatic.

In the standard neo-classical growth model (the 'Solow' model), the reason for a poor region's lower output per head is its lower capital stock per head. The mechanism through which convergence occurs is capital deepening as the higher rate of return on investment in the poor region (due to its lower capital–labour ratio) induces 'catch-up' investment. In this model convergence can fail for two reasons: first, the assumption may be false that the only difference between the two areas is their capital per head and hence that the underlying long-run steady state characteristics of the two areas is the same. Abramowitz has used the term 'social capability' to capture the idea that different countries could belong to different 'convergence clubs'.[14] In principle this could be true of regions also, with the consequence that the neo-classical model would predict convergence through the process of capital deepening but to *different* long-run levels of per capita GDP. The second reason why neo-classical convergence could fail is if market imperfections prevent the necessary investment response. Stepping outside the standard model, there may be agglomeration externalities associated with the rich region that enhance the attractiveness of investment there even though the level of capital per head is higher. The political union of a rich and a poor region allows big deviations from market-determined levels to persist for both regional factor prices and investment levels. On the one hand, government policy can raise investment in the poor region to help offset agglomeration effects or to improve 'social capability' but on the other the transfer of institutional arrangements to the poor region can undermine regional competitiveness.

The dependence of east Germany on the rest of the Federal Republic was much greater after unification than has ever been the case in Italy. The scale of the regional problem arises both from the initial conditions at unification and from the policies adopted. The relevant initial conditions were the relative decline of the productive capability of the GDR during the 40 years of separation and the loss of value of east German industry due to the precipitate collapse of the Soviet Union and other former CMEA trading partners and of the CMEA trading arrangements. Pre-war data suggests little difference in per capita GDP between eastern and western Germany – in fact, there is some evidence that it was higher in the east. By the late 1980s, the per capita GDP of the GDR fell short of that of the FRG by about 30 per cent.

The consequences of the productivity gap at unification for the scale of the regional problem were greatly exacerbated by the early agreement between government, west German unions and employers' associations to a rapid convergence of negotiated wage rates and by the extension to the east of the very generous west German social security system. The interaction of the wage agreements and the social security system, in which unemployment benefit depends on the final wage, placed a high floor under the wage, especially for workers previously employed in Treuhand firms (where union-negotiated wage rates were always paid). The early agreements for rapid wage equalisation in east Germany were implemented with little controversy or public comment in spite of the visible collapse of the east German economy and rapidly rising unemployment.[15]

As a consequence of the wage and social security policies associated with unification, the new Länder began with an enormous competitive disadvantage. Although the terms of the currency union between the GDR and the Federal Republic are sometimes identified as the source of the competitiveness problem for east Germany, this claim is not compelling. A simple way of seeing this is to consider the impact of the 1:1 rate used for current transactions (a rate less favourable to the Ostmark was used for the conversion of some savings). In the goods market, the translation of a given Ostmark price for an east German product into Deutschmarks at one-to-one typically resulted in a collapse in demand for the product with the consequence that either the Deutschmark price was sharply reduced or the product was withdrawn from sale. According to this logic, an incorrect exchange rate would, through the operation of market forces, have led to a decline in Deutschmark wages in response to the excess supply of east German labour as the labour market equilibrated. Yet an increase rather than a decrease in wages in Deutschmark was observed after the currency union occurred. The operation of market forces to correct an inappropriate initial exchange rate used for the currency conversion was impaired by the wage and social security policies, with the result that the disequilibrium in the labour market was exacerbated and not ameliorated.

An empirical examination of the evolution of the gap between per capita income in the north-centre and the south of Italy confirmed the role of the relative share of investment and the relative level of unit labour costs in industry (a measure of competitiveness). As suggested by theory, convergence is boosted by a rise in the investment effort in the poor relative to the rich region and by an improvement in regional cost competitiveness. The policies adopted at unification fostered a very high level of investment in east Germany. As argued in section 1, the method of privatisation was one that promoted this. In addition, the government provided high levels of subsidy for investment in the east. The outcome was a share of investment in GDP double that of west Germany. There is some evidence from an examination of the investment effort and productivity growth in sub-industries of manufacturing that the extent of productivity catch-up to west Germany was fastest in those sub-industries with the highest amounts of investment.

Although investment levels remain high in east Germany, the competitiveness problem persists (as is documented below). The ending of the brief phase of convergence of the Italian Mezzogiorno has been attributed to unfavourable policy and institutional changes that produced weakening of regional investment and a deterioration in competitiveness. A further factor in the Italian case appears to have been the devolution of administrative power from central to regional government that happened in the early 1970s, and which appeared to shift spending powers to a region in which there were very poorly rooted civic traditions. This opened up a greatly increased scope for rent-seeking behaviour. The pre-war success of eastern Germany and evidence on the process of administrative reform since unification suggest that the kinds of problems arising from weak administration and the possible integration of a dependence culture that appear to have been so important in Italy's persistent regional problem are unlikely to recur in Germany.

EAST GERMAN DEVELOPMENT AS A PROBLEM OF INSTITUTIONAL MISMATCH[16]

The federal government's strategy was to achieve the economic unification of Germany through the replication of west German institutional and production structures in the new Länder. It was assumed that the production profile and patterns of organisation of west German companies would be reproduced in the east alongside the transfer of the administrative, industrial relations and social security systems. The early behaviour of west German companies provided encouragement that a strategy based on the large-scale engagement by western business in the east was feasible. Of the 500 large west German firms surveyed about their investment intentions in 1990, more than 60 per cent were preparing for major investment activity in east Germany and another 20 per cent were intending to invest in the near future. The motive for large companies to undertake major investment projects through the purchase of east German companies rested on the assumed value of the markets of these enterprises in eastern Europe and the Soviet Union. A base in east Germany appeared attractive since unification eliminated the macroeconomic and political risk facing investors elsewhere in the transition countries.

The ambitious plans for private investment in the new Länder based on buoyant expectations of the value of markets in eastern Europe and of the access to them provided by east German enterprises were rapidly scaled down as the Soviet Union collapsed and the painful process of transition became apparent. The export markets of east German enterprises collapsed within a year of unification and it was clear that the demand from within east Germany could be met from the existing western capacity of German firms. Simultaneously other key components of the replication strategy – wages and social security – had been implemented. It rapidly became clear that even a more modest than originally anticipated engagement of west German companies in the new Länder would require large subsidies.

An explanation of the importance of west German business engagement in the new Länder for the prospects for convergence rests on the claim that the ability of west German firms to pay high direct and indirect labour costs and to compete successfully on international markets is dependent on specific institutional arrangements within and between firms. These arrangements have allowed German industry to retain market share in industries by making intensive use of skilled labour as the key to successful innovation. As has been confirmed by observers using a range of different empirical techniques, west German firms are especially good at incremental innovation with established technologies at the high quality end of the product range. By contrast, they are not particularly good at frontier or radical innovation in which quite new technologies are being developed.

A competitive strategy based on high quality incremental innovation entails a kind of work organisation and skills that create monitoring and incentive problems for management. One reason is that in order for the innovation process to work it is necessary for skilled workers from engineers to skilled manual workers to have a great deal of autonomy. Secondly, this kind of innovation system requires employees to have general industry technology skills that are supplemented with company-specific skills built up through decentralised problem solving. The combination of autonomy and transferable skills creates a serious problem for management of how to motivate, monitor and retain such powerful employees. Its solution requires a relational contract between managers and employees based on consensus decision making. The German works council provides a framework on the workers' side for a contract of this kind with management, but the external industrial relations system has a major role to play in guaranteeing the works council its powers and in preventing it from abusing those powers. If there is inappropriate behaviour by powerful workers within the firm, the management can turn to the employers' association, and if management fail to stick to its relational contract then the works council can turn to the union.

Whilst the macroeconomic role of the German wage setting system frequently attracts attention, its microeconomic logic is often overlooked. To appreciate the institutional obstacles to the replication strategy for the new Länder, we can see that in the absence of a sufficient presence of German companies operating in the high quality incremental innovation niche, the regional economy has taken on the cost burden of the wage-setting and social security system without reaping the micro-institutional benefits. Although the initial wage increases in east Germany were the result of union and employer association agreements, the social security system comprises part of the explanation for east Germany's persistent competitiveness problem. The reason is that negotiated ('tariff') wage increases are not legally binding. Indeed, many small firms in east Germany pay wages below the tariff rates. The problem is two-fold. The floor to such wages is set by the social security benefits and this limits the creation of low productivity jobs (for example, in the services sector or in the supply of goods or services in competition with producers in neighbouring low-wage countries such as Poland or the Czech Republic). For larger firms, membership of employers' associations is attractive because of the benefits supplied (for example, in relation to training) but brings with it the need to pay the tariff wage rate.

Two other components of the institutional basis of west German competitive success are difficult to reproduce without a sufficient presence of large German companies in the east: training and technology transfer. Companies play a major role in paying for the acquisition of general industry – as well as company-specific skills in Germany. Companies undertake training against the background of a vocational training 'expert community' of unions and employers' associations that undertake curriculum development and the monitoring of standards. Only west German-owned companies in east Germany train in the west German target range with trainees comprising six per cent of employees. Even this level is dependent on special subsidies – one-half of new in-firm places in 1994 were subsidised.

Less well known is the collaboration between companies that enables efficient technology transfer to take place. Long-term relationships between firms appear to play a major role in the translation of radical innovations (usually coming from abroad) into agreed industry standards and in the associated build-up of competences in the new technology through research institutions and research departments of large companies.

Figure 1 provides a summary of major west German institutions, the role they play in sustaining the high quality incremental innovation system in west Germany and the obstacles they present for the development of a self-sustaining growth process in the new Länder.

EAST GERMAN ECONOMIC PERFORMANCE

The east German economy has grown rapidly in the years since unification. As shown in Table 1, the average growth rate over the period from 1991 to 1996 was 6.8 per cent per annum compared with the poor performance of the west German economy in the same period, in which average growth was less than one per cent per annum. This period of rapid growth has produced an impressive amount of catch-up for the new Länder. Evaluating output at

FIGURE 1

INSTITUTIONS IN EAST AND WEST GERMANY

Institution	Role in West German High Quality Incremental Innovation System	Problems created for the New Länder
Industry-wide collective bargaining system	Employers support the tariff wage system as a counter-weight to the power of skilled workers.	Firms are unable to produce profitably at tariff wage rates. The incentive to invest is lowered.
Training system where companies pay for training in general industry skills	Tariff-wage system supports the training system by helping to prevent poaching of skilled workers and hence assists the maintenance of high levels of training. External certification and access to the internal labour market of large companies provides young people with the incentive to invest in training.	The base of companies is too small to provide sufficient in-firm training places.
Innovation and technology transfer system	Industry associations foster standard-setting and help to minimise relational problems arising from incomplete contracts when companies need to cooperate in innovation.	Long-term relationships are difficult to develop. East German 'independent' firms lack access to technology diffusion networks.

1996 market prices, the GDP per capita in east Germany in 1991 is estimated at 40 per cent that of west Germany. By 1996, east Germany was at a level of 57 per cent of west Germany. This speed of catch-up is much faster than that predicted by some early observers[17] – it is similar to that achieved by the Italian Mezzogiorno during its single decade of convergence in the 1960s. However, in the last few years, the speed of convergence has dropped dramatically: in 1997, east German growth has been provisionally estimated at 0.4 per cent below that of west Germany.

Unemployment shot up to over ten per cent soon after unification and remains at above 15 per cent of the labour force. This is well above the west German level, which has increased in the 1990s to historically high rates. Moreover it is estimated that there are another 12.6 per cent of the east German labour force in hidden unemployment (as compared to less than two per cent in west Germany).[18]

TABLE 1

THE EAST GERMAN ECONOMY

		1991	1996	1991–96
GDP growth	EG		2.0	6.8
(% p.a.)	WG		1.3	0.9
Unemployment rate	EG	10.7	15.0	
(% of labour force)	WG	5.5	9.1	
GDP per capita WG=100				
(at 1996 market prices)	EG	40.2	57.0	
Gross investment share	EG	42.5	51.0[a]	
(% of GDP current prices)	WG	22.0	18.8[a]	
Unit labour costs in industry WG=100				
(wage + non-wage labour costs per unit output)	EG	147.4	124.1[b]	
Transfers to East Germany[c]				
% of EG GDP		51.5	35.2	
% of WG GDP		3.7	4.0	

Notes:

[a] 1994 (Data is no longer published for gross investment for EG and WG separately.)

[b] 1995

[c] from OECD, Economic Survey of Germany (1997), Table 8, p.43.

Sources: Statistisches Bundesamt (1997), Volkswirtschaftliche Gesamtrechnungen, Fachserie 18, Reihe 1.3, 1996 Hauptbericht. Sachverständigenrat zur Begutachtung der gesamtwirtschaftlichen Entwicklung (1997). Jahresgutachten 1997/98. Own calculations.

The huge investment effort in east Germany that has contributed to the closing of the GDP per capita gap is reflected in a share of investment in GDP in the east of between 40 and 50 per cent over the post-unification period. The comparable figure for west Germany is about 20 per cent (see Table 1). The financing of levels of consumption and investment expenditure well beyond what could be paid for from east German GDP has come predominantly from west Germany. West Germans have been transferring between three and four per cent of GDP per annum to the east. In spite of the growth of east German output, this transfer still represented 35 per cent of east German GDP in 1996.

Although high investment has promoted the modernisation of east German industry, the catch-up of productivity still lags behind that of wages. In 1991, east German industrial labour costs were nearly 50 per cent higher than those in west Germany. By 1995, they were still 24 per cent higher.

Table 2 provides more detailed information on the state of manufacturing industry in east Germany. Manufacturing employment has halved since 1991 in absolute terms, taking the share of manufacturing in total employment from 28 per cent in 1991 to less than 16 per cent in 1996.

This is a long way below the share in west Germany. The interaction between high investment and the collapse of manufacturing employment is reflected in the increase in the stock of machinery and equipment per worker in east Germany from 28 per cent of that in west Germany in 1991 to over 70 per cent in 1996. It appears that east Germany is moving toward a manufacturing sector with a similar level of capital-intensity to that of the west, but one that is very small relative to the size of the economy.

The significance of the size of manufacturing for regional convergence is confirmed by a cross-section regression for European regions.[19] We found that there was a significant positive relationship between the share of employment in manufacturing in a region and its per capita GDP. The regression result predicts that with a manufacturing employment share of 16 per cent, east Germany would have a GDP per capita of 85 to 90 per cent of the European average. This would, of course, leave it well below the west German level.

TABLE 2

MANUFACTURING INDUSTRY IN EAST GERMANY: SELECTED INDICATORS

	1991	1996	% p.a. change 1991–96	WG
Employment ('000)	2,049	1,003	–15.7	–3.8 (% p.a. change 1991–96)
Manuf. employment/ Total employment (%)	28.0	15.9		26.7 (1996)
Stock of machinery & equipment per worker (WG=100)	28.1	72.2		100
Profitability (gross profit share in value added) (%)	–54.3	2.0		19.0 (average 1991–96)

Sources: Statistisches Bundesamt (1997) Volkswirtschaftliche Gesamtrechnungen, Fachserie 18, Reihe 1.3, 1996 Hauptbericht. Sachverständigenrat zur Begutachtung der gesamtwirtschaftlichen Entwicklung (1997). Jahresgutachten 1997/98. Own calculations.

A useful summary measure for the performance of manufacturing industry is to calculate the gross profit share in value added from national accounts data. The result of this calculation is interesting. In 1991, the gross profit share in east German manufacturing was –54 per cent, which reflected the fact that the bulk of firms were making losses as the value added was only two-thirds of the wage bill. This situation has gradually improved through two processes. On the one hand, the most poorly performing firms have been closed down. As noted in the first section, a great deal of this has occurred through the closure procedure introduced by the Treuhandanstalt. On the other hand, the profitability situation of surviving firms has on average improved as a result of continued cuts in employment and improved sales. By 1996, the gross profit share for the manufacturing sector as a whole in east Germany had turned positive. The continued seriousness of the situation is underlined by the disparity between the two per cent profit share for east German manufacturing and the 19 per cent achieved by west German manufacturing (on average over the 1991–96 period). It should be noted that the result for west Germany for this period was an historically poor one.[20]

Since the recovery of the manufacturing sector is of great importance if east Germany is to reduce its dependence on the west, the steady improvement in performance is noteworthy. The disappointing aggregate growth of east Germany in 1996–97 reflects the slowdown of the construction boom and of the early phase of rapid development of personal services.[21] This aggregate picture masks the improvement in the position of manufacturing and of one part of the services sector that has been lagging – business-related services. Another positive indicator is the evidence that east German firms are increasingly able to make sales beyond the region. A survey in 1994 showed that 52 per cent of turnover of east German firms stayed within the region; by 1996 the proportion had fallen to 43 per cent.[22] The skewed size distribution of manufacturing firms towards small and medium-size categories (see above) is one factor making the penetration of markets outside the region difficult.

CONCLUSIONS

The regional and institutional mismatch problems dominate east Germany's prospects. But an additional factor that hampered convergence was the macroeconomic policies of the Bundesbank and the federal government. Two stages of macroeconomic policy can be identified. Firstly, it was inevitable that unification would raise the level of aggregate demand in west Germany as the extra spending in east Germany pulled in goods and services from the west. This would boost employment. Inflationary pressure was bound to increase unless either there was an appreciation of the Deutschmark, which would have tended to reduce import prices and boost real wages, lessening wage inflation, or there was a negotiated agreement between the government, employers and unions as to the sharing of the burden of unification. Neither of these moves occurred. Membership of the exchange rate mechanism and the unwillingness of France and the UK to agree to a revaluation of the DM ruled out the first. The unwillingness of the federal government to accept the scale of the burden that unification would entail was at least partly responsible for ruling out the second. The result was a sharp rise in wage inflation in the early 1990s that led inevitably to the Bundesbank tightening monetary policy. The consequences of this were the collapse of the ERM and the onset of recession across continental Europe.

The second stage of macroeconomic policy centres on fiscal policy: tight monetary policy in the early 1990s was followed by a phase of very tight fiscal policy from 1994. Unification inevitably meant a rise in the fiscal burden for west Germany and therefore for the Federal Republic as a whole. A number of economists pointed out soon after unification that it should be seen as an investment project for west Germany and that deficit finance was the appropriate way to pay for it. This rationale clashed with both the dominant domestic concern with reducing the burden of national debt and with the timetable for meeting the Maastricht criteria for European monetary union, one component of which was that national debt to GDP ratios should be below 60 per cent. Even if the national case for a substantial temporary rise in the debt ratio above 60 per cent in order to smooth the costs of unification over time had been accepted, the central role of Germany in the EMU project raised a major obstacle. As a result, the balance between tax and deficit finance to pay for unification was tilted towards the former. This depressed demand in west Germany and increased the rate of unemployment required to hold down inflation there, as the evidence suggests that workers in west Germany were less willing to accept cuts in take-home pay due to unification-related tax increases than was typical for other tax rises.

The macroeconomic straitjacket has worsened the conditions for the successful incorporation of the east German economy into the Federal Republic. Weak growth in west Germany lessened the incentives for west German firms to increase capacity by purchasing Treuhand firms and setting up greenfield plants. Without a sufficient density of west German companies operating in the east technology transfer and serious vocational training on the west German model cannot work. Whilst the continuation of support from the west for investment in east Germany is necessary, institutional innovation will also be required in the east if it is to achieve self-sustaining growth.

NOTES

This paper makes extensive use of previous work that I have done – often in collaboration with others – on the economic transformation of the east German economy. The relevant references are listed as appropriate below. Since this paper is based on existing work, I have not generally repeated here the references to the literature reported there.

1. A standard source for the analysis of transition is the annual *Transition Report* published by the European Bank for Reconstruction and Development.
2. The transformation of the financial sector in east Germany and the comparison with other transition economies is discussed in W. Carlin and P. Richthofen, 'Finance, Economic Development and the Transition: The East German Case', *Economics of Transition*, Vol.3, No.2 (1995), pp.169–95.
3. For a more detailed discussion, see P. Aghion, O. Blanchard and W. Carlin, 'The Economics of Enterprise Restructuring in Eastern Europe', in J. Roemer (ed.), *Property Relations, Incentives and Welfare*. Proceedings of the IEA Conference (London: Macmillan, 1997), pp.271–318.
4. See W. Carlin and C. Mayer, 'The Treuhandanstalt: Privatization by State and Market', in O. Blanchard, K. Froot and J. Sachs (eds.), *The Transition in Eastern Europe: Volume 2: Restructuring* (Chicago: Chicago University Press and NBER, 1994), pp.189–213.
5. See, for example, EBRD, *Transition Report 1997* (London: EBRD, 1997), chapter 5.
6. For a detailed presentation of the results, in terms of ownership and control, of the privatisation process in east Germany, see W. Carlin and C. Mayer, 'The Structure and Ownership of East German Enterprises', *Journal of the Japanese and International Economies*, 9 (1995), pp.426–53.
7. For further detail, see W. Carlin, 'Privatisation and Deindustrialisation in East Germany', in S. Estrin (ed.), 'Privatisation in Central and Eastern Europe', in S. Estrin (ed.), *Privatisation in Central and Eastern Europe* (London: Longman, 1994), pp.127–53.
8. Detailed data is presented in Carlin and Mayer, 'The Structure and Ownership of East German Enterprises'.
9. The general economic argument in favour of the role of auctions in privatisation is set out clearly in K.M. Schmidt and M. Schnitzer, 'Methods of Privatization: Auctions, Bargaining, and Giveaways', in H. Giersch (ed.), *Privatization at the End of the Century* (Heidelberg: Springer Verlag Berlin, 1997), pp.97–133. An argument for the limited usefulness of auctions in the east German case is made in Carlin and Mayer, 'The Treuhandanstalt'.
10. This argument was made in Carlin, 'Privatisation and Deindustrialisation in East Germany'. A recent paper that provides comprehensive data on the Treuhand's activities including the management buy-out programme is D. Bös, 'Privatization in Eastern Germany: The Never-Ending Story of the Treuhand', in Giersch (ed.), *Privatization at the End of the Century*, pp.175–97.
11. Carlin and Mayer, 'The Structure and Ownership of East German Enterprises'.
12. For a detailed analysis of management transfer, see I.J.A. Dyck, 'Privatization in Eastern Germany: Management Selection and Economic Transition', *American Economic Review*, Vol.87, No.4 (Sept. 1997), pp.565–97.
13. This section is based on A. Boltho, W. Carlin and P. Scaramozzino, 'Will East Germany become a new Mezzogiorno?', *Journal of Comparative Economics*, Vol.24 (1997), pp.241–64.
14. M. Abramowitz, 'Catching Up, Forging Ahead, and Falling Behind', *Journal of Economic History*, Vol.46. No.2 (June 1986), pp.385–406; W.J. Baumol, 'Productivity Growth, Convergence, and Welfare: What the Long-Run Data Show', *American Economic Review*, Vol.76, No.5 (Dec. 1986), pp.1072–85.
15. K-H. Paqué, 'East–West Wage Rigidity in United Germany: Causes and Consequences', *Kiel Working Papers* No. 572 (1993), p.22.
16. This section is based on the arguments set out in W. Carlin and D. Soskice, 'Shocks to the System: The German Political Economy under Stress', *National Institute Economic Review*, No.159 (1997), pp.57–76.
17. For example, R.J. Barro and X. Sala-i-Martin, 'Convergence Across States and Regions', *Brookings Papers on Economic Activity*, No.1 (1991), pp.107–82.
18. Sachverständigenrat zur Begutachtung der gesamtwirtschaftlichen Entwicklung, *Jahresgutachten 1997/98* (Stuttgart, Metzler-Poeschel, 1997).
19. Reported in Boltho *et al.*, 'Will East Germany become a new Mezzogiorno?'.
20. Table 3 in Carlin and Soskice, 'Shocks to the System: The German Political Economy under

     Stress', p.60.
21. For a detailed analysis of the evolution of services in east Germany see Deutsches Institut für
     Wirtschaftsforschung, *DIW-Wochenbericht*, No.3 (1998).
22. *DIW-Wochenbericht*, No.32 (1997), p.552.

Employment, Welfare Support and Income Distribution in East Germany

CHRIS FLOCKTON

This survey seeks to sketch how the income level and income equality both among social groups in the new Länder, and also in relation to the position in west Germany, have evolved as a consequence of the deep restructuring since 1990, as well as a result of the welfare systems put in place by the treaties establishing unification. The paper surveys the macroeconomic evolution and the attendant deep changes in the labour market, focusing in particular on the level of wage catch-up with the west and on differentials by firm size, occupation and branch. It addresses initiatives to attack unemployment in the east and assesses the welfare safety net in the form of unemployment benefits and social assistance, as well as the pension system instituted. The relatively favourable pension provision and the broad coverage of the social benefit system have ensured that the deep economic restructuring has not led to widespread poverty, even if there is a pervasive feeling of insecurity. The effectiveness of the housing allowance system in moderating the impact of rent rises is also discussed. The paper finally addresses the question of income distribution in this rapid transition to the market, and shows that 'income poverty' has been contained to a level broadly equivalent to that of west Germany.

This survey seeks to sketch how the income levels and income inequality among social groups in the new Bundesländer, also relative to the position in west Germany, have evolved as a consequence of the slump and deep restructuring since 1990, as well as a result of the welfare systems put in place by the treaties establishing unification. The move to the market in east Germany has wrought changes deeper than most could have imagined, with unemployment affecting a majority of the workforce at some stage during the last eight years, with a prevalent feeling of insecurity, the completely new job structures and levels of remuneration, the loss of organisational support for the working woman and mother, and the harshness of unemployment which has hit harder both females and the older male worker. At the same time, the western social insurance schemes covering

Chris Flockton, University of Surrey.

unemployment, sickness and social assistance benefits and pensions, the western housing regime and housing allowances system, the panoply of labour market measures, have all been introduced. They have moderated the impact of deep restructuring in the economy, have kept incomes and consumption afloat in the east, and have brought benefits to some groups more than others, having therefore a differential impact.

Social transfers from west to east have been running at a gross DM 85 billion annually through the 1990s. These transfers are the equivalent of one-half of total income in the east, implying that local output only funds one-half of total expenditure. Such is the scale of western spending, as well as of western debt accumulation. This study therefore seeks to form a view of the level of incomes in the east relative to the west towards the end of the first decade of transformation, and to highlight shifts in relative incomes, including household poverty.

The eastern economy remains heavily dependent upon the west, in spite of gross transfers of DM 140 billion annually from federal funds alone, reaching an aggregate level of public spending of DM 1 trillion by 1997. The two treaties instituting unification in 1990 put in place the social welfare system of the old Federal Republic to moderate the severity of the profound restructuring. The key elements of the west's welfare system were rapidly instituted, with the Federal Labour Office taking responsibility for unemployment insurance from 1 July 1990, the sickness insurance schemes and the child benefit and child-rearing allowances provisions applied from 1991, and the pensions system was integrated from 1992, though with special 'social supplements' offered to top up what would otherwise be lower pension entitlements.[1]

The DM 115 billion German Unity Fund helped pump-prime the insurance funds in the east. Financial support was also given to the eastern local authorities to carry out their social assistance functions and to manage the social support facilities, housing stock and other infrastructures which had been devolved to them upon reallocation of parts of the old GDR state and Kombinat enterprise social assets. By the end of 1991, the full panoply of labour market intervention had helped soften the blow from the wholesale reshaping of the economy: short-time working covered 22 per cent of all employees, early retirement provisions affected ten per cent of the labour force, and the job creation measures and retraining provisions of the work promotion law were being expanded rapidly, given the realisation of the magnitude of the task of reform.

Given the scale of the recasting of the east German economy, it is surprising that there has not been more overt poverty and greater income differentiation than has in fact been experienced. As will be seen, the scale of so-called 'household income poverty' calculated on standard measures lies between 9.5 per cent and 12 per cent of east German households according to the comparator adopted. Clearly, the immense scale of the social transfers, the generous pension provisions, the housing allowances and long period of rent control have all contributed to this outcome. Such solidarity has helped bind the two parts of Germany, although resentment abounds, in spite of evidence that real household income levels in the east are not that far short of those in the west.

ECONOMIC EVOLUTION AND THE EMPLOYMENT/UNEMPLOYMENT OUTCOMES

The collapse in activity in 1989/90 and during the first years following unification led to a catastrophic shrinkage in the labour force and in the numbers employed. The true scale of mass unemployment was somewhat thinly disguised by all-pervasive, second labour market measures. Thus, accompanying the fall in industrial output in late 1991 to 60 per cent of its pre-unification level, there was a shrinkage in the numbers employed from 9.7 millions in 1989 to 6.6 millions in 1994. The numbers employed in industry in this heavily industrialised part of Germany fell from 3.3 million to 660,000. Overall, of those employed in 1994, only 25 per cent still worked at their original enterprise from 1990. In spite of the recovery in the fortunes of the east from 1993 to 1996, when it grew at eight or nine per cent annually, there has been no longer term improvement in the labour market, rather the reverse. The rapid growth in construction and manufacturing of 18 per cent annually during that period appeared to produce a consolidation in the labour market: there were small rises in employment in 1994 and 1995. However, the marked slowdown in 1996 and 1997, with the east growing significantly below the west's growth rate in 1997, has eradicated those employment gains, and produced a record low point in employment, worse than the depths reached in 1993.[2]

In spite of some marked successes, the evolution of the eastern economy still gives ground for concern and circumspection over what has been achieved so far. Thus, in real terms, output in the east has grown by 41 per cent over the period 1991–97, a time when the west grew in real terms by only seven per cent in total. However, as a proportion of Germany's total output, the share of the east has risen from 7.2 per cent to 11.6 per cent over this period, 1991–97: it remains too small, with a distorted economic structure which is incapable of generating self-sustaining growth.[3] The downturn in the west in very recent years and the crisis in the construction industry have taken their toll, such is the lack of balance in the eastern economy.[4] Thus, it was primarily the construction industry which made a very strong contribution in hauling the eastern economy out of slump from

1992 to 1994, and manufacturing began to achieve strong growth rates from later in 1993 onwards. The slowing and then shrinkage of the construction sector, following the expiry at the end of 1996 of highly generous tax allowances for construction investments under the *Fördergesetz,* dragged the regional economy into a slow growth phase and exacerbated the unemployment crisis. Since construction contributed 16 per cent to GDP in 1996, compared with 14.6 per cent for manufacturing, the fact that manufacturing was still expanding its output strongly could only moderate the negative impact on output and employment.[5] In 1996, the eastern economy grew at only 1.9 per cent and at 1.6 per cent in 1997. In January 1997, there were 158,000 unemployed construction workers in the east.[6] In respect of the private services sector, this has grown only relatively weakly since 1995, after growing at eight per cent in the period 1992–95. Thus, in spite of making up 30 per cent of regional output, it has done little to help absorb the mass of the unemployed.

The manufacturing sector in the east suffers from a smaller firm size, poorer product development and marketing skills than the west, and is burdened with labour costs which make profitability something of a distant prospect.[7] On average, eastern manufacturing enterprises employ only 95 workers, compared with 140 in the west; they suffer from a marked shortage of own capital; and their weak market presence, relative lack of competitiveness and poorer technological level mean that they export from the region only 15 per cent of output, compared with 33 per cent by west German firms. Goods exports from east Germany make up only three per cent of total German goods exports. In such a situation, finding the resources and the innovation to generate self-sustaining growth is an extremely difficult task. Investment rates per employee in industry have been good, with levels in the east one-half higher than those in the west in the period 1991–96, and, in fact, running at double the western rate since 1993. Financially, though, firms have been crippled by the high labour charges and the low productivity. As a result of the wage harmonisation agreed in the autumn and winter of 1990/91 by the west German trade unions for eastern firms, often in Treuhandanstalt hands, a staged progression of eastern collective wage rates to the full western rate was agreed for the period to 1994. After strikes in 1993 over employers' attempts to delay the staged harmonisation, it was agreed that the full harmonisation would take place by negotiation by 1996. Thus east German wage costs rose by 33 per cent in 1992 and by 15 per cent in 1993. Although the situation varies by sector, tariff wage costs at the end of 1997 varied between 85 per cent and 100 per cent of the German level and, even in 1996, hourly wage costs in manufacturing were 50 per cent higher in east Germany than in the UK. Of course, it is not the wage cost itself which is critical for competitiveness, but the unit labour cost, which expresses labour costs in relation to productivity, or output. At the end of 1996, east German productivity per head was in total only 58 per cent of the western level. For all sectors in the east, unit labour costs were 23 per cent above the western level in 1997, after being 50 per cent above in 1991.[8] The position differed markedly by sector, however. Thus, in 1997, unit labour costs in eastern manufacturing had fallen to only five per cent above those of the west, while in private services they were 35 per cent above and in distribution, transport and communications, 23 per cent above.[9] Such high unit costs signal poor competitiveness and weak or non-existent profit margins.

Returning then to the level of employment, it will be clear that cost pressures in both manufacturing and services have made expansion of their workforces a difficult prospect in the face of rapid labour shedding in the construction industry. 1997 was the first year since unification in which no sector in the east generated job growth, and in December 1997 employment reached only 71 per cent of that of the first quarter in 1991. Employment was lower than in the trough of 1993. It is hardly surprising that 400,000 easterners commuted to the west for work. By sector, the following applied:

- employment in private services rose from 1 million to 1.4 million in the years to 1994, but since late 1996 all branches of private services have been shedding labour;
- there was a rapid expansion in public services employment to 1.5 million by the end of 1991, but staffing per inhabitant is 45 per cent higher than in the west, and large cuts in the staffs of general administration, health and social security are expected;[10]
- the numbers of new self-employed had risen to 510,000 in the period 1990–95 and stabilised subsequently;[11]
- new entrepreneurs, setting up their own firms, make up about seven per cent of the self-employed, compared with approximately ten per cent in west Germany.

The impression gained, therefore, is the rather gloomy picture that no alleviation of the poor labour market position in the east can be foreseen in the medium term: manufacturing, even if it sustains an economic upturn, may not generate many new jobs, and other sectors can be expected to continue to shed staff. In 1997, total employment fell again, by 200,000 to 6.05 million.

Turning to the unemployed, there has been a very marked rise in recent years, to reach an average, seasonally adjusted level of 1.49 million in 1997, or 18.1 per cent, compared with 15.7 per cent in 1996. The rate therefore stands at double that in the west. The evolution in the unemployment rate is not solely a function of demographics and employment creation, it also is heavily influenced by the special labour market measures, which reduce the unemployment count. As mentioned earlier, in the period to the end of 1992, the 1.6 million beneficiaries of short-time working pay (often when they had 'zero' work) and the 750,000 beneficiaries of early retirement assistance kept unemployment down to approximately 1.2 million. In later years, such as at the end of 1995, half a million were in receipt of training, job creation and special wage subsidy measures. The rise in registered unemployment since then reflects both the underlying economic forces, together with a marked shrinkage, particularly of early retirement assistance, but also of second labour market measures (where there were cuts of 50,000 in job creation places and of 95,000 in further training places).[12]

Women have borne much more of the brunt of unemployment, with an average unemployment rate of 22 per cent in 1997. According to a Bundesbank report of 1998, they make up 56 per cent of the unemployed, compared with 42 per cent in the west.[13] This points to gendered recruitment and redundancy practices which prejudice the chances of women, as well as the differential shrinkage in what are more traditional female occupations. However, it also reflects the very pronounced labour market participation of women, which reaches 90 per cent of the working age group, compared with 70 per cent in the west. This pushes up overall participation rates, and, for an equal supply of employment in east and west, this higher participation would have the effect of raising the eastern unemployment rate possibly ten percentage points above that which would occur in the west.

WAGES AND WAGE DIFFERENTIALS

In 1997, the rapid pace of wage equalisation with western levels slowed markedly, in spite of the *Stufenverträge* (wage harmonisation agreements). At the end of 1991, the collective wage level had stood at 60 per cent of the west, at 89 per cent at the end of 1996, and at the end of 1997, it stood at 89.5 per cent. However, this far from reveals the wage cost burden, since there are longer hours worked and lower benefits paid in the east. For example, in the east, the weekly hours worked are two hours longer (which extends machine running times, even if it does not affect hourly wage costs), and there are western benefits which are not paid in the east, such as the 13th month wage, some holiday pay, employee savings/share accounts, and, in particular, employers will tend not to pay above the tariff wage, which is common practice in the west. The effective wage paid in the west is often considerably more than the collective wage. Rather, the practice of paying less than the collective wage in the east is far more typical. Legally, firms may pay less than the collective wage, either if the firm is not a member of the employers' federation for the branch/region which negotiated the agreement, or if the firm has a firm-level agreement with union representatives, which expressly allows for less than tariff wage in certain circumstances – these are normally for the recruitment of the long-term unemployed (opening clauses), or where the firm faces financial difficulty (hardship clauses).

In the east, it is thought that approximately 60 per cent of firms, with 50 per cent of the workforce, are not covered by a collective agreement, only by a firm-level agreement. The east German electrical and engineering industries have only 30 per cent of their firms covered by such collective agreements, admittedly it is the larger firms which are members, while the *Mittelstand*, medium-sized firms, tend to have firm-level agreements. In Saxony, for example, 65 per cent of firms in these industries have left collective bargaining. The gain for a firm which is in a dire financial position is clear: while the tariff wage lies at broadly 90 per cent of the western level, the non-tariff wage lies at 77 per cent. Lastly, in the construction industry, in the face of a wave of bankruptcies, and the distortions to competing cost structures posed by the widespread use of foreign 'loan workers' at low rates, many firms pay less than the tariff wage, or they re-classify their staff into the lower paid job groupings. As a result of the 'Posted Workers' Law (*Entsendegesetz*), a minimum wage has applied for two years on construction sites in the east, however, this minimum level lies at only 60 per cent of the collective wage level, and so allows widespread undercutting of the tariff wage. Such is the force of financial exigency, when firms face bankruptcy. In recent years, there have been strikes in the east, in the building and engineering sectors, seeking to force through 100 per cent of the western wage, but reality at the level of the firm continues to impose itself. As will be seen below, firms have sought a much greater flexibility in the collective wage agreement system, which would allow, via hardship and opening clauses, as well as arrangements for more flexible working, for firm-level agreements to flesh out considerably the collective agreements, and so attain provisions which reflect more closely the financial and operating requirements of the firm. In particular, the 'Common Initiative for More Jobs in East Germany' of May 1997, agreed on a tripartite basis, awakened hopes of this kind. As will be seen, this led to disenchantment, as did earlier attempts at a greater flexibility in the east, to reflect better the poor competitive position of eastern manufacturing.

In terms of the level of income for those in work, we have to consider the average effective wage/salary level paid, the net level (taking account of the lower tax incidence), and the real income per household, given that the price level remains ten per cent lower in the east for a standard household.

Thus, in mid-1996 the average effective wage and salary lay at 78 per cent of the western level, and at 87 per cent net of tax and deductions. Per standardised household, incomes lay at only 72 per cent of the west in nominal terms, but at well over three-quarters in real terms. This lower cost of living relates primarily to lower rent levels, lower administered prices for heating and transport, and lower personal services costs.[14] However, for some groups of households, real incomes now approximate those in the west: this is the case for four-person worker/clerical households, and in the case of two-person pensioner households it may be that the real income is greater than their western equivalents.[15]

How has the wage distribution changed between social categories within the labour force? Of course, there were wage differentials even in GDR times, which reflected university education status and the skilled/unskilled division. The largest part of income inequality lies within socio-economic groups rather than between them. Pre-existing GDR differences have since been amplified by differential pay on the basis of performance, motivation, adaptability, and so on. There are, however, interesting gender differences in respect of the evolution of skill wage premia. For males, their inherited skill premia have been lost, following unification, such that there are not now such pay differentials for university education and skilled status. In a sense, the human capital acquired under socialism has been devalued, or written off, and the clearest example lies in the wholesale early retirement or redundancy of the older workers, who, when they remain in the labour market, face large falls in income relative to their earlier expectation. In the case of women, no such loss of differential has been experienced, and education, skill and experience in some expanding branches are key factors in their career progress.[16] Other key influences on differentials are whether the firm is large or small, and whether the firm is in a sector exposed to extra-regional competition. Clearly, large firms pay more, and this may relate to their paying at the tariff wage, but large firms may also be exposed to international competition, which depresses the wage rate. In the public sector, there is no evidence of market impacts on wage rates, as would be expected, rather the greatest impact on differentials has been an adjustment to the western civil service job hierarchy, which has widened inherited differentials.[17] Average gross incomes in farming lay close to the western level in mid-1996, those in public services lay at 85 per cent, and in services at 78 per cent. In manufacturing, however, they lay at only 68 per cent at that time.[18] This clearly shows the extent to which the enterprise is exposed to competition impacts upon the relative wage level.

Overall, then, it is clear that the catch-up in wage levels with the west has slowed, and that key influences on wage levels and differentials are the membership or otherwise of the collective wage agreement, the size of the firm, the exposure to extra-regional competition and the sectoral differences associated with this. In real terms, the gap between real household incomes in east and west is far less. A much lesser element in incomes, however, is formed by interest and dividend income from savings. Over the time-scale 1990–96, household monetary holdings have risen by 2.5 times and lie at one-third of the western level, compared with one-fifth in 1990. Rent incomes from property ownership must be far lower than in the west, given that home ownership and property ownership is much less developed in the east.[19]

WELFARE SUPPORT: UNEMPLOYMENT ASSISTANCE, BENEFIT PROVISIONS AND PENSIONS

The labour market programmes and social support budgets represent the lion's share of federal spending in the new Länder, although the eastern Länder and local authorities themselves bear a significant share of the burden, particularly in the form of social assistance itself. Two-thirds of the total transfers to the east still take the form of income support payments, whether unemployment benefit and unemployment assistance, social assistance, housing benefit, pensions, or health- and nursing care assistance: the scale of these transfers accounts very largely for the recurrent fiscal crises and contemporary pressures on German welfare provision. From a purely west German viewpoint, in spite of the record western unemployment levels of recent years, the west German unemployment, pension and health insurance funds have been in surplus through the 1990s and so it is these surpluses, the rise in contribution rates, and the increasing scale of federal indebtedness, which have funded the income support transfers to the east.[20] As shown above, in response to the unemployment crisis in the east there has been a succession of high-profile political initiatives to moderate the impact of restructuring, to promote reskilling and the transfer of labour to new activities and into early retirement. Together this labour market and social support has required a DM 84 billion transfer annually to the east in each of the years from 1996 to 1998, and forecasts foresee a continuation of support at this level.

In a succession of initiatives, the federal government has sought to bring employers, investors and trade unions together, in combination with its own federal programmes, to create jobs and generate the conditions in which a labour market upturn would be possible. The Solidarity Pact of 1993 was the first of these, in which banks and employers undertook to raise their investment levels in the east, while the unions promised to pursue collective agreements which more reflected the condition of mass unemployment (without, however, reversing their push for wage harmonisation, which was one of the most damaging influences on employment). The Eastern Alliance for Jobs of 1995 included further such commitments, and, in particular, union commitments to include hardship clauses and entry clauses in their collective agreements, so as to provide some relief to crisis-hit firms. The Common Initiative for More Employment in the East of May 1997 carried further the commitment by the unions to open up more flexibly their collective agreements by offering greater scope for firm-level agreements: here, the government and employers accepted the objective of stabilising employment in the east in 1997 and of raising employment levels by 100,000 in 1998. Lastly, the February 1998 Stimulus for more Jobs, announced by the federal government in an election year, reversed the large-scale cuts in job creation places experienced in 1997 and provided for an additional 100,000 places in the eastern Länder in 1998.

In May 1998 the trade unions cancelled their participation in the Eastern Alliance for Jobs: this was evidence of deep resentment and disappointment on their part. These feelings were in fact shared by all agents. The unions claimed that the employers had not invested, had not preserved jobs and that the federal government was cynically manipulating job creation programmes in an election year. Criticism of the trade unions was also very widespread: they were pursuing sometimes sizeable real wage increases and further reductions in working time, and they had interpreted flexibility clauses very restrictively indeed, even though they were suffering a haemorrage of members due to the employment crisis. The federal government, for its part, can be criticised for electioneering in its policy reversal over the scale of job creation programmes in the east. It has also tightened the eligibility conditions for the continued receipt of unemployment benefit: in particular, through the Stimulus for more Jobs of February 1998, it has linked the award of social assistance for the able-bodied to acceptance of a job creation position, or training post (see below). However, in aggregate, the government has withstood much of the criticism in the west over the scale of its financial support to the new Länder, and it has carried forward largely unchanged its assistance programmes (implying total federal net transfers of at least DM 94 billion annually) until the end of 2004.

In terms of direct labour market expenditure, total spending by the Federal Labour Office and the federal government in east Germany reached DM 50.1 billion in 1997, of which the government paid directly one-quarter. In net terms, only the payment by the Labour Office can be disaggregated and it amounted to DM 26.3 billion, with one-third of all expenditures flowing to the east, but only one-sixth of revenues arising there. In addition, the federal government funds the office's deficit and pays directly for unemployment assistance, *Arbeitslosenhilfe* (payable once eligibility for unemployment benefit has expired) and for early retirement assistance for those otherwise unemployed (*Altersübergangsgeld*). More than 60 per cent of labour market expenditure in the east takes the form of passive transfers, namely, unemployment and early retirement income support, while 38 per cent is devoted to so-called active labour market measures, which comprise primarily job creation and retraining measures, with a small proportion of the funding devoted to direct wage subsidies for the previously long-term unemployed. The scale of job creation places has fallen from a high point of 390,000 in 1992, to a low of 155,000 in 1997, although this has been inflated by the exceptional extra 100,000 for 1998, mentioned earlier. Under such schemes, the wage costs are paid to 98 per cent of the total by the Labour Office, but it funds a minor proportion of the capital costs. This in itself favours labour-intensive activities, with little capital equipment. Typically, the organiser of the programme meets only 11 per cent of the total costs.

A marked characteristic of the pervasive job creation schemes in the east has been that the majority have been offered by local authorities anxious to lower local unemployment: the vehicle adopted has been that of the 'employment enterprise', the ABS or *Beschäftigungsgesellschaft*. This organisational form was intended by the Work Promotion Law as a transitional arrangement to permit the retraining of workers shed by a large employer. The trainees remain in an employment contract and therefore receive 100 per cent of their previous earnings level, paid by the Labour Office (compared with 63 per cent or 68 per cent for the unemployed). The employment enterprise was first introduced in the east in 1991 in failing enterprises of the *Treuhandanstalt*, but since 1992 it has become almost a permanent institution of local authorities, to manage much of the labour shedding locally. Under special regulations for east Germany, local authorities could utilise employment enterprises to fulfil many of their legal functions, such as environmental improvement, maintenance of playgrounds and sports facilities, and so on. Two prime difficulties could have been foreseen at the outset. Firstly, such wholly subsidised enterprises are attractive to local authorities (for whom the financial commitment is minor) but they undercut the tenders for work by private service providers, and, since they maintain the previous wage level, they make even more rigid the wage conditions in the east. From a market viewpoint, the mechanism is therefore one of a distortion of competition. Secondly, and equally seriously, the training offered in these schemes is of poor technical level, since the capital stock is weak or non-existent, and one-half of participants are engaged in gardening and environmental clean-up tasks. They are no better placed on the open labour market than are unskilled workers. The renewed work promotion law, which applied from April 1997, sought to

address some of these deficiencies. Firstly, it forbade unfair competition and
stressed that job creation measures should primarily be funded in
commercial organisations. The law also expanded the area of tasks to
include all renovation and restoration of monuments and buildings, and it
introduced a range of direct subsidies to employers, in the form of
recruitment and wage subsidies, initial trial employment contracts and
special training measures, all designed to absorb the older and longer term
unemployed. The total number benefiting from wage subsidies in these
various forms amount to 80,000 in the new Länder.

The Stimulus for More Jobs of February 1998 addressed the situation of
social assistance (*Sozialhilfe*) recipients in the east: it channelled more
funds to local authorities, and at the same time also tightened the conditions
for personal eligibility for assistance. Using *Kreditanstalt für Wiederaufbau*
funds, the federal government sought to allocate several billion
Deutschmarks to local authorities in the east, to enable them to organise an
extra 100,000 job creation places for social assistance recipients, to induce
the latter to re-enter the labour market. This would be in addition to the
200,000 work scheme places already organised by the municipalities. On
such schemes, recipients receive DM 3 per hour in addition to the social
assistance benefit, or a total of DM 1,500 monthly, but where individuals
refuse to participate benefit is refused: it is therefore the element of
compulsion which has attracted most criticism, as well as the implication
that such schemes establish a low wage floor for unskilled work. However,
upon completion of a one-year scheme, the participant re-establishes a
claim to the relatively favourable German unemployment benefits.

The numbers of social assistance recipients (that is, those receiving
direct income support) in east Germany rose from 217,000 in 1991 to
306,000 at the end of 1996 and reached 14 per 1,000 inhabitants. This
compares with 20 per 1,000 in the west. In several ways, there are important
differences between west and east Germany. The proportion of foreigners in
receipt of assistance, at 6.4 per cent, is far lower than the 26 per cent share
in west Germany. Secondly, the share of young people (those younger than
25 years) is markedly higher in the east (at 54 per cent compared with 45
per cent in the west).[21] Furthermore, a prime reason why there is a markedly
smaller proportion of social assistance recipients among the general
population in the east lies in the fact that far fewer retired people benefit,
since pension provisions reflect lifetime employment and leave east
Germans – women in particular – relatively well provided for. Lastly,
among recipients of working age, 54 per cent were unemployed, the greater
majority of these having exhausted their unemployment benefit and
assistance. Of the 150,000 recipients of income support in its narrowest
definition, 38 per cent were single, and 27 per cent constituted single

mothers. Overall, a net DM 4.7 billion was paid in social assistance in the new Länder in 1996, with an average monthly payment of DM 641, compared with DM 819 in west Germany, where, in particular, rent levels are higher.[22] Finally, the east German social assistance level is approximately three-quarters of that of the west, and, in the east, it guarantees an income level which is 87 per cent of the average east German wage. From these statistics one might conclude that the system of social assistance is well targeted and that, in principle, it affords a safety net which is quite favourably placed in relation to average incomes.

Concerning pensions, there can be little doubt that east German pensioners are among the main beneficiaries of German unification. Under the GDR, pensioners received a pension which guaranteed only a subsistence level of existence, although rents, transport and energy, as well as basic foodstuffs and other items of everyday consumption were very heavily subsidised.[23] The Treaty on Economic, Monetary and Social Union provided for the full application of the west German pension system, and recognised the years of service accumulated by employees under the socialist regime. The first revision to eastern pensions took place in January 1991 with a 45 per cent rise, and so 20 per cent of all east German households automatically benefited. Measured in terms of the reference pension ('*Eckrente*') payable after 45 years, east German pensions have risen from 30 per cent of western in 1990 to over 90 per cent in 1995 and to even higher levels since. Of particular benefit have been both the recognition of the longer years of working in the east and the crediting of extra years of service granted by the GDR, the so-called '*Auffüllbeträge*'. Since both males and females had longer work histories than their western counterparts, and, particularly, since females were credited favourably under the socialist family policy with years spent in their children's upbringing, the east Germans have significantly longer years of service. Men, for instance, have 46.6 years of pensionable service in the east, compared with 39.3 years in the west. Under the German pension insurance scheme, pensions are linked to years of service, to the final salary averaged over a number of years and they are 'dynamic' in the sense that the pension grows with the cost of living. Given that more years of service are credited, this gives the result that pensions for females tend to be on average ten per cent higher than in the west, in spite of the lower final salary. For males, the pension level is 91 per cent of the western level. The recognition of the extra years credited, the *Auffüllbeträge*, is costly and affects 2.2 million of the 4.3 million pensioners in the east. It is not surprising that there are voices heard for a consolidation of these advantages by their incorporation in future annual pension increases. The CDU pensions expert, Andreas Storm, called, for instance, for slower rises in the east than otherwise justified by a mechanical calculation, since were wage levels to be equalised between east and west then the eastern male pension would lie at 11.5 per cent above the equivalent western level.[24] It is clear, therefore, that pensioners as a group have fared well since unification and can be seen as clear winners in the redistribution of incomes since 1990. One might also conclude from this discussion of unemployment and social assistance provisions that, broadly speaking, the social coverage is wide, of relatively long duration and is, in the early years of benefit, income-related to an acceptable level. This is not to say that unemployment is not a source of deep misfortune in the east, but only that a social safety net is in place. Those who slip through the net do so on account of particular personal circumstances.

RENTS AND HOUSING ALLOWANCES

The housing situation and housing policy in east Germany is treated in some detail in a separate chapter in this volume, and contained there is a discussion of the rent rises which have taken place since unification. The focus of interest here is placed more on the distributional aspects of the housing allowances paid to moderate the impact of the rent rises. Briefly, large-scale rent rises had to take place after unification, given the fact that rents had been heavily controlled in the GDR, and, in the case of the pre-war housing stock, they had been held at the level last set under the Nazi regime in 1936. Rents of DM 1 per square metre were commonplace, and the total lack of incentive for owners to modernise, as well as the almost total neglect of the pre-war housing stock by the authorities as a matter of policy, meant that with the move to the market, controlled rent rises would be needed to generate the incentive to modernise and to renovate an often decaying stock.[25] The Unification Treaty provided, though, that rent rises could only be implemented as incomes grew, and so a long period of controlled rents was foreseen. The first Basic Rent Decree, applicable from 1 October 1991, together with the Housing Running Costs Decree, permitted monthly rent rises according to condition and equipment of the property of from DM 0.70 to DM 1.30 per square metre of living space. The running costs could rise by up to DM 3 per square metre monthly. In parallel, the Special Housing Allowance Law came into force to moderate the rent rise impact. The Second Basic Rent Decree came into force on 1 January 1993, and rents rose substantially. Lastly, legislation inaugurating the transition to the west German system of 'comparable rents' was passed in June 1995, coming into effect in August 1996. This *Mietüberleitungsgesetz* provided for the abolition of the existing rent control system in the east by the end of 1997 and for the introduction of a 'rent mirror' in towns and cities, which would form the basis of a comparable rents system from January 1998.[26] Throughout the period, special housing allowances accompanied this large-scale rent rise, with the Special Housing Allowance Law applying to the end of 1996, and the subsequent Housing Allowance Transition Law applying to the end of 1998. This last legislation has been extended for a further two years to the end of 2000.[27]

Turning to the impact of the rent rises on disposable incomes, and the distributional impact of the housing allowances, it is clear firstly that, in spite of the doubling of rent levels on average over the period 1992–97, the share of net income spent on rent has been contained. The 1997 Housing Allowance and Rent Report states that, inclusive of heating costs, rents in the east represent 23 per cent of net incomes compared with 27 per cent in the west.[28] Rapid wage catch-up and the allocation of housing allowances have made the situation tolerable. However, one must bear in mind the smaller size of eastern dwellings and their often poorer level of equipment with all facilities: average rents are DM 500 monthly, compared with DM 742 monthly in the west, but this reflects the smaller size of dwellings, whereby, with an average floorspace of 62 square metres, dwellings in the east are fully ten square metres smaller than in the west. At first, in 1991, only 132,000 eastern households drew housing allowances, and these tended to be owners, who after unification had had to pay much higher interest charges, running and repair costs. Once the rent rises took effect, however, the special housing allowances were payable and, in 1992, two million households, almost every third household, drew the allowance. In the intervening period, to the end of 1996, the numbers eligible fell, reaching 627,900 households, or 9.2 per cent of the regional total, compared with 6.9 per cent in the old Länder. Allowances averaged DM 83 per inhabitant compared with DM 73 in west Germany. A particularly favourable feature of the calculation of the allowance in the east has been that it included heating and warm water costs (excluded in the west), and relatively favourable maximum upper cost limits applied in the calculation of the allowance payable. One-third of the permissible housing costs are therefore covered by the housing allowance in the east, compared with only 22 per cent in the west.

If we look at the distributional impact, then it is apparent that the composition of the recipients of housing allowance has changed markedly over time. The 1992 Socio-Economic Panel reveals that, in that year, more than 28 per cent of households received housing allowance, and that of the 20 per cent of poorest households, two-thirds received the allowance. Among pensioner households in this lowest income category, 70 per cent received the allowance.[29] The coverage of the allowance was therefore in general appropriate, even if a more exhaustive programme might have been desirable. A study by the Federal Statistical Office reveals that, over the years 1991–96, the proportion of pensioners among housing allowance recipients has fallen by well over one-half to 22 per cent and of that of the employed by one-third to 20 per cent: large rises in the shares of the unemployed to 36 per cent and of social assistance recipients to 14 per cent can be seen.[30] Thus, the allowance has, as would be expected, reflected the relative evolution of the incomes of different social groups. Pensioners are relatively well placed, as are those in work: poverty tends obviously to be associated with lack of employment and with one-parent family status: the sick and handicapped form smaller groups among the social assistance recipients of the separate, fixed-sum housing allowance (*pauschaliertes Wohngeld*). As noted in the chapter on housing in this volume, the freeing of rents according to the west German comparable rents system is not expected to lead to large rent rises, for perhaps three main reasons. The comparable rents in the east are heavily influenced by the legacy of controlled rents, there is a sizeable overhang of property, given the earlier construction boom, and, in the case of the many dwellings still requiring modernisation, there is an upper limit on monthly rent rises of DM 3 per square metre in the case of comprehensive renovation of the property. Evidently, the requirement in the Unification Treaty that rent rises be permitted only as incomes grow has been observed as a general principle. Larger rent rises occur once a rent contract has expired and is re-issued. It is true that rents now form a significantly larger part of eastern incomes than they did in the GDR, but, nevertheless, they are lower as a proportion than in the west, and the application of housing allowances does appear to have been well targeted. The widespread antagonism in the east to the rent rises must therefore be seen primarily as deriving from a desire for the old certainties under the GDR and as a further source of worry among a population scarred by unemployment.

INCOME DISTRIBUTION AND 'INCOME POVERTY'

From the foregoing it will be clear that, while income equality for those in work has not yet reached the levels of the west (in terms of the effective wage paid), nevertheless the gap in terms of income net of tax and deductions has narrowed. Furthermore, real household incomes show a much closer alignment on western real incomes, both for four-person worker and clerical households and for two-person pensioner households. There have been substantial changes in the relative income positions of social groups in east Germany over the last eight years (even if changes within groups tend to be larger), because of differences by branch and firm size, and by whether the employer is sheltered from or exposed to competition. Broadly speaking, among the principal gainers from this redistribution have been the retired, for the reason that pension arrangements have benefited those with many accumulated years of service, and for the reason that western, 'dynamic' pensions are far more favourable than the existence-level pensions of the GDR years. Also prime beneficiaries are the self-employed, who may have benefited from the currency exchange, the restitution of property, and from the extremely favourable investment allowances and grants of the past eight years. In the GDR, there were 83,000 craft enterprises in 1989; in 1996 there were 120,000, while employment in them had risen by one million to 1.4 million. The total number of self-employed is 1.4 million.[31] The losers, without any doubt, are the many unemployed (which include a high proportion of females), single mothers, who also face much worse employment and childcare conditions, and the older worker who experienced repeated stretches of unemployment without effective prospects of continuous employment again. For these, forced early retirement may have curtailed the individual's final pension prospects through an abbreviated working career, or those continuing in the labour market face a succession of job creation schemes and poorer paid work in relative terms. In this latter case, individuals have lost the skill premia they once could command and their interrupted work histories also seriously affect their future pension entitlements. Finally, there are the poor who have irregular work histories and who were poor under the old GDR as well as in the new Germany.[32]

The depth of the restructuring has wrought fundamental changes in the relative labour market position of individuals and groups, and some have risen, while others have fallen. Thus, measures of income differentiation, which aggregate and average these movements, disguise the full scale of the relative shifts. This is the case with the commonly accepted measure of income poverty, which in this context seeks to test whether there has been much greater income differentiation, leading to a greater incidence of poverty. As will be seen, such measures lead to the conclusion that the scale of income differentiation has been held in check, and that income poverty is still less in the east than in West Germany. By convention, income poverty is defined as the proportion of households (standardised for statistical reasons) which have a net household income of less than one-half the average household income: those with less than 40 per cent of the average net household income are said to suffer 'strict poverty',[33] one can gain a sense of the extent of poverty relative to the average. Studies here of the Socio-Economic Panel of test households measure income poverty of households in relation to (a) the average household income within east Germany, (b) the west German average, and (c) the household income judged satisfactory by west Germans. Here, the purpose is to assess income differentiation within the region, by comparison with the west, or against a subjective western income target. Adopting a comparison within east Germany itself, the proportion of households lying below the threshold net income rose from 3.5 per cent in 1990 to 7.9 per cent at the end of 1994 and then with little change through 1995. If the comparator is the subjective measure of a satisfactory income in west Germany, then 10.4 per cent of eastern households are to be regarded as income poor. Finally, in a comparison with west German household incomes, the income poverty rate stands at 12 per cent of households, a statistic comparable with conditions within west Germany.

CONCLUSION

This survey of the relative catch-up of eastern labour incomes with the west, of the all-pervasive labour market measures and early retirement in the east, so as to alleviate mass unemployment, of the mass of transfer incomes in the form of unemployment benefit and social assistance, of housing assistance and rent controls, points to a very considerable buffering (*'soziale Abfederung'*) of the devastating effects of slump and economic transformation which have touched the great majority of east Germans. The relatively generous benefits and the controlled freeing of rents and administered prices have all helped to soften the harshness of the adjustment and have established a solidaristic unity, even if the west resents the scale of the costs and the east hankers somewhat nostalgically after the past. Certainly, there are huge resentments in the east and only a grudging acknowledgement of the financial burden which the west has assumed. The living standards in the new Länder are now approximating those in the west for large groups in society, and the growth of income differentiation has been kept in bounds, with limited growth of income poverty. However, the unemployment and insecurity persist, together with a sense of loss of identity and of apparently more equitable social arrangements.

NOTES

1. S. Mangen, 'The Impact of Unification', in J. Clasen and R. Freeman, *Social Policy in Germany* (London: Harvester, 1994); E. Owen Smith, *The German Economy* (London: Routledge, 1994).
2. 'Zur Wirtschaftslage in Ostdeutschland', *Deutsche Bundesbank Monatsbericht* (April 1998), p.48.
3. 'Zur wirtschaftlichen Lage in den neuen Ländern und in Berlin-Ost', *Wirtschaft und Statistik* (March 1998), pp.183–212.
4. 'Zur Wirtschaftslage in Ostdeutschland'.
5. 'Zur wirtschaftlichen Lage in den neuen Bundesländern'.
6. *Handelsblatt*, 14 Jan. 1997.

7. *Deutsche Bundesbank Monthly Report* (June 1998).
8. 'Zur wirtschaftlichen Lage in den neuen Ländern'.
9. 'Zur Wirtschaftslage in Ostdeutschland'.
10. 'Öffentlicher Dienst: starker Personalabbau trotz moderater Tarifanhebungen', *Deutsches Institut für Wirtschaftsforschung (DIW) Wochenbericht*, No.5 (1998), pp.87–97.
11. 'Neue Selbständige in Deutschland in den Jahren 1990 bis 1995', *DIW Wochenbericht*, No.41 (1997), pp.749–53.
12. *Deutsche Bundesbank Monthly Report*, various issues.
13. 'Zur Wirtschaftslage in Ostdeutschland'. See also 'Women, Work and Family' in this volume.
14. *Handelsblatt*, 14 Jan. 1997
15. 'Zur Wirtschaftslage in Ostdeutschland'.
16. V. Steiner and P. Puhani, 'Economic Restructuring, the Value of Human Capital and the Distribution of Hourly Wages in East Germany 1990–94', *DIW-Vierteljahresheft zur Wirtschaftsforschung*, No.1 (1997), pp.197–204.
17. 'Weitere Annäherung der Arbeitseinkommen in Ost- und Westdeutschland: ostdeutsche Lohnstückkosten nach wie vor über Westniveau', *DIW-Wochenbericht*, 7 (1997), pp.119–25.
18. *Handelsblatt*, 17 March 1998.
19. 'Zur Wirtschaftslage in Ostdentschland'.
20. Details in C.H. Flockton, 'Germany's Long-Running Fiscal Crisis: Unification Costs or Unsustainability of Welfare State Arrangements?', *Debatte*, Vol.6, No.1 (1998), pp.79–93.
21. 'Zur sozialen Lage in den neuen Ländern und Berlin-Ost', *Wirtschaft und Statistik* (April 1998), pp.285–314.
22. 'Sozialhilfeempfänger und Empfänger von Leistungen nach dem Asylbewerberleistungsgesetz', *Wirtschaft und Statistik* (Oct. 1997), pp.720–26. Also, 'Ergebnisse der Sozialhilfe und Asylbewerberstatistik 1996', *Wirtschaft und Statistik* (June 1998), pp.509–19.
23. C.H. Flockton, 'Economic Transformation and Income Change', in E. Kolinsky (ed.), *Social Transformation and the Family* (London: Macmillan, 1998).
24. *Handelsblatt*, 14 April 1997.
25. G. Hallett, *Housing Needs in West and East Germany* (London: Anglo-German Foundation, 1994).
26. 'Zur sozialen Lage in den neuen Ländern und in Berlin-Ost'.
27. Bundesbauministerium, *Presseinformationen*, 27 May 1998.
28. Bundesbauministerium, *Presseinformationen*, 27 March 1998.
29. 'Die Einkommensverteilung nach Haushaltsgruppen in Deutschland seit der Mitte der achtziger Jahre', *DIW-Vierteljahresheft zur Wirtschaftsforschung*, Nos.3/4 (1993) .
30. 'Zur sozialen Lage in den neuen Ländern und in Berlin-Ost'.
31. *Handelsblatt*, 3 June 1996.
32. K. Müller *et al.*, 'How Unemployment and Income Inequality Changed in East and West Germany Following Unification', *DIW-Vierteljahresbericht zur Wirtschaftsforschung*, Nos.1/2 (1994).
33. For the following, see 'Ostdeutschland: 5 Jahre nach der Einheit', *DIW-Wochenbericht*, Nos.51/52 (1995); 'Löhne und Gehälter in Ost und Westdeutschland gleichen sich an, Lohnstückkosten jedoch nicht', *DIW-Wochenbericht*, No.8 (1996); 'Wohnungsmieten in Deutschland im Jahre 1995', *DIW-Wochenbericht*, Nos.22/3 (1996).

The Impact of German Unification on the German Industrial Relations System

KARL KOCH

The paper places the institutional transfer of employers' associations and trade unions from west to east in the framework of the systems concept of industrial relations. In response to the social and economic consequences of unification, industrial relations in the east have been subject to significant adjustments from the social partnership model in the west. Works councils in east Germany have expanded their role and developed co-operative relationships with management, leading to the establishment of micro-corporatism at plant level. This has, however, evolved in an interlocking configuration between works councils and the existing arrangements the collective bargaining partners have at sectoral/industry level.

A distinct characteristic of the unification process in Germany was the transfer of institutions from west Germany to east Germany. Institutional transfers were part of the overall transformation process of east Germany. A key institutional transfer was to be in the area of industrial relations. The analysis of this process has focused on the institutional dimension, that is, the agencies and actors in the field of industrial relations. However, industrial relations can be regarded in terms of a social sub-system which is constructed from both the variables acting on it as well as agencies and actors within it. The advantage of this approach is that it allows a more holistic analysis and includes the complexity of industrial relations as a system. It is, of course, recognised that the original industrial relations system concept has undergone numerous modifications to move it from a static model to a dynamic model. This facilitates a more contextual analysis of the multiple difficulties and consequences of the German unification process than just focusing on institutional transfer. The latter approach certainly influenced the pessimistic results of some researchers in regard to the ability of, for example, employers' associations and trade unions to adapt to the eastern German environment.[1] At the macro-level the original Dunlop model was limited by the selected number of factors which shaped the environment of the system. Thus industrial relations actors were seen to interact within three interrelated contexts:

Karl Koch, South Bank University.

The technology, the product and factor markets or budgetary constraints and the power relations in the larger community, and the derived status of the actors. An industrial relations system and its larger setting create an ideology or a commonly shared body of ideas and beliefs regarding the interaction and roles of the actors that helps to bind the system together.[2]

Constructing an extended, and more sophisticated, model provides a useful insight into the transformation of east German industrial relations to the west German framework. In this respect the ideal model would include all possible variables, but in practice there has to be some selection. This means that significant factors may well be omitted. For example, as Hyman has shown, the addition to the external environment of the societal and cultural heritage of the German Democratic Republic (GDR) is of considerable importance.[3] But this is a difficult dimension to include in an industrial relations systems framework.

The debate of the nature of industrial relations systems is concerned with interpretation and explanation of these sub-systems. Thus, for west Germany the contribution that industrial relations made to *Modell Deutschland* was summarised under the concept of corporatism. Corporatism as a concept is by no means consistent but varies according to the emphasis analysts ascribe to the mix and balance of the features that constitute it. However, included in the features are the organisational characteristics of trade unions and employers' associations, and how these relate to and interact with each other and how collective bargaining is conducted with, or without, the aid of the state. In this respect the systems approach can be welded on to Lehmbruch's definition of liberal corporatism:

By the term 'liberal corporatism' we mean a special type of participation by large organised social groups in public, especially economic policy making. Consultation and co-operation among administrations and organised interests is, of course, common in all constitutional democracies with a highly developed capitalist economy. But the distinguishing trait of 'liberal corporatism' is the high degree of co-operation among these groups themselves in their shaping of public policy.[4]

This view is compatible with the autonomy granted to employers' associations and trade unions to regulate the arena of collective bargaining, both at macro- and micro-level, and to do so within a co-operative framework. The question, therefore, arises of how successful the transfer of the west German industrial relations to east Germany was in preserving these features.

CHARACTERISTICS OF WEST GERMAN INDUSTRIAL RELATIONS

The main characteristics of the west German industrial relations model can be summed up as follows. Firstly, there is a clear legal framework within which the system has to operate. The legal norms define the parties to collective bargaining and specify the outcome in terms of the standing of collective agreements. Through voluntary machinery between the collective bargaining parties on arbitration and conciliation norms are extended into the arena of conflict resolution. The norms define the relationship of plant-level industrial relations through the Works Constitution Act (1972). These specific provisions form part of an extensive labour code, supported by a labour court arrangement ranging from federal to local level. These extended legal provisions have led to the German system being labelled a juridified one.

Secondly, employers' associations and trade unions demonstrate a high degree of organisational concentration. Employers' associations achieved a remarkable organisational density in industry, banking and insurance of 80 per cent, covering over 90 per cent of employees in west Germany. Trade unions, based on the principle of industrial unionism and a 'unitary' trade union movement, remained unaltered until the 1990s. Covering large industrial sectors, trade unions were able to create, with employers' associations, an institutionalised balance of power between labour and capital.

Thirdly, the organisational predispositions of the social partners and the legal stipulations of *Tarifautonomie* formed the basis of co-operation and consensus between the parties to collective bargaining independent of state involvement.

Fourthly, this co-operation has been nurtured and fostered by the ramified legal system of co-determination. As this system regulates the relationship of employee representation from enterprise level to plant level it has been responsible for sustaining a co-operative relationship between labour and capital.

Finally, the German 'dual' industrial relations system is characterised by the separation of plant-level industrial relations from industry/sectoral arrangements. The former operate within the Works Constitution Act and are dominated by works councils, elected by all employees in an establishment, and their mediation with management. The latter area is the prerogative of the trade unions and employers' association in determining wage rates and employment conditions for large bargaining units.

Placing these characteristics within the broader political and socio-economic framework of Germany, two major features for economic and political decision making emerge. First, Germany's institutional setting allows clear checks and balances by interest groups on political and economic decision-making groups. This is very evident for the industrial relations system in Germany with its characteristic legal nature defining the nature and action of industrial relations actors and agencies. Second, German industrial relations facilitate the process of consultation and the mediation of conflicts through distinct conflict avoidance procedures.

This pattern is visible in both the political and economic sphere. For the political system in Germany this has been summarised by Katzenstein with the concept of the 'semi-sovereign state'.[5] That is, there is a sharing of power among the representatives of different interests from whom some agreement must be obtained. At the economic micro-level this is illustrated by the curtailment of power of management at enterprise level through supervisory boards and at plant level through works councils. The political and economic spheres, therefore, have prerequisites driving them towards consultation. In the economic arena this has resulted in an emphasis and support for consensus, and this in turn has supported institutional arrangements with formal and informal mechanisms for securing consensus.

A study of the industrial relations transformation processes in the former GDR is, therefore, one which focuses on the question of how the transferred institutions have been able to sustain the west German characteristics. Articulated differently, it is the question of what adjustments have been made to the transferred system and what efficacy these adjustments have demonstrated.

INDUSTRIAL RELATIONS IN THE GERMAN DEMOCRATIC REPUBLIC

The GDR's centrally planned economy, functioning under the ideology of socialism, included none of the essential elements which composed western democratic industrial relations systems. Instead of collective bargaining, wages and conditions of employment were determined through central plans dictated by the Politburo or appropriate ministries and supported through an extensive system of socialist legislation. The industrial relations actors were integrated within the monolithic state and the ruling Socialist Unity Party (SED) apparatus. Thus trade unions were highly centralised within the Freier Deutscher Gewerkschaftsbund (FDGB), the GDR trade union federation, whose main function was not membership representation in the western, pluralist sense. Instead it provided an extensive social benefit framework for its constituency. In addition it acted as a transmission organ for SED ideology and policies. In this respect it performed an important function to both legitimise and anchor socialist economic policies.

At plant level there was some representation in terms of workplace trade union representatives acting as a pressure group for their constituents *vis-à-vis* 'management'. However, the primary function of trade union representatives, who were mostly SED party members, was to support the implementation of economic plans and achieving output targets. Despite the ideological involvement of the old plant-level representatives (*Betriebs-gewerkschaftsleitungen*), a considerable number were to be the core of the new west German works council, even before the first election to the latter in 1991.[6] The rank and file membership were under the tight control of delegated FDGB union officers – a system that was based on the political control mechanism of centralised socialism. The fact that it was effective was demonstrated by the evident schism between the trade union hierarchy and their constituency with the inability of the latter to articulate their concerns.

PRESSURES ON THE INDUSTRIAL RELATIONS SYSTEM

The major external influences on the transferred industrial relations system to east Germany were the concomitant economic development and the massive privatisation programme. The most significant influence on the evolution of the industrial relations system in east Germany has, of course, been the introduction and implementation of the social market economy. The complex process of transforming east Germany from a centrally planned economy to a market economy commenced with the German economic, social and monetary union in 1990. From the perspective of industrial relations the two crucial elements were, and continue to be, the massive privatisation programme and the development of the east German economy, particularly the labour market. In addition, the disparity between east and west German economic performance influences the industrial relations evolution in Germany, particularly the collective process. For Germany as a whole the end of 1997 marked an economic upswing; however, the rate of economic growth had decreased. In the important manufacturing sector output in the last quarter of 1997 rose by under 0.5 per cent.[7] This reflects the fact that the economic upswing in Germany had, as so often in the past, been driven by exports. In 1997 the intensification of the Asian economic crisis, with its associated uncertainties, caused some restraint for the German export market. However, it is not only slower market growth but also the fiercer competition in the international market-place that provides considerable problems for industrial sectors of German industry.

Certainly, since unification the east German economy has to a considerable degree become integrated into the structures of the market economy and the international division of labour. However, this has not been a linear process and since 1995 the east German economy has lost considerable momentum. Since 1991 there has been an annual average rise of just under six per cent in real GDP in eastern Germany. The first period of system transformation in 1990 was marked by a deep slump as a consequence of the disastrous legacy of the inherited socialist economy. As Table 1 reveals, this was followed by a steep increase in economic growth, peaking at a growth rate of 9.6 per cent in 1994.

The industrial relations system was, therefore, subject to considerable variation arising from macro-economic influences. Table 1 also suggests that the eastern German economy has entered a new phase in its adjustment process. For the first time since 1991 economic growth in eastern Germany in 1997, with 1.6 per cent, was below the corresponding rate of growth in western Germany, which was 2.2 per cent. These trends in eastern Germany reflect the decline of the impact of financial support from western Germany. They also reflect the integration of the eastern German enterprises into the competitive German and global markets, thereby initiating new problems.

TABLE 1

ECONOMIC GROWTH IN EASTERN AND WESTERN GERMANY:
CHANGE FROM PREVIOUS YEAR IN % – GDP AT 1991 PRICES

Year	Germany	East Germany	West Germany
1991	+ 2.8	- 19.0	+ 5.0
1992	+ 2.2	+ 7.8	+ 1.8
1993	- 1.2	+ 9.3	- 2.0
1994	+ 2.7	+ 9.6	+ 2.1
1995	+ 1.8	+ 5.2	+ 1.5
1996	+ 1.4	+ 1.9	+ 1.3
1997	+ 2.2	+ 1.6	+ 2.2

Source: Data from Deutsche Bundesbank, Monthly Report April 1998

The central problem in eastern Germany, however, remains the labour market. The transformation process from the socialist economy to the market economy resulted in a fall of employment from 9.7 million employed in 1989 to 6.2 million employed by 1993 – a loss of around 3.5 million employment places in four years. This affected around 36 per cent of all employees in east Germany. However, 1995 saw an increase in the employed to 6.4 million, falling again to 6.1 million in the first quarter of 1997. But employment is a problem for the entire Federal Republic of Germany.

TABLE 2

UNEMPLOYMENT IN GERMANY

	1997	1998	1999
		In '000	
West Germany	3.021	2.945	2.810
East Germany	1.364	1.435	1.405
Total for FRG	4.385	4.380	4.215
		In % Rate	
West Germany	9.8	9.5	9.1
East Germany	18.4	19.4	19.1
Total for FRG	*11.5*	*11.4*	*11.0*

Source: Calculated from the Estimates of the *Wirtschaftsforschungsinstitute*, 9/5/1998.

Table 2 provides bleak evidence that in the near future Germany can, at best, only expect marginal decrease in unemployment. For eastern Germany the expectations are a continuation of an unemployment rate of around 19 per cent, a figure which will undoubtedly impact on the wage setting process. The gains that eastern German industry made in productivity and curbing costs was in part paid for by the increase in unemployment. Unemployment rates vary, of course, amongst the new federal states, with Brandenburg, Thuringia and Saxony performing better than many of the others. Nevertheless, unemployment rates in November 1997 were 18.7 per cent in Saxony and 21.7 per cent in Saxony-Anhalt.

There are also marked sectoral differences. Thus construction has slowed down and the marked slowdown of economic growth in the service sector has aggravated the economic situation in eastern Germany. Construction was a major component in the east German economy and as infrastructural provisions, in particular housing, approached western standards this sector was bound to slow down. Manufacturing, on the other hand, which had a difficult initial stage of restructuring, has seen an expansionary course since 1993. Output was up by just under nine per cent in 1997 – a consequence of the expansion of export business. This also reflects an improvement in east German companies' competitiveness and their continuing integration into the international division of labour.

Privatisation of the socialist industrial stock, land and agricultural holdings was to have an impact on industrial relations as it determined the later industrial landscape of the new federal states. The process of privatisation in east Germany was through sale or re-privatisation to previous owners. The legislation of 17 June 1990 gave the Treuhandanstalt (TH) the brief of privatising the GDR's people's property. From 1990 to the end of 1994 the TH largely concluded the privatisation of 13,200 former state-owned companies (*Volkseigene Betriebe – VEB*) with over four million employees and converted them into independent companies. As a result of privatisation and the change of ownership one can differentiate between three main types of enterprises in east German industry.

Firstly, the so-called 'cathedrals of the deserts'. These are new subsidiaries of prominent western firms built with financial state subsidies agreed with European Union support. Secondly, small and medium-sized enterprises (SME), producing for the domestic eastern German market but also owned by western companies. Thirdly, small and medium-sized companies producing for specific market niches. The number of companies, excluding agriculture, rose in the new federal states from 178,000 in 1991 to 353,000 in 1995; that is, 133 new companies per 10,000 employees were being created annually. This compared with 67 new companies per 10,000 employees in the old Länder.[8] This was a redeployment of the labour force in eastern Germany as at the same time the inherited *Kombinate* shed their labour force.

Industrial relations, obviously, vary according to the firm/company structure. In particular, there is a relationship between both enterprise/plant size and the adherence to collective agreements. As Ettl and Heikenroth revealed in their analysis, those enterprises which fell under the TH paid agreed collective agreement rates. Those companies which were bonded to west German ones, or dominated by foreign investments, held to agreed rates in 89 per cent of the sample, but 29 per cent of privately owned companies paid below the rate. However, reprivatised companies or those exclusively in the management of eastern German hands in 46 per cent of cases paid below agreed rates.[9]

An even more significant finding was that in 97 per cent of the sample companies with 500 or more employees paid agreed rates, but in 68 per cent those with fewer employees paid below. Even more striking was that in two-thirds of the cases small firms, with less than 49 employees, did not adhere to collective agreements.

The TH played a controversial role in the east German transformation process, not least because of the former TH companies' employees, 2.8 million were either unemployed, had taken early retirement, moved into growth sectors such as services, insurance and banking, or had emigrated from the east German labour market.

EMPLOYERS' ASSOCIATIONS

There were very few private enterprises in the GDR; most were incorporated into the architecture of the state and the centrally steered

economy. Consequently, there was no base, unlike trade union
organisations, on which employers' associations could build. Remarkably,
this did not impede their organisational evolution in east Germany. By mid-
1990 employers' organisations had a sufficient base for west German
employers' associations to take an active part in industry/sectoral
contract negotiations.[10] The Bundesvereiningung der Deutschen
Arbeitgeberverbände (BDA, Federation of German Employers'
Associations) played a crucial role in these early developments. The BDA
plays no direct part in collective bargaining but has been central in co-
ordinating collective bargaining strategies. It provided, through a system of
partnerships at regional level, resources for the emerging employers'
associations in east Germany. The BDA also resisted the formation of
specific east German employers' associations. Because of the strength and
experience west German employers' associations were able to supply, local
employers' associations failed to establish themselves. Nevertheless, the
very heterogeneous groups of 'employers', some organising from January
1990 in the Unternehmerverband der DDR (UV der DDR) and some in the
'Bund der Selbständigen der DDR', provided a dynamic for the
privatisation of companies which had been taken over by the SED state.

The west German *Landesfachverbände*, in particular in the crucial
metal- and electro-industries, amalgamated and absorbed the developing
east German employers' associations. On this basis, around 100 employers'
associations had been formed by the beginning of 1991. Henneberg
concluded from his case study in Saxony and Thuringia that west German
employers' associations simply extended their regional organisations to the
new federal states and recruited new members. The speed of the unification
process allowed the west German organisations to transplant the details of
structure and function of their organisations to the new federal states, and in
a considerable number of cases personnel. In particular, the collective
bargaining structures, which had developed over decades within the social
market framework of west Germany, became applicable in east Germany as
early as 9 March 1990, with the acceptance of the *Tarifautonomie* principle.
The net result was that the social partners were thereby provided with the
elements necessary for retaining the consensual collective bargaining model
which had served west Germany for so long. The tempo of unification did
not allow an alternative to this model to develop, not even a modification of
the model, with the result that the collective bargaining model in the long
term has generated considerable antagonism from employers and their
associations in east Germany.

The problems for the employers centred around the twin issues of labour
costs and labour productivity. Labour costs continue to be a central problem
for major industries and their strategies to increase their profitability but

also their competitiveness on both the domestic and international market. Collective wage agreements in the iron and steel, metal-working and electrical engineering industries, and private banking reached west German levels by the beginning of 1998. Taking the average level of collective wage and salary agreements, eastern German levels had achieved 90 per cent of the comparable wage and salary level of western Germany. This was a massive shift compared with wage differentials of 53 per cent at the beginning of 1991. However, an east–west comparison of pay and income, as Table 3 reveals, underlines the disparity between the new and old Länder.

TABLE 3

COMPARISON OF EAST–WEST GERMAN PAY AND INCOME IN 1997 (%)

Income Category	East–West Ratio
Basic negotiated pay	89.5
Monthly rate of pay*	87.0
Hourly rate of pay*	83.0
Actual earning	77.0

Note: * Including ancillary agreements – holiday pay and Christmas bonuses

Source: Data taken from Deutsche Bundesbank, Monthly Report, April 1998.

The economic process of reconstruction in eastern Germany has been characterised by a steep increase in labour productivity; real GDP per employee increased by 9.3 per cent annually between 1991 and 1997. This compared with 1.9 per cent in western Germany. Productivity has slowed down since 1995 but it has been responsible for increasing the competitiveness of companies in the new federal states. As a result, the disparity compared with firms in western Germany was reduced, although it still amounted to one-third in April 1998.

These endogenous pressures on the industrial relations model were to lead to changes in east Germany; gains in productivity being offset against an increase in the number of unemployed. The employers' associations, especially in the industrial sector, are subject to the pressures discussed earlier. There is a difference of emphasis in these pressures between west Germany and east Germany. The former has been exposed to the full complexities of the globalisation process, with its stress on competitiveness, and the accompanying drive towards flexibility and cost minimisation by enterprises. The latter is influenced by the continuing economic and social problems associated with the integration and transformation process.

In both cases employers have questioned the efficacy of employers' associations in addressing their problems and responding to change. Organisational density in *Gesamtmetall*, employers organised in the crucial investment sector of engineering and metal working, has declined from 58 per cent in 1980 to 42 per cent in 1998. In the Verband Deutscher Maschinen und Anlagenbau (VDMA) almost 60 per cent of employers are no longer subject to sectoral/industry collective agreements. In the east German printing industry organisational density was down to 30 per cent in 1998.[11]

Changes in employers' association density were by no means unregulated but were conducted within the framework of the principles of *Tarifautonomie*. Thus employers left employers' associations using the procedures laid down by the Collective Agreement Act. This meant that extant collective agreements were still binding for the period of their original validity and legal provisions further included arrangements for a 'bridging phase'. The juridified German system of industrial relations has imposed a regulated withdrawal mechanism for employers legitimising the process.[12]

TRADE UNIONS

The west German trade unions had a complex relationship with the GDR prior to 1989. This in part explains the somewhat uncertain, confused and hesitant policy of the DGB immediately after November 1989. However, after March 1990, the west German trade unions had to respond with a clear strategy. As Czada has pointed out, the response was an institutional transfer along conservative lines to confirm organisational stability and to exercise control over the integration process.[13] A universal policy of the west German trade unions was the rejection, partly for political and legal reasons, of fusions with the trade unions organised under the umbrella of the FDGB. However, this did not exclude some of the FDGB constituents contributing, and becoming part of, the new trade union organisations being established in east Germany.

Towards the end of 1991 the then 16 industrial trade unions within the DGB had transferred their west German organisational structure at regional and local level to the new federal states. The success of this initial phase can be judged by the development in trade union membership figures. The DGB membership showed an increase of nearly 50 per cent, moving from eight million in 1990 to 12 million in 1991. These dramatic increases were to be short lived; from 1991 to 1996 there was an absolute decline of 1.8 million trade union members in the new federal states, while in the same period the west German trade unions lost 600,000 members. In east Germany it was not only the massive decline in unemployment which was responsible for this loss but also the disillusionment with trade unions' ability to provide the economic improvements hoped for. Trade union density for employees covered by the industrial unions in Germany, as Table 4 demonstrates, declined to 27 per cent in 1995. Total trade union density at the beginning of 1998 is estimated at around 29 per cent.

TABLE 4

TRADE UNION ORGANISATIONAL DENSITY – PERCENTAGE

	1991	1992	1993	1994	1995
DGB Total	33.1	31.3	29.4	28.0	27.0
DGB West	29.6	28.9	27.6	26.8	26.2
DGB East	42.2	38.2	35.2	32.0	29.5

Source: Data from M. Fichter, Institutional transfer and the transformation of labour relations in east(ern) Germany: lessons for central and eastern Europe? , Transfer, 2/1997, p.397.

TABLE 5

DISTRIBUTION OF UNEMPLOYED 'IG METALL' MEMBERS

Region	% of Total Membership
Berlin	19.3
Brandenburg	24.9
Mecklenburg-Vorpommern	25.6
Saxony	33.0
Saxony-Anhalt	36.1
Thuringia	29.0

Source: Data from IG Metall, Direkt, Der Info Dienst der IG Metall, No.4, 18 Feb. 1998.

The analysis of trade union membership trends suggests that the development of union density has become normalised after the initial surge in 1990. It reflects the general difficulties of persuading white collar workers, female employees and young workers to become trade union members. In addition, membership decline has accelerated because of an ageing population and the dramatic increase in unemployment. The latter development has had an enormous impact on the IG Metall membership in the new federal states: Table 5 summarises the distribution at the beginning of 1998 of 325 000 unemployed members.

For German trade unions these trends are leading to an increase in trade union amalgamations For example, the IG Metall merged with Textile and

Clothing and Woods and Plastics, while in 1997 the three industrial unions, Mining and Energy, the Leatherware Union, and Chemicals, Paper and Ceramics merged, thus reducing the industrial trade unions from 16 to 11. But what will transform the German trade union landscape is the proposed fusion of six trade unions in the service sector, including the organised white-collar employees. This will not only reduce the trade unions under the umbrella of the DGB to five but set new challenges in both eastern and western Germany.

COLLECTIVE BARGAINING CHANGE AND PLANT-LEVEL DEVELOPMENTS

Crucial to developments in eastern Germany was the deterioration in the economy in 1993. It was at this time that employers' associations did not only distance themselves from the harmonisation of wages and salaries between east and west Germany when they cancelled the *Stufentarifvertrag* on 18 February 1993, but they expressed their disagreement with the political promise of a speedy wage harmonisation and hoped to achieve realistic labour costs. This was a reversal of the policy which had been formulated in the important engineering and electronic industry sector in July 1990, when the IG Metall and the regional employers' associations had signed collective agreements dealing with wage and salary rates and other issues. This was to lead to the significant collective agreement of 7 March 1991 which set out the incremental evolution of east German wages, the *Stufenplan*, to harmonise with west German wage levels by 1994.

In addition employers' associations wanted to exercise pressure on the west German collective bargaining policy and emphasise that the relationship between plant-level bargaining and the *Flächentarifvertrag* required a new form of regulation. The employers from the metal working and electro industry sector have emphasised that the existing framework of sectoral collective agreements should be retained but needs modernisation, with clear flexibility stipulations to operate at plant level. Employers' associations argue that a total shift of wage setting to plant level would destroy the existing conflict resolution model of collective bargaining.[14] What is envisaged is a 'collective agreement pyramid'. At the base, minimum terms and conditions of employment are determined for employees at plant level; in the middle, collective agreed standards provide the possibility for enterprise specific plant agreements between management and works council; and at the apex are joint recommendations by the collective bargaining partners.

In fact it is the relationship between the *Flächentarifvertrag* and plant-level institutions which the empirical evidence suggests has not only sustained the existing model of German industrial relations but is providing both continuity and stability. The DGB affirms its adherence to the sectoral/industry collective agreement but accepts that there is a need for regulated and legal flexibility at plant level.[15]

There are arguments that the strengthening of the works council as a bargaining agent had its genesis in 1984 when the collective agreement in the metal industry on the reduction of the 40-hour working week included an 'opening clause'.[16] This widened the scope of bargaining for the plant-level actors, management and works council, and subsequent to this agreement around 10,000 plant agreements, on the issue of working time, were concluded in the metal industry. Although works councils are formally separated from trade unions, in practice there is a tight linkage. Furthermore, evidence from researchers such as Kotthoff demonstrate that works councils have gained in power and status over the last decades.[17]

There is support for the view that the scope of works council competencies is being extended.[18] The IG Metall and the employers' association agreed during the wage harmonisation plan that some companies could forbear wage increases under certain circumstances – the so-called 'hardship clauses'. These specific opening clauses allowed the social partners to retain control through a complex mechanism by which companies were required to seek approval to implement their plant-specific bargaining. In fact, the hardship clauses were used moderately. In the metal-working industry there were 167 applications for the five eastern collective bargaining regions, of which 81 were agreed.[19]

The point is that the locus of bargaining had shifted to plant level. But the point also is that the German model has been flexible enough to allow this because of the subtle relationship between bargaining structures, bargaining procedures and works councils. Collective agreements reflect this trend as increasing numbers of agreements, in western and eastern Germany, include provisions for variations of regional/sectoral collective agreements at enterprise and plant level. The variations have been broad, thus SMEs have been able to apply certain conditions in respect to payments such as bonuses or gaining exemption from some wage levels for specific sectors of their workforce.[20] Opening clauses are, therefore, not only a response to the changes in the economic environment but also a strategy by the collective bargaining parties to contain pressures towards decentralisation. In particular, both employers' associations and trade unions do not wish to encourage plant-level wage determination. However, particularly in east Germany economic pressure increasingly expands the role of works council activity. On the other hand, these same pressures have driven east German companies to abandon membership of employers' associations, leaving them free to determine specific company wage agreements. In those cases where the wage rate is subject to negotiations between management and works council the trade unions strongly oppose this. Trade unions view this breach of sectoral/industry agreement, outside an agreed framework of applicable opening clauses, as seriously detracting from their power.

A study in the east German textile industry provides an example of works councils which have evolved co-operative attitudes towards management, 'in particular in firms with "new" management and "new" councillors'. These developments are new arrangements within the new transferred industrial relations structures and not legacies from GDR patterns of behaviour. But, in contrast to some studies, the data indicated that 'not only were the works councils formally installed but also the "substantive" or "normative" establishment was successful in terms of the acceptance, legitimation and support of the actors, i.e. workers, involved'.[21]

Kreißig's study in the vehicle and vehicle sub-contractor industries confirmed the presence of active works councils in even the SME.[22] In his sample there was evidence that works councils frequently continue a tradition of co-operation with management based on pre-unification patterns. However, there was also evidence of a 'generation' change in the composition of the works council. The works councils are evolving, both in composition of membership and ability to adapt to the specific conditions generated by the economic prerogatives of the new federal states.

It is too early to judge the final shape of plant-level industrial relations in east Germany, but studies reveal an internal evolution which is adjusting plant-level relations to the specific needs of the east German economic and social environment. The interesting question is whether this will result in the co-management pattern establishing itself in west Germany, or whether a 'new' arrangement between works council and management will emerge.

CONCLUSIONS

So how has corporatism fared in eastern Germany? Lehmbruch argues that corporatist strategies of the old Federal Republic have contributed to cushion the crisis unleashed by the transformation process and has strengthened the institutional framework of the introduced market economy.[23] He rightly points out that effective corporatism in west Germany depended on the key centralised institutions' abilities to incorporate the constituents in the process of regulation, in the case, for example, of negotiations. Lehmbruch's conclusion is that it is by no means clear whether the case of eastern Germany can be answered in a differentiated way. There is a schism between sectoral/industry collective bargaining processes and plant-level developments, but it is bridged by regulated mechanisms. This relationship becomes evident when institutions and industrial relations actors are placed within an analysis of the industrial relations system. What manifests itself is an interlocking configuration, defined by the legal paradigm of *Tarifautonomie* and Works Constitution Act, between employers' associations and trade unions at the macro-level, and the works council at the micro-level.

The institutional transfer of the west German industrial relations system to the east has been accomplished, but this only tells part of the story. Employers' associations and trade unions are in a period of adjustment brought about by both endogenous and exogenous factors. The specific architecture of east Germany's economy has dictated an accelerated tempo of change in collective bargaining strategy and location. A consequence of this has been the significant evolution of plant-level structures, in particular the works council. As evidence from empirical research reveals, works councils are establishing themselves as significant bargaining partners at plant level, but there is not the integration between trade unions and works councils which is part of the system in west Germany. Nevertheless, a linkage between the sectoral/industry level and plant-level institutions has evolved.

Deregulation and flexibility have been features of the west German industrial relations system for some time. In west Germany these developments have been generated from internal driving forces, that is, the initial pressure from the trade unions for a 35-hour working week. The dramatic changes occurring in the structure of both employers' associations and trade unions are accelerating the adjustment. In east Germany, moves towards deregulation and flexibility came from external driving forces, primarily the economic recession and restructuring of industry as a consequence of unification. Compared to west Germany this process has occurred within a short time-frame. The process has been underpinned and supported by the development of micro-corporatism at firm level.

The forces on the transferred system of industrial relations in east Germany are creating adjustments to the system. But the system has demonstrated remarkable flexibility, and creativity, in this adjustment. German institutions provide effective and strong mechanisms to create consensus. The shift of collective negotiations to enterprise/plant level in east Germany reflects this and substantiates the argument that micro-corporatism is evolving at this level.

NOTES

1. W. Ettl and H. Wiesenthal, 'Tarifautonomie in de-industrialisiertem Gelände. Analyse eines Institutionentransfers im Prozeß der deutschen Einheit', *Kölner Zeitschrift für Soziologie und Sozialpsychologie*, Vol.46, No.3 (1994).

2. J.T. Dunlop, *Industrial Relations Systems* (Boston: Harvard Business School Press, rev. edn., 1993), p.283.

3. R. Hyman, 'Institutional Transfer: Industrial Relations in Eastern Germany', *Work, Employment and Society*, Vol.10, No.4 (1996).

4. G. Lehmbruch, 'Consociational Democracy, Class Conflict and the New Corporatism', in P. Schmitter and G. Lehmbruch (eds.), *Trends Towards Corporatist Intermediation* (London: Sage, 1979), p.54.

5. P. Katzenstein, *Policy and Politics in West Germany: The Growth of a Semisovereign State* (Philadelphia: Temple University Press, 1987).

6. For details see L. Kirschner *et al.*, 'Transformation von Interessenwahrnehmung und Mitbestimmung. Fallstudien aus Unternehmen und Betrieben der neuen Bundesländer', *KSPW, Graue Reihe* 303 (Halle, 1992).

7. Economic Data in paper taken from Monthly Reports of the Deutsche Bundesbank, January 1998 to June 1998.

8. Data from Nürnberger Institut für Arbeitsmarkt und Berufsforschung (IAB), 1997.

9. W. Ettl and A. Heikenroth, 'Strukturwandel, Verbandsabstinenz, Tarifflucht: Zur Lage der Unternehmen und Arbeitgeberverbände in ostdeutschen verarbeitenden Gewerbe', *Industrielle Beziehungen*, Vol.3, No.2 (1996).

10. F. Henneberger, 'Transferstart: Organisationsdynamik und Strukturkonservatismus westdeutscher Unternehmerverbände – Aktuelle Entwicklungen unter besonderer Berücksichtung des Aufbauprozesses in Sachsen und Thüringen', *Politische Vierteljahreschrift*, Vol.34 (1993), p.653.

11. G. Schaub, 'Wege und Irrwege aus dem Flächentarifvertrag', *Neue Zeitschrift für Arbeitsrecht*, No.12 (1998), p.621.

12. For a legal discussion, see H.M. Frieges, 'Der Verbandsaustritt: Unwägbarkeiten und verfassungsrechtliche Grenzen der zwingenden Fortgeltung von Tarifbestimmungen', *Neue Zeitschrift für Arbeitsrecht*, No.12 (1998), pp.630–33.

13. R. Czada, 'Schleichweg in die "Dritte Republik", Politik der Vereinigung und politischer Wandel in Deutschland', *Politische Vierteljahresschrift*, Vol.35 (1994), p.248.

14. W. Franz, 'Der moderne Flächentarifvertrag', unpublished Discussion Paper given at ME-Forum, Die Unternehmer der Metall-und-Elektro-Industrie, Berlin, 5–7 March 1998.

15. See Grundsatzprogramm des DGB 1996, No.14.

16. K. Koch, 'Regulatory Reform and German Industrial Relations', in K. Dyson (ed.), *The Politics of German Regulation* (Aldershot: Dartmouth, 1992).

17. H. Kotthoff, *Betriebsräte und Bürgerstatus* (München/Mehring: Rainer Hampp Verlag, 1994).

18. K. Koch, 'The German Works Council and Collective Bargaining Development Since Unification', *German Politics*, Vol.4, No.3. (1995).

19. S. French, 'Necessity or Opportunity? The Undermining of Multi-Employer Bargaining in the New Länder', *IGS Discussion Papers Series Number 98/2 in German Studies*, University of Birmingham, 1998, p.6.

20. R. Bispinck, 'Deregulierung, Differenzierung und Dezentralisierung des Flächentarifvertrags', *WSI-Mitteilungen*, 8 (1997), pp.551–61.

21. C.M. Frege, 'Co-operative Workplace Relations in East Germany? A Study of Works Councils in the Textile Industry', *Industrielle Beziehungen*, Vol.4, No.3 (1997), pp.196–215. See also C.M. Frege, 'Union Membership in Post-Socialist East Germany: Who Participates in Collective Action', *British Journal of Industrial Relations*, Vol.34, No.3 (1996), pp.385–413.

22. V. Kreißig, *Kombinate, Privatisierung, Konzerne, Netzwerke* (München/Mehring: Reiner Hampp V, 1996).

23. G. Lehmbruch, 'Die Rolle der Spitzenverbände im Transformationsprozeß: Eine neo-institutionalistische Perspektive', in R. Kollmorgen *et al.* (eds.), *Sozialer Wandel und Akteure in Ostdeutschland* (Opladen, Leske & Budrich, 1996), p.142.

Housing Situation and Housing Policy in East Germany

CHRIS FLOCKTON

This paper assesses the poor physical state and supply of housing in east Germany at the time of unification and discusses the fundamental transformation of the eastern state-controlled housing regime to the western, heavily regulated market system. It discusses in detail the inherited problems of physical fabric, housing organisation debt and disputed ownership title. The housing policy regime instituted granted very favourable tax reliefs to investors in real estate, and so created the construction boom, which kick-started the east German economy. It also instituted a phased adjustment of the extremely low east German rents to the western system and level, with the express objective of attracting investment to modernise the run-down stock. As the counterpart to the partial alleviation of the inherited debts of the housing associations, privatisation targets were set for rented property, but the Zwischenerwerber model has had to be instituted given the limited interest in the east in owner-occupation of older apartments and Plattenbau dwellings. The effect of housing allowances in moderating very large rent rises is assessed. Finally, the paper speculates on the potential impact in the east of the housing policy changes planned under the Kohl government in 1997/98.

FROM STATE CONTROL TO CLOSE REGULATION IN A SOCIAL MARKET

Enormous transitional problems were posed by the challenge of restructuring and adapting the GDR housing regime, since it formed the nexus of some of the most intractable problems arising from the abolition of the command economy. State ownership and control had been all-prevalent, much of the stock was in serious decay, and yet the rents had tended to be held at 1936 levels. Exhibiting all of the problems of disputed ownership, weighed down by inherited debts, and scarcely privatisable in their existing condition, much of the state and co-operative housing in the east would have to be transferred to housing organisations created under FRG

Chris Flockton, University of Surrey.

legislation, whose purpose would be to renovate and manage the housing stock, while meeting social commitments to their tenants. The disputed titles to property, the inherited debt burden and the rent controls would clearly weigh heavily on the ability to borrow and invest. From the tenants' viewpoint, however, the threat of eviction in favour of an earlier property owner, and, particularly, the scale of rent increases which could be envisaged, were all deeply unsettling at a time when the population was threatened with redundancy and loss of livelihood. To square the circle, it was inevitable that the state would have to bear much of the cost in the form of social housing subsidies, housing allowances, attractive tax reliefs to new investors, and through a write-off of a significant proportion of the inherited debt burden. All of this would cost the federal government alone well over DM 100 billion, if not far, far more.

The Munich Ifo-Institut estimated in 1992 that the total cost of new house building, fundamental repair and modernisation lay at approximately DM 1,000 billions (in 1990 prices) to achieve FRG standards within a 15-year period.[1] Certainly until 2005, they estimated the investment needs at DM 65 billion annually. This calculation omits any reference to the social security costs involved in shielding the tenants from the large rent rises, which would threaten ever greater social differentiation, poverty and homelessness for those hit by the full force of transformation in the labour market. In fact, as will be shown below, after serious early difficulties, when little new construction and investment took place, east Germany experienced a construction boom. This covered modernisation, new construction for rent and home-ownership, and speculative retail and commercial property development on an unimagined scale, all fuelled by tax reliefs amounting to DM 33 billion – the 'tax give-away of the century', according to Finance Minister Waigel.[2] The boom ended with the expiry of the tax allowances at the end of 1996: the subsequent deep recession in the construction sector then depressed the east German economy, which depended so heavily on building activity, and helped create an unemployment rate of over 21 per cent in early 1998. However, in spite of the obvious waste of resources in the form of empty office and retail developments, and of upmarket rental accommodation beyond the reach of most east Germans, there has, nevertheless, been a very visible transformation of the housing stock and of regional city centres over the last eight years.

The housing statistics testify to the very considerable improvements which have taken place in the new Länder. In the period to 1997, the rates of modernisation and of new building cannot fail to impress. A total of 3.51 million dwellings were modernised (or roughly one-half of the housing stock), and 500,000 new dwellings were constructed. The rate of home ownership rose by five percentage points to 29 per cent and, for tenants, the improvements were conducted without unaffordably large and sudden attendant rent increases. The space per dwelling rose to an average of 70 square metres (compared with 88 square metres in the west) and 60 per cent of all eastern dwellings now all have sanitary facilities, together with central heating. This contrasts with the poor physical situation in 1990, when the situation of the housing stock resembled the FRG in the 1950s, in terms of fabric and facilities.[3] As will be seen, these improvements were accompanied by phased rent rises and a transition to the west German system of 'comparable rents', but the impact was moderated by housing allowances and rent rise ceilings on modernised properties. This is not to detract from the anxiety felt by those who had to face the loss of their property which was given back to previous owners, nor to the bulk of the working population who faced job losses and job change. However, looking ahead, after such a rapid rate of housing construction and with the appearance of excess supply of new housing, it is clear that the problems for the future lie in the need for continued renovation of inner city and of panel-built housing (*Plattenbau*): further ahead, possible reforms to housing policy could have an impact on the rent levels paid by the broad mass of the population.

This fundamental transformation of the state-controlled housing regime in the east to a western, heavily regulated social market system, which itself was in transition at the time of unification, is discussed in some detail below, with particular reference to the inherited problems of physical fabric, debt and disputed title. The policy on rent levels, housing allowances and their impact on incomes is analysed, and the current housing policy reform debate in the Federal Republic is discussed briefly with a view to highlighting the potential impact on regional incomes. The agenda for the future, which focuses primarily on inner city renewal, will finally be addressed.

THE INHERITED SITUATION IN 1990

Until the end of the 1960s, the GDR had a more favourable space allocation per head in its housing than did the FRG, partly for the reason that the east had suffered less from war damage and partly as a result of the population decline by approximately two million people from 1948 to 1989.[4] Rents in older, pre-war property had been frozen at their 1936 levels and there had been very little housing investment, with the result that serious decay was arising in the inner cities and in old property in rural areas, starved of materials for repair. War damage was still apparent and bomb sites could still be seen. Many homes remained in private ownership, although there was no active property market, and owners sometimes made over their property to be managed by the state housing organisations. These had taken over expropriated properties from those denounced as 'war criminals' and from those who had fled the country. After the fall of Walter Ulbricht in 1971, Erich Honecker, the new General Secretary of the Socialist Unity Party (SED), gave special emphasis to mass housing construction as one of the 'key tasks' of his new programme. This was designed to raise the material living conditions of the population, and so mass, industrialised building in the form of panel-built blocks (*Plattenbau*), located generally on the fringes of the built area, came to be the dominant mode of house construction. The highly ambitious target of 2.8–3 million dwellings by 1990 was set, and the housing budget was devoted to the soulless housing estates, with few amenities and badly sited, while decay continued uninterrupted in the pre-war housing stock. The state housing organisations managed these vast apartment blocks, and rents were held at broadly one-fifth of the actual cost. Overall in the GDR rents stood at 0.80–1.25 Ostmarks per square metre, and water and energy costs were equally heavily subsidised.[5] Only from the mid-1980s was there some reorientation of policy towards inner city renewal, designed partly to give some sense of urbanity to what were commonly called the 'grey cities' of the GDR.

In 1990, the space allocation per head in the east lay well below that of the west, at 28.1 square metres compared with 36.5 square metres. The physical state of the stock was also poor. Of the approximately seven million dwellings, 1.5 million required urgent, fundamental repair and, in general, the two-thirds of the housing stock which was older than 1968 suffered from considerable neglect. Ten per cent of dwellings were regarded as uninhabitable, 24 per cent of dwellings had no internal toilet, and 53 per cent had no modern heating system.[6] Even the *Plattenbau* tower blocks suffered from substantial defects in the quality of their construction and required very heavy repair expenditures. For renovation and repair alone, the West German Association of Housing Organisations calculated that DM 550 billion would be required.[7] Concerning the age of the housing stock, less than 50 per cent of dwellings were constructed post-war (compared with 70 per cent in the west) and more than one-third were constructed before 1914. The stock is therefore considerably older. In terms of ownership structures, 40 per cent of properties belonged to state and co-operative organisations, and only 40 per cent of the stock was privately owned (compared with 80 per cent in the west). Only 24 per cent of dwellings were actually in owner-occupation.[8]

At the time of unification, the state housing associations had to be split up, the critical questions of inherited housing system debts and of restitution to former owners resolved, and the west German system of housing support put in place.[9] The unification treaty specified that 'people's housing enterprises' (*Kommunale Wohnungsunternehmen*), together with their debts, should be vested in local authorities, which, in keeping with the thrust at the time of FRG housing policy, would be free to transfer the housing to private companies wholly or partly owned by themselves, or could then sell them to tenants. The GDR co-operative housing organisations would retain ownership of their housing, and the accompanying debts. However, in accordance with GDR law, co-operatives did not own the land underneath the buildings, and this would therefore have to be sold to them by the local authorities, on behalf of previous owners. It will be clear that these provisions concerning debts and land stored up considerable problems, which would be a prime obstacle to any rapid renewal and reinvestment in housing by these organisations.[10] This is amplified by the frequent lack of secure title to properties: without an entry in the Land Register, a housing organisation cannot raise a bank loan for improvement purposes.

THE RESTITUTION PROBLEM

Against the express wishes of the last GDR government under Prime Minister de Maizière (CDU), which stood out for monetary compensation for previous owners who had been expropriated in the period from 1949, the federal government had included in the unification treaty the provision for restitution of expropriated property to owners, rather than compensation. Only where land had subsequently been built upon would monetary compensation be made. Clearly, apart from the fact that later tenants could be evicted, this would have highly harmful effects on investment, as indeed it would have in the case of commercial property. The number of claims for restitution of dwellings to former owners numbered approximately 1.3 million, which included 600,000 dwellings administered by local housing companies.[11] There were also 200,000 dwellings administered by the former state enterprises as trustees, such dwellings having been voluntarily handed over to the enterprises by private owners. The treaty provided that the responsibility of local housing organisations for these properties would cease from the end of 1992, leaving the properties with effectively no owner.

Obviously, the settling of claims for restitution and of the many disputed titles has seriously delayed renewal. By September 1992, for example, only 11 per cent of claims had been settled. The reasons for slowness were given as disputes among several claimants, the destruction of land registers in the GDR, the GDR legal distinction between state ownership of the land and the right of use to be awarded to a user, and simply the sheer volume of complicated cases. Of particular concern was and is the case of pre-war housing, often the inner-city apartment blocks, where ownership is unclear or disputed. In many cases, previous owners are old and do not have the means for modernising their property: the limits on permissible rent increases are also perceived by them as a serious hindrance to the very expensive renovation needed, which may cost DM 40,000–60,000 per flat. (The costs of renovation for panel-built housing may rise to DM 80,000–100,000.)[12] Considerable alleviation of this problem was offered by the renewal of the *Vermögensgesetz* and the *Investitionsgesetz*, which came into effect in July 1992. These modified the principle of restitution before compensation to the extent that, where potential investor-purchasers can demonstrate a sustainable investment plan, and the former owner cannot do so, the property can be sold to the investor, and the former owner would be compensated financially at the sale price. Where the owner is not known, the local authority may act as an effective agent of the missing owner. Even by mid-1997, however, the slowness of the procedures concerning clarification of property title meant that one million dwellings held by the housing organisations had not been entered in the Land Register, and a further 313,000 of their dwellings still had disputed title: these still represented 50 per cent of the dwellings managed by the housing organisations for which title was or had been disputed.[13]

THE INHERITED DEBTS

There has been considerable dispute over the status of the GDR housing debt of DM 36 billion, which was translated at an exchange rate of 2:1 under the monetary union, and which was allocated to the local authority housing organisations under the unification treaty. The federal government took the view that these were normal commercial debts, while the local authorities and housing associations argued that, under central planning, these had no economic function but were merely a bookkeeping entry. Since 1990, however, the debts accumulated interest rapidly, even though repayment of interest was not to commence until 1995. The debt level would have accumulated to DM 50 billion by then, and would have forced rents higher than those in west Germany, if both renewal of the fabric and debt amortisation were to take place.[14] These weighed heavily upon the finances of the 1,100 housing associations, which manage approximately 60 per cent of the east German housing stock: together with the restitution question, this debt problem explains much of the failure to undertake new building and substantial renovation in the early years. As part of the Solidarity Pact discussions in March 1993, it was agreed that DM 31 billion of this inherited debt would be written off by the federal government. A significant *quid pro quo*, however, contained in the *Altschuldenhilfegesetz* (Inherited

Debt Assistance Law), was that the housing associations could only benefit from a 45 per cent write-off of their debt if they undertook to privatise 15 per cent of their housing stock by the year 2003. As will be seen, this represented a challenge, given the need for prior renovation of property before it is sold, and the relatively low demand for home-ownership of this type of property.[15] In particular, the prospects for sale of panel-built apartments in tower blocks were slim indeed.

In the very early years following unification, the scale of new building remained very low and the giant building combines left from the GDR days had to concentrate on repair and renovation. Even by the end of 1992, the scale of housing investment per head in the east reached only 40 per cent of the western level, due primarily to the unresolved ownership and debt problems, but also to the deep slump which the region was undergoing.[16] By December 1992, the Federal Building Minister announced that one-quarter of the seven million dwellings in east Germany were undergoing state-subsidised repair and renovation, that 25,000 dwellings were being rebuilt with assistance from the *Aufschwung Ost* programme and from the federal government's own *Kreditanstalt für Wiederaufbau*, and that 20,000 new homes were under construction with the assistance of social housing subsidies.[17] These results can be considered somewhat meagre, given the scale of the problem, and since a rebuilding initiative would clearly pull the east German economy out of its deep slump. However, a boom must have been in the making. Alongside the huge state investments in infrastructure and public buildings, special housing programmes were also budgeted by the federal government. State subsidies to foster the purchase of privatisable dwellings were allocated at the rate of DM 14 million in 1991 and DM 64.3 million in 1992, in the hope that privatisation would speed modernisation and repair of properties both directly and indirectly, and as a way of alleviating the crushing inherited debts of the housing organisations.[18] The federal government budgeted an extra DM 800 million for 1992–93 for housing modernisation in the east, and it raised the lending limits of the *Kreditanstalt für Wiederaufbau* for housing modernisation in the east by DM 10 billion to DM 30 billion. It also made legal changes to speed the zoning and preparation of building land in the east by local authorities.[19] The highly favourable tax relief of a 50 per cent amortisation for investors in building projects in the east, under the *Fördergesetz*, proved an enormous attraction to investors. Finally, the staged rises in rent levels on 1 October 1991 and 1 January 1993, and the announcement that the east German rental system would adapt to the west German 'comparable rents' system, must have generated investor interest, even if these rent adjustments were heavily controlled and were accompanied by housing allowances for the tenants (see below).[20]

The boom in construction was certainly apparent by 1993 and continued to the end of 1996, when the highly favourable tax reliefs came to an abrupt end. By mid-decade, record levels of construction of dwellings had been achieved, and there was a clear trend towards the construction of both more single family houses, and of dwellings for home-ownership. In 1996, 143,366 dwellings were constructed, a rate per inhabitant 50 per cent higher than in the west. Of these, 36 per cent were single-family houses, and 34 per cent were constructed for home-ownership. The size of dwellings constructed, therefore, was far larger than those in the GDR, reaching 83 square metres, or one-third larger in their floor area.[21] The absolute shortage of housing was therefore largely at an end as a result of this boom in construction. However, whether the construction was well targeted is somewhat doubtful. In particular, the highly attractive tax reliefs offered under the *Fördergesetz*, amounting to DM 100,000 per dwelling and totalling DM 33 billion in aggregate over the years, had led to considerable misdirection of investment. There was an excess of higher quality rental accommodation, which most east Germans could not afford, and the developments were often poorly sited. Many smarter housing blocks remain vacant. Of course, this criticism can be extended even more to other tax-financed commercial developments, whether of speculative office and retail space constructed in inner cities, or the new shopping malls on the outskirts of east Germany's major cities. Unlet new office space in Berlin and Leipzig, for example, accounts for one-half of all the unlet office space in the whole of Germany, with a vacancy rate of 34 per cent in Leipzig, where rents are expected to fall by 25 per cent. Likewise in the case of retail space, Berlin (primarily East Berlin) will have a floor area in the year 2000 which will meet forecast demand only by the year 2010, such is the excess.[22] Returning to the question of the adequacy of new dwelling construction to meet demand, however, it is clear that such tax-favourable schemes do not meet the demand among households having only average earnings, who are on the threshold of affording home ownership.

The privatisation programme clearly has not met fully the expectations of more economically liberal housing ministers. By the end of 1996, 220,414 dwellings had been privatised, of which 173,322 had been sold in the three years of 1994–96. In this recent period, almost 60,000 had been sold directly to tenants, but 88,000 were sold to co-operatives and 'interim owners', which must sell on one-third of their stock at a later date. A total of 2,074 housing organisations had benefited from the relief of inherited housing debt and sales of dwellings by the end of 1996 represented 60 per cent of the sales required by 2003 under the *Altschuldenhilfegesetz*.[23] The 'interim owner' model was first introduced in legislation of December 1995 to hasten the sale of housing by housing associations. The latter are obliged to use the funds raised by sales firstly to reduce their indebtedness, and then to raise loans to that amount, to help pay for the rehabilitation of their remaining housing stock. Overall, this has added to an investment volume of DM 130 billion, expected to rise to DM 200 billion by the year 2003. The role of the 'interim owner' in speeding privatisation and renewal can be seen in the fact that only between one per cent and five per cent of tenants of the panel-built tower blocks have been willing to purchase their flats.[24]

THE RENT QUESTION AND HOUSING ALLOWANCES

Large-scale rent rises had to be undertaken with the move to more market-based relations, particularly if incentives were to be created for more investment and modernisation of the decaying housing stock. However, a shift from the DM 1 per square metre rent levels of the old regime would have to be accompanied by generous housing allowances, as well as by a long period of controlled freeing of rents. The unification treaty itself specified that rent rises could only be instituted as incomes rose, and so a long period of controlled rents was foreseen. Phased rent rises were instituted on 1 October 1991 and 1 January 1993, and legislation inaugurating the transition to the west German system of 'comparable rents' was passed in June 1995. This latter, the *Mietüberleitungsgesetz*, provided for the abolition of the existing rent control system by the end of 1997 and the introduction of a 'rent mirror' in the towns and cities, which would form the base of a comparable rents system from January 1998.[25] Throughout this period, special housing allowances were paid in east Germany to moderate the impact of the rent rises, especially on the poorer households. The *Sonderwohngeldgesetz* (Special Housing Allowance Law) applied from 1991 to the end of 1996, and, subsequently, the *Wohngeldüberleitungsgesetz* (Housing Allowance Transition Law) to the end of 1999. To avoid deleterious effects arising from rent rises in the full application of the comparable rents system, this last legislation has been extended in full for a further two years to the end of 2000.[26]

   This transition has, as intended, been accompanied by a rapid rise in rent levels: by 60 per cent in 1992/93 and by 24 per cent from 1994 to 1997. However, much of this has been offset by a combination of rapid wage catch-up with the west, and by the housing allowances.[27] In 1992 and 1993, an estimated 30 per cent of tenants in the east and 20 per cent of owner-occupiers were in receipt of housing allowances.[28] The 1997 Housing Allowance and Rent Report states that the rent burden in 1996 was 19.7 per cent in the east and 25 per cent in the west, excluding heating costs, and 23 per cent and 27 per cent respectively, inclusive of heating costs.[29] In fact, it is the so-called 'second rent' – the cost of water, sewerage and rubbish removal – which over the period 1992–97 has risen by 70 per cent, even as rent rises have fallen back strongly. Clearly, there were considerable fears that, with the abolition of the old rent control and the move to 'comparable rents', there would be a jump in rent levels very close to western rents. In reality, of course, the rent level will depend on what the local demand for housing is, and, with an excess of property in east Germany in many locations following the construction boom, rent rises in 1998 may only reach 1.9 per cent, or scarcely higher than the inflation rate.[30] Rent rises are designed to recoup modernisation costs. There is, however, an upper limit of DM 3 per square metre on the monthly rent rises permitted following renovation, but in one-half of cases the rise has been limited to DM 1 per square metre.

THE CONTINUING NEED FOR MODERNISATION AND REHABILITATION

In many parts of east Germany there is now no absolute housing shortage and any substantial increase in new building would threaten to create excess supply. However, there remains a considerable problem of rehabilitation of older property, particularly that built pre-1945 or pre-1914, and which is located primarily as *Mietskasernen* (tenement buildings) in the inner cities. Additionally, the condition of the poorest quality panel-built blocks continues to worsen, and the threat of a 'ghettoisation' in these blocks, whereby the poorer and older households become concentrated there, becomes ever more a reality. The 1995 east German housing census showed that 40 per cent of dwellings still lacked either a bath/shower or WC, and that 11 per cent had no sanitary facilities at all. One-third of the stock still lacked central heating. Including East Berlin, 6.6 per cent of dwellings were empty, primarily for the reason that they suffered from serious deterioration, or that they were being renovated.[31] According to the Association of German Housing Organisations, which manages two-thirds of the rental housing stock in east Germany, one-third of their stock still remains to be modernised, at an estimated cost of DM 80 billion–100 billion. The particularly desolate condition of the oldest workers' tenements and of the tower blocks will entail investments of DM 120,000–180,000 per dwelling to bring them to contemporary standards.[32] In addition, the flight of the middle-income earners from the tower block estates threatens the financial and social viability of these settlements. A so-called 'Bronx effect' is feared, where a ghetto of the old and the unemployed will be created. In the example of Schwedt, on the Polish frontier, where 90 per cent of the town is constituted of panel-built blocks (*Platten*), ten per cent of the accommodation is empty and there is a fear that this may reach 15 per cent by the end of the decade. The migration of the more solvent households to the suburbs, where housing costs are no higher, leads to increasing financial charges for those remaining and a vicious circle of polarisation is set in motion.[33]

The ending of the *Fördergesetz* and subsequent policy decisions have recognised that priority should be given to renovation of the most deteriorated stock. Since, from 1997, the tax instruments for investment assistance in east Germany grant a depreciation rate of 25 per cent for new construction (which earlier stood at 50 per cent), but 40 per cent is permitted for modernisation, there is a clear incentive for inner city rehabilitation. Likewise, the extension by DM 9 billion of the Kreditanstalt für Wiederaufbau low-interest loans (at 4.5 per cent for 25 years), and the raising of the ceiling of the loan from DM 500 to DM 800 per square metre for housing modernisation schemes, focuses public support much more on renewal. From 1999, the new instrumentarium of 15 per cent investment grants for east Germany (ten per cent for new construction for owner-occupation) will then come into force.[34] The increasing rate of settlement of ownership claims now also makes possible a determined attack on the problem of decayed older property. That this extension to the Kreditanstalt programmes is expected to generate 100,000 new construction jobs in a sector in deep recession, during an election year, can only raise the attractiveness of this approach.[35]

PROPOSED REFORMS TO HOUSING POLICY

Through the 1980s and 1990s, budgetary pressures, as well as a more market liberal policy orientation, have led to significant changes in housing policy. The abolition of the non-profit housing association status, for which the scandals surrounding the trade union-owned Neue Heimat presented the second Kohl government with a pretext, was accompanied in the later 1980s by a marked reduction in subsidies for social housing construction. The high cost and poor targeting of the assistance were heavily criticised by the coalition parties.[36] In particular, the '*Fehlbelegung*', which arises where households in social housing have an income above the upper limit for access to subsidised accommodation, attracted most attention. These concerns have continued through the 1990s, and federal investment expenditure on social housing construction itself has fallen to a low point of only 15 per cent of the project costs. Meanwhile, federal expenditure on housing allowances has been frozen in real terms since 1990, in spite of a rise in rents in west Germany by 33 per cent. Future plans were for a freezing of the federal housing allowance payments at the 1997 level of DM 3.5 billion.[37] Of course, tax reliefs for owner occupation, and, after 1996, the grant to owner-occupiers constructing a house, are of approximately the same order financially as the assistance to lower income groups,[38] such that the rhetoric of poor targeting of assistance sounds somewhat hollow. The federal government has sought to move away from the construction of social housing and to favour fixed-period contracts with private builders of rental accommodation, whereby low-interest loans are made available so long as lower income households are to be housed there. Rents and the levels of assistance to landlords would reflect local and regional housing market conditions. For those whose income lies nevertheless below a threshold in relation to the subsidised rent level, housing allowance would be paid, as in the past. One particular difficulty with this approach is, and has been, that the property escaped rent control at the end of the contract and so the stock of this low rent housing shrinks. This indeed has already been the case, since many of the long-term contracts entered into in the 1950s and early 1960s are now expiring and a notable fall in the stock of social housing has been occurring.[39]

In July 1997, the then Federal Housing Minister Hans Töpfer published a 237-page draft Social Housing Reform Law, which would have built on these principles, and which, in particular, sought to abolish the so-called *Kostenmiete* (building cost-related rent) for all new social housing construction and for the social housing stock itself from the beginning of 1999. The Housing Bill also included proposals to harmonise the practice in individual Länder for levying extra rent contributions on those households with incomes exceeding the upper limit for social housing.[40] In practice, the draft law had already been much watered down during consultations with Länder housing ministries: it consequently offered a range of options for action which would permit the Länder to continue largely with their present practices unchanged. In Spring 1998 the draft was blocked in the Bundesrat for electoral reasons and so only the provision for an extension to the *Wohngeld* housing allowance in east Germany was agreed.[41] The impact of such draft legislation on east Germany, had it been voted, can only be assessed in broad terms. The most obvious effect of the abolition of the *Kostenmiete* would be to focus assistance on the poorer households, who tend to be concentrated more in the east, while raising rent levels for households whose incomes are nearer the average. The abolition of the *Fehlbelegungsabgabe*, associated with a shift to freer rent levels, might in particular affect older households, such as pensioners, who have been left in accommodation which is now larger than their requirements. However, there were nevertheless limits on rent rises of five per cent in a three-year period. Lastly, the assistance to home owners who have constructed their own houses would be affected by the removal of favourable tax reliefs, were the Tax Reform proposals of 1996/97 (which were blocked in the

Bundesrat) to be finally implemented.[42] In spite of this evident desire for radical reform, it has to be said that, in many ways, the acquisition of huge swathes of social housing in the east upon unification, which is now still very largely in the hands of large communal and co-operative housing associations, has made more perennial the subsidised, rental character of the housing market from which successive Kohl governments have sought to escape.

NOTES

1. E. Holtmann and W. Killisch, 'Wohnungspolitik im geeinten Deutschland: Problemlagen und Entwicklungsperspektiven', *Aus Politik und Zeitgeschichte*, B8–9 (1993), p.12.
2. *Handelsblatt*, various.
3. *Handelsblatt*, 12 Dec. 1996; *Handelsblatt*, 4 Sept. 1997.
4. See Holtmann and Killisch, 'Wohnungspolitik'.
5. DIW (Deutsches Institut für Wirtschaftsforschung), *Handbuch der DDR-Wirtschaft* (Reinbek: Rowohlt, 1984), p.179.
6. *Wirtschaft und Statistik*, No.12 (1996); No.5 (1997); No.4 (1998).
7. See Holtmann and Killisch, 'Wohnungspolitik'.
8. *Wirtschaft und Statistik*, No.5 (1997), p.304.
9. G. Hallett, *Housing Needs in West and East Germany* (London: Anglo-German Foundation, 1994).
10. Ibid.
11. Ibid.
12. *Handelsblatt*, 1 July 1998.
13. Ibid.
14. Holtmann and Killisch, 'Wohnungspolitik'.
15. *Handelsblatt*, 13 March 1997; *Handelsblatt*, 24 July 1997.
16. Holtmann and Killisch, 'Wohnungspolitik'.
17. I. Schwaetzer, *Bulletin*, ed. Presse und Informationsamt der Bundesregierung, No.134/S 1225 (1992).
18. Ibid.
19. Ibid.
20. Holtmann and Killisch, 'Wohnungspolitik'. Also R. Ulbrich, 'Wohnungsversorgung in der BRD', *Aus Politik und Zeitgeschichte*, B8–9 (1993).
21. *Wirtschaft und Statistik*, No.3 (1998).
22. *Handelsblatt*, 15 Jan. 1998; *Handelsblatt*, 5 Feb. 1998.
23. Bundesbauministerium, *Presseinformationen*, 23 July 1997.
24. *Handelsblatt*, 24 July 1997.
25. *Wirtschaft und Statistik*, No.4 (1998).
26. Bundesbauministerium, *Presseinformationen*, 27 May 1998; *Wirtschaft und Statistik*, No.4 (1998); 'Wohnungsmieten in Deutschland im Jahr 1998', *DIW-Wochenbericht*, No.22 (1998).
27. 'Wohnungsmieten in Deutschland im Jahr 1996', *DIW-Wochenbericht*, No.21 (1997); 'Aktuelle Tendenzen der Wohnkosten und der Wohnungsmodernisierung bei ostdeutschen Privathaushalten', *DIW-Wochenbericht*, No.40 (1993).
28. Ulbrich, 'Wohnungsversorgung'.
29. Bundesbauministerium, *Presseinformationen*, 27 March 1998.
30. Bundesbauministerium, *Presseinformationen*, 29 May 1998; 'Wohnungsmieten in Deutschland im Jahr 1997', *DIW-Wochenbericht*, No.22 (1998). See also the chapter on Employment, Welfare Support and Income Distribution in this volume.
31. *Wirtschaft und Statistik*, No.2 (1996); No.3 (1998).

32. *Handelsblatt*, 2 July 1997.
33. *Handelsblatt*, 27 Nov. 1997.
34. Bundesbauministerium, *Presseinformationen*, 8 April 1998.
35. *Handelsblatt*, various.
36. Hallett, Housing needs.
37. *Wirtschaft und Statistik*, No.4 (1998).
38. Ibid.
39. Hallett, *Housing Needs*.
40. Bundesbauministerium, *Presseinformationen*, 21 July 1997.
41. Bundesbauministerium, *Pressinformationen*, 25 June 1998.
42. *Handelsblatt*, various.

The East German Family:
Change and Continuity

MIKE DENNIS

The incorporation of the GDR into the old Federal Republic has been accompanied by some far-reaching changes to the pattern of family life in the five new Länder. These changes found their most vivid expression in a precipitous fall of the marriage, divorce and birth rates. The paper traces these developments and considers whether they signal an irreversible transformation of the east German family. It concludes that despite growing convergence with elements of the west German family model, many GDR-typical patterns and attitudes towards marriage, gender roles, the value of children and combining work employment with family duties still persist in east Germany. Despite changes in its structure and function, a distinctively east German family model exists and has a future.

The incorporation of the GDR into the political, social and economic system of the old Federal Republic has been accompanied by a series of dramatic changes to the pattern of family life in the five new Länder. These changes have found vivid expression in the precipitous fall in the marriage, divorce and birth rates of around 66 per cent, 80 per cent and 60 per cent respectively between 1988 and 1992. Do changes of this order signal an irreversible transformation of the functions and structures of the east German family? Indeed, is the traditional family form on the verge of collapse as east Germans appear to be retreating from the conjugal relationship and suspending childbearing? This paper argues, the symptoms of crisis and the many changes notwithstanding, that the east German family retains the capacity for survival and, furthermore, despite growing convergence with elements of the west German family model, many GDR-typical patterns and attitudes towards marriage, gender roles, the value of children and combining work employment with family duties still persist in the new Germany.

FAMILY PATTERNS IN THE GDR

The nuclear family, normally defined as two married adults living together with their own or adopted children, was the most popular family type in the

Mike Dennis, University of Wolverhampton.

GDR. According to the official census of 1981,[1] the last to be conducted in the GDR, a married couple living with one or more children accounted for 56.4 per cent of families, closely followed by spouses with no children (31.2 per cent). Of those families with children, 55 per cent had one child, 37.6 per cent two, 5.6 per cent three and 1.5 per cent four or more children. This conventional nuclear family unit accorded with the communist regime's own notion of the ideal family as set out in the Family Code. Promulgated in 1966, the code, although modified from time to time, remained the politico-ideological basis of family policy until the end of the Honecker era. In the preamble to the code, it was alleged that a new and lasting quality in family relations had become feasible, since socialism had eliminated exploitation at work, enhanced educational opportunities and fostered the equality of women. Although the family was deemed to be irreplacable for the upbringing and socialisation of children, the latter function was not regarded as the sole reponsibility of parents but was to be undertaken in close co-operation with state and party bodies.

In practice, the code's idealisation of the nuclear family and its aspirations for harmonious and equal relations within the family unit were undermined by a sharp increase in divorce and by the growing popularity since the later 1970s of other partnership forms, such as lone parenthood and cohabitation. Lone parents, primarily women, and their children constituted 12.4 per cent of all families in 1981; 49.2 per cent of lone parents were divorced women, 30.4 per cent single women, 10.7 per cent married women and 9.3 per cent were widows. Although lone parenthood diverged from officialdom's preferred model, the regime proved relatively flexible and adjusted social policy to accommodate lone parents' requirements for an apartment and a child-care place. The second major departure from the ideological blueprint concerned the significant number of live-in couples: according to the 1981 census, ten per cent of all unmarried persons formed a live-in relationship, and one social scientific investigation conducted in 1987 estimated that over 26 per cent of men and over 28 per cent of women aged 18 to 40 were cohabiting.

Despite the pluralisation of family types, the vast majority of east Germans regarded marriage as the most desirable type of relationship. Comparisons between east and west Germans in terms of the core values and goals in a person's life indicate that the easterners were more strongly orientated towards marriage, the family and children. The main attractions of marriage were perceived by east Germans to be the promise of security in life for couples and their children[2] and expectations of happiness derived from the emotional bond of mutual love, personal attraction and compatibility. Marriage and re-marriage rates testified to the powerful appeal of marriage, even if the high rate of re-marriage suggests that a pattern of serial monogamy was emerging in which individuals had a number of spouses in sequence. In 1989, the marriage rate was 23.4 per 1,000 inhabitants aged 18 to 40 years and the rate of re-marriage of divorcees was 71 per cent as against 18.5 and 63 per cent respectively in the FRG.[3] Not only did east Germans marry more frequently but they did so at an earlier age. In 1989, the average age at first marriage was 25.3 years for men and 23.2 years for women, about three and 2.5 years lower than in the west. The gap in the age of marriage can probably be attributed to west Germans achieving economic independence at a later age than their east German counterparts. Getting married, starting a job and having a child tended to be much more closely synchronised in the GDR than in the FRG, where a more diversified pattern existed.

CAREER AND THE FAMILY: THE GDR COMPATIBILITY MODEL

Another distinctive feature of GDR family life was the strong commitment of women to combining employment with child-rearing and household duties rather than treating a family and a job as alternatives and taking a career break. This approach was facilitated by the state's comprehensive support for motherhood and child-care. Over 90 per cent of east German women aged 16 to 60 were employed, mainly full-time; most returned to work after the end of baby year and few accepted the role model of housewife by profession. In the FRG, women tended to take a longer break after the birth of a child and a variegated pattern took shape around the variables of child-rearing and a job, pursuing a career without children, and full- or part-time employment. Under communism the high level of integration of women into the workforce was primarily determined by the SED's anxiety to exploit their labour in an economy in which labour shortages were endemic; but it also derived from one of the key tenets of official Marxist-Leninist ideology, that is, the emphasis on productive activity outside the home as a necessary precondition of equality between the sexes. From the point of view of women, employment had many advantages: not only did it provide them with an income which reduced their dependence on a male partner, but it also gave them access to a network of personal contacts and to a range of public amenities. However, although the notion of an equitable division of housework and child-rearing enjoyed widespread support among both men and women, practice was somewhat different. The traditional gender-based division of family labour exacerbated the difficulties arising from the multiple roles which women performed; in consequence, many women felt obliged to sacrifice promotion in order to cope with the demands of motherhood and housework. Furthermore, many parents were worried that they devoted too little attention to their children.[4]

FAMILY FUNCTIONS IN THE GDR

Given the high level and wide range of public transfers to the family household in the form of subsidies for childcare, family allowance and interest-free loans for couples with children under 16 years of age and given the adequate level of income from employment, the GDR family virtually lost its function as a unit of production. It retained, however, a vital economic function as a unit of consumption with respect to the way income was spent on consumer durables and other items.[5] Another traditional function, the family's responsibility for socialising the young, was much reduced by the active engagement of pre-school institutions, schools, mass organisations such as the Thälmann Pioneers and the Free German Youth and by the intervention of the state-controlled media in the various stages of a child's development. Most children were cared for in crèches (from 29 per cent of those under three years of age in 1970 to 80 per cent in 1989) and kindergartens (from 64 per cent to 95 per cent over the same period), and a high proportion of time was spent there, averaging 20 hours per week in the former and 35 hours in the latter.[6] Despite these constraints, the family was by no means redundant as an agent of socialisation. Parents played a crucial role in the educational achievement of their children and young people valued them as advisers in such matters as child-rearing, the choice of a career and clothes and as confidants in emotional matters.[7]

Not only did the nuclear family's role as the main agent of demographic reproduction come under serious challenge during the Honecker era, but its position as the only legitimate place for sexual relations also collapsed. The normative barriers against pre-marital sex were dismantled, the average age at which sexual intercourse commenced fell to under 17 years of age and the number of illegitimate children increased. Whereas in 1965 the proportion of children born outside wedlock was only 9.8 per cent, by 1989 it had escalated to almost one-third of all live births (only one in ten in the FRG), and much of the stigma attached to illegitimacy had long disappeared. In sharp contrast to the surge in illegitimacy, the birth rate plummeted during the later 1960s to 10.5 live births per 1,000 inhabitants in 1975. The GDR was failing to reproduce itself. Although the SED regime's pro-natalist measures, such as the baby year, fostered a temporary baby boom in the late 1970s and early 1980s, they failed to prevent a subsequent decline from 14.6 in 1980 to 12.0 in 1989. The low birth rate was not the result of any antipathy to children, but the outcome of changing attitudes to the value of a large family, the increase in the use of contraceptives, the legalisation of abortion in 1972, the lack of spacious accommodation and a conscious attempt by women to alleviate the heavy burden of their multiple roles.[8]

THE TRADITIONAL FAMILY IN RETREAT?

Although the institution of marriage lost little of its theoretical appeal during the Honecker years, the GDR nevertheless had one of the highest divorce rates in the world. Divorce rose sharply from the mid-1970s, reaching 30 per 10,000 inhabitants in 1986 (as against 20 in the FRG); by the end of the decade, the chance of a marriage being terminated had risen to 45 per cent (30 per cent in the west). Conjugal relations were overloaded by the high expectations of a partner, and reality often diverged from the notion of romantic love attached to marriage. More women than men petitioned for divorce (69 per cent of all petitions in 1989), in part a reflection of women's economic independence. Among the factors contributing to divorce were inadequate accommodation, sexual disharmony and sexual infidelity, arguments with parents, and women's dissatisfaction with the division of labour in the family.[9]

As in west Germany during the 1970s and 1980s, marriage appeared to be in partial retreat as different ways of ordering sexual and parental relationships spread. Although the number of people cohabiting was high (153,173 according to the 1981 census), cohabitation was often not dissimilar to the kind of joint household operated by married partners. About 50 per cent of live-in couples had children and cohabitation was normally the prelude to marriage. In the 1987 *Kinderwunsch* survey, only 7.4 per cent of over 4,000 respondents fully agreed but as many as 60 per cent disagreed with the view that cohabitation was preferable to marriage as a lasting type of partnership. The average duration of a live-in partnership before marriage was one year less in the GDR than the 3.5 years in the FRG.[10] Similarly, although about one in ten east Germans lived alone in 1981, 'single' households did not constitute a significant threat to the primacy of the traditional marital relationship. Widowhood and divorce were the main reasons for living alone; 'singles', who consciously pursue their own individual lifestyle, were, unlike in the FRG, a rarity in the GDR.[11] At the end of the 1980s, the most common life form among young west German adults was living alone, whereas in the GDR it was a working couple with at least one child.[12]

Lone-parent households were more widespread in the GDR than in the FRG. Although lone parenthood was often the result of a desire to enjoy greater freedom of decisionmaking and to put an end to conflicts with a partner, many lone mothers regarded it as a temporary phase before marriage or re-marriage. The official 1981 figure of 358,000 lone parents raising at least one child under 17 years of age exaggerates the incidence of lone parenthood, as about half may have been living with an unmarried partner, partly because personal circumstances and the GDR housing situation made it desirable to retain separate apartments.[13] Although lone parents' income was about 20 per cent lower than the average per capita income of two-parent family households and, in retrospect, many lone mothers consider that their financial position was difficult, they were nevertheless economically self-sufficient, due in no small part to state support.[14] The problems of lone parenting should not be underestimated, however. Combining a job with bringing up children alone and with limited opportunities for social communication is a demanding task. One sign of the difficulties which might ensue from lone parenting was that 70 per cent of the children in a *Heim* during the later 1980s came from lone-parent families.[15]

THE GDR FAMILY ON THE EVE OF UNIFICATION

Although the marital unit – with or without children – was undoubtedly under challenge from other types of relationship, the preceding discussion points to the retention of its dominance in theory as well as in practice. Furthermore, certain GDR-typical features were well entrenched: the early age at first marriage, women's commitment to combining a job with a family, the high value attached to children as part of family life, and a low birth rate. Another characteristic was the exceptionally high divorce rate, a testimony to the burdens imposed on marriage by the unfulfilled ideal of emotional love and the burdens borne by employed mothers. Although these and other differences were, on balance, of greater significance than the similarities with the pattern of family life in the FRG, convergence was observable in the spread of alternative 'life forms' such as cohabitation, the small number of lone fathers and the infrequency of households in which several generations lived together.

In the GDR's highly politicised and intrusive system even society's 'smallest cell' was not impervious to interference by the state and its agents. Stasi informers – sometimes relatives and friends – might spy on the everyday activities of individuals who had come under suspicion, and the regime's economic and social policies shaped family structures and the lifestyle of members. Nevertheless, east Germans were not passive conduits of regime policy. Two examples of their capacity to frustrate external pressures were the decline in the birth rate, despite the pro-natalist measures of the SED, and a diversification of family forms which was scarcely congruent with the 1966 Family Code's preference for the nuclear family. There are also many indicators of a widespread retreat by family members into a semi-private life. Survey data suggest that this may have increased from the later 1970s onwards as opportunities contracted in the public sphere for useful and rewarding activity. One study conducted in 1988 by the Institute for Sociology and Social Policy among 500 employees found that a high proportion of free time was associated closely/very closely with other family members and with bringing up children. In the GDR more disposable free time was spent in the family than in the FRG, partly because of the more limited range of leisure activities and partly because the family provided some shelter from the pressures in the public domain.

DEVELOPMENTS SINCE THE *WENDE*

The transition from the old administrative-command system with its high level of predictability and relative security to the political system and social-market economy of the FRG has proved far more painful and protracted than many east Germans had originally anticipated. Everyday life has been transformed. Although '*Ossis*' enjoy new opportunities for travel, consumption and political participation, they have been confronted by unfamiliar social cleavages and by the loss of secure employment, early retirement and the collapse of old social networks. Between 1989 and 1994, the number of employees plunged from 9.7 million to 6.6 million, with women being far harder hit than men. In November 1994, only 25 per cent of people who had been in employment in 1989 still worked at their original enterprise. A plethora of new regulations and institutional structures have been introduced and many integral aspects of the old social welfare system have undergone radical change: the monthly 'household day' off work on full pay and the baby year have disappeared, the amount of time allowed off to care for sick children has been reduced, and the comprehensive system of organised holidays for children has been dismantled.

Although neither attitudes to the value and role of the family nor the internal structures of the family have undergone the degree of radical change which has occurred in the political, economic and legal systems of the GDR, the family has not been immune to the transformation shock, as can be seen in (a) a precipitous decline in the birth, divorce and marriage rates (see Table 1); (b) a significant increase, by the mid-1990s, in the average age at first marriage by about four years, to 27 years for women and 29 years for men; (c) an appreciable fall in the number of abortions and out-of-wedlock births; and (d) a reconfiguration of the role of the family as an agent of socialisation and as an emotional and economic resource.

A DEMOGRAPHIC REVOLUTION?

Nicholas Eberstadt of Harvard University, an expert on demographic developments in the former communist bloc, has argued that the steep fall in the birth rate to 5.1 per 1,000 inhabitants in 1993 is unprecendented for

an industrialised society in peacetime and that 'Eastern Germany's adults
appear to have come as close to a temporary suspension of childbearing as
any large population in the human experience'.[16] With the birth rate
collapsing and the mortality rate stabilising, deaths have exceeded births, by
94,658 in 1991 and 94,248 in 1995. The overall population of the new
Länder, taking into account outward migration, declined from 16.666
million in 1988 to 15.541 million in 1996.[17]

TABLE 1

MARRIAGES, LIVE BIRTHS AND DIVORCES IN THE NEW LÄNDER, 1989–95

Year	Marriages	Live Births	Divorces
1989	130,989	198,922	50,063
1990	101,913	178,476	31,917
1991	50,529	107,769	8,976
1992	48,232	88,320	10,312
1993	49,252	80,532	18,361
1994	52,429	78,698	22,908
1995	54,184	83,847	83,847

Sources: Wirtschaft und Statistik, No.1 (1997), p.21; Wirtschaft und Statistik, No.12 (1995),
p.887; Statistisches Jahrbuch 1997 für die Bundesrepublik Deutschland (Stuttgart: Metzler
Poeschel, 1997), p.79.

To what extent this decline can be reversed depends very much on
whether the present childbearing cohorts have merely postponed the timing
of births and to what extent future cohorts will increase fertility. Although
the age at which women in the new Länder bear their first child has risen to
almost 27 years and few married couples under the age of 25 have children,
east German women in the main childbearing cohorts continue to give birth
at a younger age than those in the west.[18] The question as to whether and/or
when the east German fertility rate will recover and attain that of west
Germany is a matter of much speculation. The Federal Statistical Office
predicts that the rates will converge in 2005 and that the overall population
will rise to between 14,995.3 and 15,614.1 in 2010. Other estimates tend to
be more cautious: Münz and Ulrich, for example, predict that the population
of the new Länder in the latter year will be as low as 13,900.0.[19]
Demographic developments will depend very much on variables which are
difficult to predict, such as the degree of convergence between east and west
German economic and social structures and east Germans' perception of
their personal economic situation.

The 'birth shock' should not be attributed to a sudden aversion towards
children. Not only does the wish to have children remain high, with most

east Germans desiring to have between one and two children, but a high value continues to be attached to children as a source of happiness and personal fulfilment. Opinion surveys find that a family with children is ranked among the two highest items on east Germans' scale of core values in life.[20] There are, however, indications of a shift in attitude. A minority of those aged 18 to 25 reject the idea of having children, and an investigation conducted in 1993 in the new Länder and east Berlin found that fewer women under 25 than women in general (41 per cent as opposed to 51 per cent) regarded children as very important on their scale of personal values.[21] Moreover, although most east Germans regard a stable partnership as a precondition for having a child and the nuclear family as the optimal form of family, cohabitation and lone parenthood are widely accepted as valid forms.[22]

The frequency of out-of-wedlock births during the 1980s has continued into the post-communist era. Although such births fell by 54 per cent between 1989 and 1993, the even greater fall in legitimate births (by 64 per cent) has meant that out-of-wedlock births as a percentage of all live births grew from 33.6 per cent to 41.1 per cent.[23] The rise in the illegitimacy rate indicates that the economic and political transformation of the GDR has not been accompanied by a shift towards childbearing within marriage. However, as under the SED regime, many live-in couples tend to marry soon after the birth of a child.

The high incidence of illegitimacy and cohabitation signals that sexual activity continues to be decoupled from the institution of marriage. Virtually all young east Germans favour pre-marital sexual relations, and sexual intercourse begins on average at about 17 years of age for both men and women. This sexual liberation of young east German women, which the latter statistic implies and which is sometimes also measured according to their high orgasm frequency, has been interpreted positively by some observers as an indication of the GDR's lead over the FRG in equality between the sexes; others depict it in negative terms as an expression of uninhibited and primitive '*Ostlust*'.[24]

WHY HAVE BIRTH AND MARRIAGE RATES FALLEN?

What lies behind the fall in the marriage and birth rates? Should it be interpreted as the consequence of the wider range of choices and a greater individualisation of lifestyles within a less conformist and a more open society? Although the pluralisation of family forms, the delay in having children and the increase in single households can be attributed, in part, to the new opportunities for travel, consumption and a career as well as to the general pressure on young people to adapt to new values, a rational

economic calculation emerges from the considerable corpus of research as
the main determinant of the rapid fall in births and marriages. A turbulent
labour market and a high level of unemployment, especially among women,
and anxiety about their personal economic situation have dissuaded many
east Germans from the 'risk' of having children and committing themselves
to an early marriage. The average age at first marriage – which rose by 1.25
years between 1970 and 1989 to 25.3 years for men and 23.2 years for
women – had increased by another four years by the mid-1990s.

With women's unemployment running higher than that of men at the
same time as so many women remain firmly committed to the notion of a
career, young children may be seen not only as a constraint on occupational
mobility and the time available for training but also as a burden on the
family budget.[25] Social Economic Panel (SOEP) data from investigations
carried out in April 1991 and March 1992 suggest that women's anxiety
about the general economic situation had little impact on fertility, but that
those who were worried about their own economic position were about four
times less likely to elect to have a child than those who did not share this
concern.[26] Surveys by the Social Scientific Research Centre Berlin-
Brandenburg confirm that these anxieties are not unfounded: couples living
in households without children have a level of income 13 per cent above the
average, whereas those with children are 14 per cent below average; this
gap falls to 26 per cent in households with three or more children.[27]

In view of the climate of economic and social uncertainty and of the
dismantling of the GDR's generous provision for children, it is not
surprising that the financial outlay, especially when children are older,
emerges as one of the main reasons for not having a child. Some idea of the
kind of weighting attached to the various factors is obtained from a study of
several hundred people which was undertaken in the town of Gotha in 1991
and 1993. Economic insecurity was given as the main reason for the fall in
the birth rate (by 86 per cent of the men and by 78 per cent of the women),
followed at a considerable distance by other reasons such as the problems
in securing suitable child-care facilities and the cost of raising children.[28]

THE SURVIVAL OF THE TRADITIONAL GDR FAMILY MODEL
AND ALTERNATIVE FAMILY FORMS

Despite the collapse of the GDR's employment society, the determination of
east German women to remain in the labour market – whilst simultaneously
caring for their family – provides a clear demonstration that certain deeply
embedded social norms have proved highly resistant to legal and
institutional changes. Studies have shown that only a tiny minority of
women regard the role of a full-time housewife as an appropriate alternative

and a clear majority favour employment underpinned by full-time care for their children. In a survey conducted in 1995 by the Berlin-Brandenburg Social Scientific Research Centre, over 90 per cent of the men and the women deemed work to be very important or important. Among the women aged 18 to 59, 58 per cent desired full-time and 38 per cent part-time employment. Another investigation, conducted in May 1996 by the same organisation, found that only 24 per cent and 23 per cent of east German men and women respectively, as against 56 per cent and 49 per cent of west German men and women believed that a woman ought to take a long break from or give up work altogether in order to bring up children.[29] According to an ALLBUS report, east Germans are far more likely than their counterparts in the west (57 per cent to 32 per cent) to believe that a child benefited if the mother worked.[30] Not only do such findings testify to east Germans' more positive attitude towards institutional child-care provision, but also underscore the persistence of another traditional GDR social norm: the desire to combine work with motherhood and homemaking. Yet although the family-career model retains its pivotal role, even among younger east German women, investigations by the German Youth Institute suggest that an important shift may be taking place. The second generation of young women were, at least temporarily, subordinating plans for starting a family to a career, a development which might lead to a job and a family being viewed as alternatives rather than as complementary aspects of life.[31] Part-time employment has also emerged as a more viable alternative than under the communist system and is another indication of the ways in which the juxtaposition between employment and family in the GDR is being transformed into a more diversified model.

Surveys of popular attitudes as well as official statistics show that the conjugal family is not only the most popular form of partnership in theory but that it also remains the major arena of private life for most east Germans. Moreover, as before the *Wende*, other forms such as lone parenthood and cohabitation are both legitimate and popular alternatives, while households in which grandparents live with their children and grandchildren continue to be a rarity (see Table 2). The existence of numerous lone-person households should not be interpreted as an indicator that 'singles' represent a widespread phenomenon in the new Länder. Most of the households consist of people who are either widowed or divorced and many are over 55 years of age. These are categories whose motivation and situation are not normally associated with the individualistic life of a 'single'. 'Singles' are far less common than in west Germany, partly because of the difficulty in obtaining an apartment and partly because of the higher level of commitment in the east to marriage and children. However, as the old family and work norms dissolve, an increase can be anticipated in

TABLE 2

FAMILY PATTERNS IN EAST GERMANY, 1993 (IN %)

Family Type	%
Married couples with children	35.5
Married couples without children	28.3
Live-in couples with children	3.2
Live-in couples without children	2.8
Single parents	4.1
Parents with unmarried children	8.6
Persons living alone	15.6
Others	1.6

Source: Drauschke and Stolzenburg, 'Familie', in G. Winkler, *Sozialbericht 1995* (Berlin: Sozialwissenschaftliches Forschungszentrum), p.285.

'singles' and in more flexible arrangements such as 'living apart together'.

With 728,000 east Germans cohabiting in 1993, a considerable increase since the 1981 GDR census, live-in partnerships remain a normal phenomenon, especially among young east Germans not previously married. Cohabitation is, however, still regarded primarily as an informal engagement before entering into a marriage and should therefore be regarded as an alternative to marriage at a particular phase in life, not as a rejection of a marital relationship. A higher proportion of east Germans aged 18 to 25 cohabit than do their western counterparts (13.4 per cent to 7.6 per cent in 1993) and the eastern live-in couples are far more likely to be divorcees.[32] A comparative study of newly-wed couples undertaken by the University of Bamberg discovered that 80 per cent of the east Germans had lived together before marriage and that, as before 1989, they married after a shorter period of cohabitation than did the west Germans in the sample. Forty per cent of the east German live-in couples had married within one year and only one-quarter had delayed marriage by more than two years; the latter had been the case among half of the west German cohabitees.[33]

The vast majority of lone-parent households are headed by women. According to the Federal Statistical Office's 1994 microcensus, there were 464,000 lone mothers and 58,000 lone fathers.[34] They constituted 10.8 per cent of all households and 14.8 per cent of all families with children under 18 as opposed to 7.7 per cent and 11.8 per cent respectively in the old Länder. In east Germany 39.5 per cent of women were unmarried as opposed to 26.1 per cent in west Germany, but with a less marked difference of 45.8 per cent to 45.1 per cent among divorced mothers.[35] Lone parenthood retains its attraction for many lone mothers as it promises them greater latitude in running their own lives and freedom from the tensions and arguments in a partnership.[36] What is not clear from the data, however, is the proportion of lone mothers who have a regular partner and regard lone parenthood as a temporary arrangement.

In many respects, lone mothers can be regarded as the main casualties of the transformation process for, despite their entitlement to a new parents' right to paid leave, cutbacks in family support have made it increasingly difficult for them to realise their high level of commitment to a career. Whereas in a 1995 survey 73 per cent stated that they wished to work full-time, 15 per cent part-time and only five per cent not at all, only 29 per cent had a job and 20 per cent were unemployed.[37] As lone parents with children are more likely to be unemployed than those without children and as many do not receive the maintenance payments for their children to which they are entitled, a vicious circle is created. Difficulties in accessing child-care facilities – despite a higher level of provision in the new than in the old Länder – may lead to problems at work and the subsequent loss of employment, which in turn enhances the risk of poverty and reliance on income support. A significantly higher proportion of lone parents are concentrated in the lower income brackets than all other groups except those living alone. In 1995, 40 per cent of lone parent households were in the 1,000 DM to 1,999 DM net income bracket compared to six per cent of married couples with children and nine per cent of married couples without children.[38] Interviews with lone mothers in receipt of *Sozialhilfe*, the lowest level of social security benefits, in the east Berlin district of Friedrichshain revealed that those in financial difficulties turned first to their parents for help. They did not, however, regard it as a satisfactory solution as long-term assistance from parents was not feasible; many preferred instead to rely on their own resources.[39]

FAMILY FUNCTIONS REINVIGORATED?

Since the *Wende*, several traditional family functions have been reinvigorated. Investigations in the early 1990s revealed that most east Germans felt that the family unit had become more important as regards the provision of material security and psychological support for its members at a time of economic uncertainty.[40] There are also indications that the dismantling of the state's agencies of political indoctrination and socialisation has enhanced parents' role in the upbringing of their children. For example, a longitudinal analysis of several young children in east Berlin established that parents were more frequently involved in helping their children with their school work, advising them on the pursuit of leisure activities and selecting a suitable school.[41] However, to what extent the role of the family as an agent of socialisation and as a source of emotional support has undergone fundamental change requires longitudinal and comparative studies which take into account the GDR family's role in these areas.

After an initial fall caused, for example, by an increase in the cost of a divorce and by east Germans' unfamiliarity with the new legal provisions, the divorce rate rose so sharply from 1993 onwards that by 1996 it had reached the high level of the 1980s. Women's dissatisfaction with the uneven division of labour in the family is one of the main reasons for marital collapse, a testimony to the persistence of patriarchal norms. In 1996, women filed two-thirds of petitions for divorce.[42] However, not only is the post-unification family beset by these older problems but new difficulties have also emerged. Conflict among family members arises from several sources: the loss of self-esteem experienced by those out of work, anxiety about the ever-present threat of unemployment, and the readjustment of the family division of labour to the changing situation.[43] Not only have surveys established that unemployment has resulted in a sharp increase in conflicts and irritability between partners but also that it has had a negative impact on children's emotional well-being, especially in families beset with serious financial problems.[44] Children's upbringing is another source of stress. One study of over 60 families in east Berlin in 1991 revealed that some mothers were experiencing serious difficulties in coping with the conflict between their role as young children's primary reference person and the uncertainties surrounding their own career.[45] The great strain on sheltered places for battered women and maltreated children is an indicator of the darker side of family life and of the potential for violence and abuse in east German families.[46]

CONCLUSION AND PROGNOSIS

Despite the high divorce rate and the spread of alternative types of personal relationships, the conjugal unit, with or without children, remains dominant and bears witness to the survival capacity of this form of relationship under both communism and market conditions. Other elements of continuity with the GDR past include the low number of 'singles' and the determination of many east German women, including lone mothers, to shape their own biographies. To what extent, however, is the east German family model undergoing structural and functional convergence with the western system? The current development may best be described as one of divergence within convergence. Elements of convergence were already observable before 1989, partly because the two German states shared some of the assimilation experiences associated with highly industrialised societies and with the broad cultural changes relating to women's employment, gender equality, family size and the legitimacy of alternative family forms. Divergence, however, remains pronounced since certain entrenched patterns of behaviour and attitude have proved resistant to the powerful assimilation impulses inherent in unification. Among the basic differences which persist today are the stronger desire by east German women to continue in work and to combine employment with homemaking, the lower number of young '*Ossis*' living alone, the higher level of lone parenthood in the east, the greater utilisation of pre-school institutions in the new Länder, and the easterners' higher valuation of marriage and children.

While the differences are unquestionably profound, the implanting of the legal, social and economic structures and institutions of the Federal Republic in the former GDR is combining with earlier homogeneous tendencies to erode the trends in the east towards earlier marriage, higher marriage and re-marriage rates, the shorter duration of cohabitation and the simultaneity of leaving the parental home, starting work and forming a stable partnership. With the birth rate falling, the size of eastern households will undoubtedly draw closer to that of the west, as will eastern patterns of fertility, though probably only from the 1980 cohort onwards. While women's life courses will become more diversified, the 'housewife only' model will continue to encounter much resistance. Finally, although convergence can also be anticipated with an increase in 'singles' and 'living apart together' arrangements, for example, among commuters to the west, the family itself, albeit with many changed features, can be expected to retain its primacy among partnership forms and not suffer the fate of its GDR parent state.

NOTES

1. M. Rueschemeyer, 'New Family Forms in a State Socialist Society: The German Democratic Republic', *Journal of Family Issues*, Vol.9, No.3 (Sept. 1988). For a recent overview of family development in the GDR see M. Dennis, 'Family Policy and Family Function in the German Democratic Republic', in E. Kolinsky (ed.), *Social Transformation and the Family in Post-Communist Germany* (London/Basingstoke: Macmillan, 1998).
2. Surveys conducted during the 1980s revealed that between 70 and 75 per cent of young men and women wished to marry. In the *Kinderwunsch '87* investigation 57 per cent fully and 26 per cent partly agreed that it was better for children if parents were married. See S. Menning, 'Geburten- und Heiratsverzicht in den neuen Bundesländern – Abschied von der Familie?', in H. Sydow, U. Schlegel and A. Helmke (eds.), *Chancen und Risiken im Lebenslauf: Beiträge zum gesellschaftlichen Wandel in Ostdeutschland* (Berlin: Akademie Verlag, 1995), p.143.
3. N.F. Schneider, *Familie und private Lebensführung in West- und Ostdeutschland. Eine vergleichende Analyse des Familienlebens 1970–1992* (Stuttgart: Ferdinand Enke Verlag, 1994), pp.178–9.
4. J. Gysi and D. Meyer, 'Leitbild berufstätige Mutter – DDR-Frauen in Familie, Partnerschaft und Ehe', in G. Helwig and H.-M. Nickel (eds.), *Frauen in Deutschland 1945–1992* (Berlin: Akademie Verlag, 1993), p.141.

5. N.F. Schneider, *Familie und private Lebensführung*, pp.249–52.
6. Statistisches Amt der DDR (ed.), *Statistisches Jahrbuch der Deutschen Demokratischen Republik '90* (Berlin: Rudolf Haufe Verlag, 1990), pp.57, 92; N.F. Schneider, *Familie und private Lebensführung*, pp.164–5.
7. O. Kabat vel Job, 'Familiensozialisation im Jugendalter – Familie als Resource', in U. Schlegel and P. Förster (eds.), *Ostdeutsche Jugendliche. Vom DDR-Bürger zum Bundesbürger* (Opladen: Leske & Budrich, 1997), pp.65, 70.
8. G. Henning, *Kinderwunsch = Wunschkind? Weltanschaulich-ethische Aspekte der Geburtsregelung in der DDR* (East Berlin: Dietz Verlag, 1984), pp.84–92. The 'baby year', which was introduced in 1976, was at first applied to mothers with two or more children and extended ten years later to those giving birth to their first child. Employed mothers could obtain release from work on pay equivalent to between 65 and 90 per cent of their net earnings. In some cases, the provisions could encompass other carers.
9. A. Pinther, 'Junge Ehen in den 70er und 80er Jahren', in W. Hennig and W. Friedrich (eds.), *Jugend in der DDR. Daten und Ergebnisse der Jugendforschung vor der Wende* (Weinheim/Munich: Juventa, 1991), p.164.
10. J. Gysi, 'Familienformen in der DDR', in *Jahrbuch für Soziologie und Sozialpolitik 1988* (East Berlin: Akademie Verlag, 1988), p.60.
11. Schneider, *Familie und private Lebensführung*, pp.120–22.
12. K.P. Strohmeier and H.J. Schulze, 'Die Familienentwicklung der achtziger Jahre in Ost- und Westdeutschland im europäischen Kontext', in B. Nauck, N.F. Schneider and A. Tölke (eds.), *Familie und Lebensverlauf im gesellschaftlichen Umbruch* (Stuttgart: Ferdinand Enke Verlag, 1995), p.33.
13. T. Meyer, 'Struktur und Wandel der Familie', in Rainer Geißler (ed.), *Die Sozialstruktur Deutschlands* (Opladen: Westdeutscher Verlag, 1992), p.277.
14. M. Möhle, 'Alleinerziehende in den neuen Bundesländern', in R. Hauser and T. Olker (eds.), *Soziale Sicherheit für alle?* (Opladen: Leske & Budrich, 1997), pp.313, 323.
15. Kabat vel Job, 'Familiensozialisation', p.66.
16. N. Eberstadt, 'Demographic Shocks in Eastern Germany, 1989–93', *Europe-Asia Studies*, Vol.46, No.3 (1994), p.521.
17. Statistisches Bundesamt (ed.), *Statistisches Jahrbuch 1997 für die Bundesrepublik Deutschland* (Stuttgart: Metzler Poeschel, 1997), p.70.
18. R. Leibscher, S. Menning and E. Nowossadeck, 'Bevölkerungsentwicklung und Bevölkerungsstrukturen', in G. Winkler (ed.), *Sozialreport 1995. Daten und Fakten zur sozialen Lage in den neuen Bundesländern* (Berlin: Sozialwissenschaftliches Forschungszentrum Berlin-Brandenburg, 1995), p.75; R. Münz and R.E. Ulrich, 'Depopulation after Unification? Population Prospects for East Germany, 1990–2010', *German Politics and Society*, Vol.13, No.4 (Winter 1995), p.13.
19. B. Sommer, 'Entwicklung der Bevölkerung bis 2042. Ergebnis der achten koordinierten Bevölkerungsvorausberechnung', *Wirtschaft und Statistik*, No.7 (1994), p.497; Münz and Ulrich, 'Depopulation after Unification?', p.31.
20. J. Dorbritz, 'Sozialer Systemwandel und die Folgen für die Familienbildung', *Berliner Journal für Soziologie*, Vol.3, No.3 (1993), p.363; L.A. Vaskovics and H. Rost, 'Junge Ehepaare in den alten und neuen Bundesländern – Ein Vergleich', in Nauck *et al.* (eds.), *Familie und Lebensverlauf*, pp.150–51. Details on the views of the 1,956 persons in the 1993 investigation carried out by the Institut für Sozialdatenanalyse appear in U. Schröter, 'Ostdeutsche Frauen zwischen Verlieren und Gewinnen', in H. Bertram, S. Hradil and G. Kleinhenz (eds.), *Sozialer und demographischer Wandel in den neuen Bundesländern* (Berlin: Akademie Verlag, 1995), p.145.
21. Leibscher *et al.*, 'Bevölkerungsentwicklung', p.77; M. Möhle, 'Frauen in den neuen Bundesländern', p.288.
22. Menning, 'Geburten- und Heiratsverzicht in den neuen Bundesländern', pp.147–8.
23. Leibscher *et al.*, 'Bevölkerungsentwicklung', p.76.
24. K. Starke, 'Partner- und Sexualverhalten ostdeutscher Jugendlicher und gesellschaftlicher Umbruch', in H. Sydow (ed.), *Entwicklung und Sozialisation von Jugendlichen vor und nach der Vereinigung Deutschlands* (Opladen: Leske & Budrich, 1997), pp.182–3 and 197–9.

25. Möhle, 'Frauen', 'Alleinerziehende in den neuen Bundesländern', pp.285, 288.
26. G. Wagner and J.C. Witte, 'Zur ökonomischen Rationalität des Geburtenrückganges in Ostdeutschland', *DIW Wochenbericht*, Vol.60, No.45 (1993), pp.662–3.
27. D. Dathe, 'Einkommen', in Winkler (ed.), *Sozialreport 1995*, p.179.
28. P. Franz and U. Herlyn, 'Familie als Bollwerk oder als Hindernis? Zur Rolle der Familienbeziehungen bei der Bewältigung der Vereinigungsfolgen', in Nauck *et al.* (eds.), *Familie und Lebensverlauf*, p.99. Multiple responses were permitted. Although pre-school provision in the crèches and kindergartens remains at a high level in east Germany, some parents experience problems with the increase in costs and are inconvenienced by the reduction in places at enterprises.
29. K. Andruschow *et al.*, 'Arbeitsmarkt und Bildung', in Winkler (ed.), *Sozialreport 1995*, p.91. Details of the 1996 survey of 872 east and 720 west Germans are to be found in S. Frister, H. Liljeberg and G. Winkler, *Arbeitslosenreport 1996. Daten und Fakten zur sozialen Lage Arbeitsloser in den alten und neuen Bundesländern* (Berlin: Turm Verlag, 1996), p.167. Material considerations, contact with other people and the development of their personal skills are the main reasons given by east German women for outside employment. According to the Schering study of 2,644 west and 1,711 east German women from the age of 14 years interviewed in 1992, about two-thirds regarded their earnings from employment as enabling them to achieve greater independence. The need to contribute to household income was greater, however, among the easterners (43 per cent to 23 per cent) as was the appreciation of the value of social contacts at work (64 per cent to 41 per cent). See Institut für Demoskopie Allensbach (ed.), *Frauen in Deutschland. Lebensverhältnisse, Lebensstile und Zukunftserwartungen. Die Schering-Frauenstudie '93* (Cologne: Bund-Verlag, 1993), pp.32–4.
30. Schröter, 'Ostdeutsche Frauen', p.144. According to a 1995 survey, fewer east than west Germans (16 per cent to 48 per cent) believe that the kindergarten damages the development of young children: see Frister *et al.*, *Arbeitslosenreport 1996*, p.168.
31. L Böckmann-Schewe, C. Kulka and A. Röhrig, '"Es war immer so, den goldenen Mittelweg zu finden zwischen Familie und Beruf war eigentlich das Entscheidende." Kontinuitäten und Veränderungen im Leben von Frauen in den neuen Bundesländern', *Berliner Journal für Soziologie*, Vol.5, No.2 (1995), p.217.
32. P. Drauschke and M. Stolzenburg, 'Familie', in Winkler (ed.), *Sozialreport 1995*, p.277. The statistics, which are derived from the 1993 Federal Statistical Office's microcensus, probably underestimate the number of cohabitees. A live-in relationship is defined by the office as comprising two partners who live together and maintain a common household: see F. Niemeyer, 'Nichteheliche Lebensgemeinschaften und Ehepaare – Formen der Partnerschaft gestern und heute', *Wirtschaft und Statistik*, No.7 (1994), pp.505–6 and 513.
33. Vaskovics and Rost, 'Junge Ehepaare in den alten und neuen Bundesländern', pp.140, 142. The survey encompassed 350 east and west German married couples.
34. Drauschke and Stolzenburg, 'Familie', p.281.
35. R. Hauser *et al.*, *Ungleichheit und Sozialpolitik* (Opladen: Leske & Budrich, 1998), p.265.
36. H. Großmann and S. Huth, 'Sozialhilfeabhängigkeit Alleinerziehender als Folge des gesellschaftlichen Umbruchs', in Bertram *et al.* (eds.), *Sozialer und demographischer Wandel*, pp.175–6.
37. Drauschke and Stolzenburg, 'Familie', pp.287, 290.
38. Ibid., p.295.
39. Großmann and Huth, 'Sozialhilfeabhängigkeit', pp.167, 171. The research was carried out in 1992.
40. Menning, 'Geburten- und Heiratsverzicht', p.148; Frister *et al.*, *Arbeitslosenreport 1996*, p.97.
41. D. Kirchhöfer, 'Veränderungen in der alltäglichen Lebensführung Ostberliner Kinder', *Aus Politik und Zeitgeschichte*, B11/96 (1997), pp.32, 38. The children were born in 1980 and the observations were conducted over a period of several days in 1990, 1992 and 1994. The main leisure activities of east German families, according to investigations carried out in 1991, 1994 and 1995, were shopping, the company of friends, and helping friends and relatives: see Drauschke and Stolzenburg, 'Familie', p.321.

42. Statistisches Bundesamt, *Statistisches Jahrbuch 1997*, p.79. Allensbach Institute data show that the household remains the domain of women, though to a lesser extent in the new than in the old Länder. In the latter, only 26 per cent as opposed to 42 per cent in the east stated that their husband/partner helped frequently with housework: Institut für Demoskopie Allensbach (ed.), *Frauen in Deutschland*, pp.50–51. Care must be taken not to overemphasise the family division of labour as a source of conflict as some surveys have identified only a low level of outright dissatisfaction with its distribution: Drauschke and Stolzenburg, 'Familie', pp.315–16.

43. Franz and Herlyn, 'Familie als Bollwerk oder als Hindernis?', p.98.

44. Frister *et al.* (eds.) *Arbeitslosenreport 1996*, p.99.

45. L. Ahnert and A. Schmidt, 'Familiäre Anpassungsbelastungen im gesellschaftlichen Umbruch: Auswirkungen auf die frühkindliche Entwicklung', in Sydow *et al.* (eds.), *Chancen und Risiken im Lebenslauf*, pp.166–7.

46. Drauschke and Stolzenburg, 'Familie', p.279.

Women, Work and Family in the New Länder: Conflicts and Experiences

EVA KOLINSKY

Drawing on published statistical accounts and personal testimony, the paper argues that east German women generally were disadvantaged after unification for reasons of lower pay, occupational status or non-transferable qualifications, with motherhood the biggest employment disadvantage of all. Most at risk of unemployment have been single mothers, and households with children headed by a woman are in the lower income brackets. Their employment motivation unabated, east German women of all age groups have developed active strategies of combating unemployment through retraining, participation in employment creating schemes and, among younger women, by postponing childbirth. In the GDR, it was the woman who was expected to change her employment to accommodate family responsibility; in the risk society since unification, this individual resourcefulness and adaptability has become a crucial means of fighting labour market exclusion.

Recasting the GDR economy into a social market economy dismantled established structures of centrally planned production or administration and the labour market that was linked to them. Within less than a decade, eastern Germany experienced a transformation from an industrial into a service society which historical precedence suggests should have taken half a century or so. Accelerated by outmoded technology, products without markets and exorbitant costs of production, de-industrialisation devastated whole industries, depriving many regions of their economic base. Although some observers expect the new Länder to overtake the old and emerge as the most modern region of Germany,[1] by the late 1990s there was little to support these expectations. After a momentous first phase of system transfer, social transformation has reached a second phase of 'problematic normalisation'.[2] By 1994, the legal framework and institutional structures that had been modelled on the west were in place and functioning while everyday living conditions remained challenged by social and economic uncertainties. Employment which had been accessible and even obligatory for all in the GDR now became unpredictable and unemployment a major

---

Eva Kolinsky, Keele University.

social risk in defunct sectors of the economy and in particular for vulnerable
social groups.

Women in eastern Germany were such a vulnerable group. Although the
GDR seemed to have overcome gender discrimination and integrated
women as frequently as men into the workforce, they have been threatened
in greater numbers than men by labour market exclusion in the transformed
social and economic climate of the 1990s. Indeed, gendered treatment that
had been hidden by women's apparently equal employment participation in
the GDR years disadvantaged women after the system transformation.
Although there is evidence – anecdotal and research-based[3] – of personal
discrimination and a preference for men over women in the labour market,
women as a group found themselves in a situation of 'structural
disadvantage' on account of their employment status and activities, their
income levels and family commitments. While the collapse of the socialist
order removed the stranglehold of political conformity and enabled
individuals to exercise options from travel or consumption to educational
participation and careers, it removed the certainty of finding and retaining
employment. Above all, it shattered the GDR *'Muttipolitik'* of social policy
measures to reduce the conflict between employment and motherhood for
women. The privatisation of the economy also privatised this conflict,
leaving it to individual women to develop strategies of combining two areas
they had taken for granted in the GDR era and continued to see as two facets
of their daily lives: employment and motherhood.

This chapter reviews 'structural disadvantages' arising from GDR
women's policy and examines how women fared with regard to
employment opportunities and income in the transformed economy.
Children constitute one of the most significant obstacles to labour market
participation and postponing childbirth is one of the most important
strategies of recasting biographies. The chapter concludes that east German
women remain distinctive in their employment orientation and confidence
in their ability to cope with the challenging conditions around them.

POST-COMMUNIST DISADVANTAGES

The near-complete employment participation of women in the GDR did not
result in equal starting positions after the system transformation had taken
effect. Women had been directed by the state into women's jobs either in
certain branches of industry, such as textile production, or at inferior levels
of seniority. Most middle and top management positions were occupied by
men. Although women were represented more strongly at the lower levels
of management, their access to leadership functions fell short of their
employment participation. In her research on the career orientation of east

German women, Barbara Bertram observed that most did not aim for top functions but were content at a more modest level.[4] Since advancement in the GDR was linked to political activism and often required membership in the ruling SED, many women either did not have the time in addition to their family commitments or lacked the inclination to get involved.[5]

Less obvious at the time was that women were paid less than men. From the outset, the GDR had proclaimed equal pay for equal work. Yet, even within the same wage or salary group, the majority of women tended to be paid at the bottom end, the majority of men at the top end.[6] When the GDR collapsed, women's average pay was one third lower than that of men. While the wage differences may not have mattered much in a low-wage economy with comparatively uniform income levels, it did begin to matter and turn into a disadvantage once income differentiation got under way.[7] The wage discrimination of women was also obfuscated by the 'second wage package' of child-related benefits. Comprising child allowances, child-care subsidies and other financial support to which mothers were entitled in the GDR, the 'second wage package' was generous in comparison to the low wages. At the end of the month, a woman with children seemed to have as much money in her pocket as her male colleagues and had no sense of being disadvantaged materially. It was only after the 'second wage package' disappeared that women's actual income fell by about one-third and their lower income from employment alone determined their material circumstances. In addition, the GDR had contributed at least 80 per cent of child-care costs through a system of state-run facilities from birth to the age of ten, holiday centres, youth clubs and leisure activities. After unification, all these institutions – if they survived at all – were placed on a market footing and the cost for their services charged to the users. The abolition of state funding for child-care exacerbated the deterioration of women's financial situation after unification without even taking traumatic experiences such as unemployment into account.

In the transformed labour market, women were less competitive than men. On the one hand, women's qualifications tended to be different from those of men and could be regarded as less valuable. On the other hand, women had often been employed in areas with low levels of modernisation and with tasks designed to compensate for technological deficiencies. Although female employment in key areas of economic restructuring, such as services, retailing and administration, should have placed women in an advantageous position after transformation, the type of work they had carried out within these sectors was not required once the GDR ceased to exist. With special reference to banking and insurance – both predominantly female areas of employment in the GDR – Hildegard Maria Nickel has shown the displacement of women by men as well as the success of some women who were kept on, upgrading their skills and even obtaining management positions which would have been inaccessible to them before.[8]

No amount of education or qualification could have prepared women in eastern Germany to counteract the most serious of the structural disadvantages to surface after unification: the structural disadvantage 'family'. The life plans of women in the GDR included as 'normal' to be a working woman and to have children, that is, be a working mother. More than 90 per cent of women aged between 16 and 60 were in employment and an equally high percentage had at least one child. Combining employment and motherhood was the rule in GDR society and widely accepted by women and men as a social norm in their daily lives.

The market principles that came into effect with unification clashed with this norm. In the GDR, the state and its citizens had viewed women as 'working mothers' and expected them to live by combining employment and motherhood. The west German economic model views women as would-be housewives who withdraw from the labour market to care for their children during the so-called 'family phase'. In this perspective, employment and motherhood are separate, conflicting commitments. If a woman wishes to participate in the labour market, the requirements of the labour market take priority and sorting out family commitments are her own, private responsibility. Women who are childless and living alone are better prepared to meet these demands than women with families and children.

Repercussions of market economic principles were quick in coming. Even before currency union took effect, several east German enterprises closed their child-care facilities. In an economic environment where women had to make their own arrangements if they chose to combine motherhood and employment, child-care provisions turned from an unquestioned service into an insupportable cost factor. As the economic system transfer gathered momentum, employers in the new Länder closed all child-care provisions and dismissed the – mostly female – staff who had run them.

Fears that child-care institutions would collapse and force women with children to give up work and concentrate on homemaking were largely unfounded. Although companies withdrew from provision, the governments of the Länder were from the first committed to supporting women's labour market participation by utilising public funds to administer the child-care sector which the privatised economy had abandoned. On paper at least, all Länder have succeeded in meeting demand by offering a place to every child between birth and school age who is registered for care. As in the GDR, child-care facilities are open daily and for the duration of a full working day. As west German regulations about staffing and equipment were applied in the east, and as facilities were relocated from the workplace into properties owned or administered by local authorities, actual provisions changed to such an extent that the sector has been perceived as in decline and at risk. In smaller towns and in the countryside, child-care facilities may be too far away to be accessible while even in cities women can no longer expect to find a place near their home or place of work. Overall, however, the political will to sustain the established full-time child-care system sets the east German Länder apart from their western counterparts and ensures better access to full-time care facilities in the east than in the west.

No less important is that full-time child-care remains accepted and used. In 1996, 80 per cent of east Germans in employment and 84 per cent of east German women in employment used full-time child-care facilities to have their child or children looked after. Even 51 per cent of the unemployed used full-time child-care.[9] Winkler's *Frauenreport* of 1990 showed that attendance at a crèche or kindergarten rose to over 90 per cent for pre-school children over the age of three. For one to three year olds, it stood around 70 per cent. Most east German women made use of the 'baby year' and cared for their children at home during the first year of life, although one in three children under the age of one were also placed in full-time day-care facilities.[10] Unless a woman had more than one child in close succession, east German women were impatient to return to work and did not normally relish their time as full-time mothers:

> I was quite sure that I would stay at home during the baby year, for the good of the child ... and for the good of the whole family and I managed it because it made sense, but during the second part of the year it was already quite unbearable for me. I noticed such things as I would stand in the stairwell talking with neighbours about the goods on offer just then in the co-op or in the evening, when the husband finally returns from his studies or from work, telling him how often and where the baby crawled a few yards, and to notice that he is not the least bit interested – well I realised then that I absolutely loathed the whole situation.[11]

Using child-care facilities is more than a mere necessity in eastern Germany. Some 55 per cent believe that full-time day-care does not harm a child in its development. In western Germany, an even higher proportion (62 per cent) believe that all care of a small child outside the family inflicts harm and should be avoided.[12] In eastern Germany, 64 per cent are even convinced that children benefit from being looked after in full-time child-care facilities, with women as positive as men in their assessment of its effects. In western Germany, just 21 per cent regard child-care as beneficial, with women more outspokenly negative than men.[13] Younger women tend to be more open minded and willing to endorse child-care, older women more critical. In 1996, a majority (55 per cent) of east German women aged 60 and over rejected child-care outside the home, a view that may pave the way for a new role for older, non-working women to support their children by looking after their grandchildren. In Saxony Anhalt, an estimated one in three women in early or full retirement were involved in this way in 1994.[14] In the new Länder as a whole, 63 per cent of only children who were of pre-school age in 1995 were regularly looked after by their grandparents, usually the grandmother. In families with more than one child, the caring role of grandparents was less central.[15]

FROM NORM TO RISK: WOMEN AND CHILDREN

With regard to children, GDR normality no longer applies. Then, women were in their early twenties when their first child was born; today the average age of first-time mothers is 27 years. This is not to say that young women in east Germany do not want children. The wish to have children remains at 80 per cent, and is higher than in the west in all age groups. In east Germany more women than men want to have children of their own. A majority (61 per cent) would like to have two children.

TABLE 1
WOMEN WITH CHILDREN IN THE OLD AND NEW LÄNDER
BY AGE GROUPS (%)

Own Children	Under 25	25–29	30–39	40–49	50–59	60 & Over	Total
(a) Old Länder							
Yes	5	29	68	81	89	87	65
No	95	72	32	19	11	13	35
(b) New Länder							
Yes	7	60	89	92	96	93	78
No	93	40	11	8	4	7	22

Source: *Gleichberechtigung von Frauen und Männern*, ed. Bundesministerium für Familien, Senioren, Frauen und Jugend (Stuttgart: Kohlhammer 1996), p.17.

Since unification, motherhood among women under the age of 25 has plummeted to the low levels familiar from west Germany (see Table 1). In all other age groups, however, more east German women have children than in the west. Although the birth rate in the GDR had fallen, the social policies designed to support motherhood and put into place from the mid-1970s onwards reduced the decline. When the transformation of the labour market turned children into a risk factor and potential employment liability, only younger women who had not completed their families could respond by recasting their biographies and postponing or foregoing child bearing. In the age group 25 to 29, these personal strategies were clearly visible in 1996, although even here the proportion of women with children in east Germany was twice as high as west Germany (see Table 1). Faced with the privatised conflict between employment and family, east German women tried to obtain their qualifications and secure their career before venturing into motherhood. Women with children, of course, faced no option but to cope with adversity. Women without children at the time of system transformation perceived motherhood as an incalculable risk:

> As far as I personally am concerned, I was still single before the 'Wende' and wanted a child and, actually, I still would like to have a child. Only today I am afraid of it because of the financial and social situation. I would practically have to stop working and could not be sure what would happen to me … if I had to write off my job. Well, this would be the end for me and I am really afraid of this. This is why there is the wish to have a child, this was normal then but today it has become a luxury, I should say, to be able to afford a child.[16]

The report *Women in the Land Brandenburg* speaks of a '*Wende*-break' parallel to the 'Pill-break' of the 1960s. In 1990, the ratio of children born to women in the region was 1,531 per 1,000. Three years on, it had fallen to 737.[17] In 1995, the birth-rate in the new Länder was 842, in the old Länder 1,338. The slight increase resulted from the fact that women over the age of 25 now had a child – usually a first and possibly an only child. Recasting their biography and having a child at a later stage than they would have done had they lived in the GDR has been a key aspect of personal adjustment to the transformed social environment.

Traditional views of women's role in society tend to see marriage and child bearing as successive stages of a normal biography. In the GDR, and even more strongly in the new Länder since unification, they have constituted separate options.[18] Motherhood without marriage had been on the increase before 1990 and single mothers enjoyed an array of special protective measures to enable them to combine employment and child rearing. It seems that east German society did not attach any stigma to unmarried motherhood. As a family type or choice of lifestyle, single motherhood before the system transfer resulting from unification neither entailed the risk of unemployment nor a risk of poverty arising from low income. These risks now exist.

There are several reasons for the potentially precarious social and economic situation of single mothers. The social order which took effect in the new Länder from 1990 implemented a version of the male breadwinner

model of the family. Tax legislation, child benefit and other policy devices
favoured households based on marriage and with one dominant provider.
There are no measures targeted to supporting women in their biographical
decision to become single mothers. Women who enter single parenthood as
a result of divorce are affected in the same way. Other than the minimal
provision of benefit payment at subsistence level, social policy offers no
safeguards that could enable single mothers to combine employment and
family duties.[19] There is only one exception to the social policy preference
for married couples: educational leave, the right for new mothers to
withdraw from the labour market for up to three years without losing the
right to resume their employment at the same level of seniority, has been
extended since unification to include unmarried mothers. In east Germany,
most new mothers make use of their right to educational leave but most
return to work after one year – as they would have done in GDR times. In
west Germany, most new mothers utilise the full three-year period of
educational leave. The right to re-enter the labour market, however, does not
protect women with children from redundancy and dismissal after the
statutory protection of their job has ceased.

Despite a social policy framework designed to favour married couples
and breadwinner-model families, east German women have retained a
preference for lone motherhood. In the GDR, opting for single motherhood
signalled that women valued their independence, were prepared to face risks
in their private lives and confident that they could manage better on their
own (or with a partner not married to them) than with a husband and the
traditional role expectations associated with marriage. The research into
attitude changes conducted by the Socio-Economic Panel showed in 1995
that single mothers viewed their own future more optimistically than single
adults without children or married couples with children.[20]

Beyond personal perceptions and hopes for a better future, however,
single motherhood today entails the highest risk of social exclusion of any
social group. In his analysis of poverty in contemporary German society,
Walter Hanesch observed in the early 1990s that women with children were
most affected by material under-provision in one of the four key areas of
income, education, housing and employment.[21] The Socio-Economic Panel
reached similar conclusions: 'Single parents suffer from a comparatively
unfavourable income situation ... paired with a high degree of inequality in
income distribution. Among this group of people, the risk of slipping into
poverty through low income is particularly high.'[22]

Yet the trend towards single motherhood remains as strong as ever. In
1996, 45 per cent of newborn children in the region of Mecklenburg-
Vorpommern were born to unmarried mothers. In large cities such as
Leipzig and Berlin, the proportion of unmarried mothers was even higher.[23]

Although the statistics do not show how many unmarried mothers lived with a partner when their child was born, differences from west Germany are striking. Here, couples tend to cohabit until a child is on the way and marry before it is born; in eastern Germany marriage and childbirth remain more distinct options. In Mecklenburg-Vorpommern, unmarried mothers even outnumbered married mothers among women under the age of 25.[24]

FAMILY STRUCTURES TRANSFORMED

Marriage itself has been in decline since unification. In 1990, for example, 22,000 marriages took place in the Brandenburg region; in 1991 their number had fallen by half and by 1995 by 60 per cent to just 8,775.[25] Other regions experienced similar developments. For 1989, Mecklenburg-Vorpommern reported 8.5 marriages per 1,000 inhabitants; for 1995, it was only 3.3. The low point had been reached between 1991 and 1993, with just 2.9 marriages per 1,000 inhabitants.[26]

During the same period, the average marital age rose to 31 years for women and 34 years for men. For first marriages it stood at 27 years for women and 29 years for men, four to five years higher than at the end of the GDR.[27] This rapid increase in the marital age within so short a period shows how drastically the generation who experienced the system transformation and its social consequences as young adults recast a core aspect of their biographies. Not unlike motherhood, marriage – if it is an option at all – is postponed until personal career plans, qualifications and integration into the labour market have been accomplished or appear transparent. Further research is needed into the employment status of women on marriage and the prospects in the labour market of mothers who had postponed childbearing in a bid to secure their employment integration.

Divorces developed in a somewhat different way. Unification itself resulted in a dramatic drop in numbers to an all-time low in the post-war era. While every fourth marriage ended in divorce in 1989 and the GDR had one of the highest divorce rates in Europe, marriages became uncommonly stable with just one in five ending in divorce in 1992. The sudden durability of marriage had nothing to do with a more secure status of the institution, but reflected the uncertainties surrounding the changes in the legislation and the impact of the west German divorce law on east Germans. After the clean-break tradition that had prevailed in the GDR, the maintenance and asset-sharing provisions of its successor acted as an effective, albeit short-lived, deterrent. From 1993 onwards, the divorce rate has stood at a record high. In 1996, 45 out of 100 marriages ended in divorce, more than at any time during the GDR era.[28]

Now, as then, more women than men tend to file for divorce. In 1991, two out of three divorces were initiated by women; in 1995, three out of four.[29] For the GDR years, attempts to explain women's active part in seeking a divorce have pointed to persistent, unequal gender roles in the home and women's reluctance to endure them.[30] This discrepancy could still apply today. In 1996, 12 per cent of east German men living in a marriage or partnership did not contribute to household chores but left women to cope with the unpaid work in the family.[31] Of course, one of the contradictions of GDR society had been that women's full integration into the labour market hardly modified gender-specific family roles or made partners share household and child-care duties more evenly.[32] Women remained solely or predominantly responsible for traditional domestic and caring tasks; even in the transformed conditions of unified Germany, gender roles and stereotypes persisted inside the family. They also influenced the expectations about women's employment. In 1993, for instance, 23 per cent of east Germans believed that occupational success was more important for men than for women. In working class milieus, the view was particular widespread that men's employment was more important than that of women, and women's main realm of duty was in the home.[33] Three years on, however, the gendered perspective on women, employment and home had declined. Just ten per cent continued to rate men's employment higher than that of women. In the meantime, persistent unemployment and employment insecurities had played havoc with many established role distributions and diminished the number of two-earner households to less than half the total.

The changed biographical decisions about marriage, births and divorce resulted in an increase in one- and two-person households. In the Brandenburg region, for example, the number of households with three or more people declined while smaller households with just one or two members increased from 8.4 to 11.4 per cent between 1991 and 1995. Households of more than two people declined especially sharply in the age cohort which was in a position to draw personal consequences from the system transformation: the under-35s.[34] Increases in numbers were strongest for one-person households of single or separated individuals and for households with more than one member where the head of household was a single person.[35] Nine out of ten such households were headed by a woman.

If we take the number of children rather than the number of households, the changes in family structure are even more evident. Between 1991 and 1995, the number of children living in families with parents married to each other declined by nine per cent, while the number of children living with just one parent rose by 20 per cent.[36] In the same period, the number of children growing up in one-parent families increased by 24 per cent. Some of these developments can be traced to the rising divorce rate, but the most important factor was the continued increase of births out of wedlock and the emergence of single motherhood as an accepted family type in eastern Germany.

DUAL EXCLUSION: UNEMPLOYMENT AND LOW INCOMES

Since the system transformation that put an end to the GDR-style employment society, unemployment and employment uncertainties have become daily risks. In families with three or more members, employment decreased between 1991 and 1995 while unemployment rose by 40 per cent. In the same period, the number of households headed by a woman without employment grew from 59 per cent to 64 per cent while households with an employed woman as head decreased from 41 per cent to 36 per cent. The number of households headed by an employed man also fell a little but remained high at 63 per cent.[37] Families with children fared worst. Here, unemployment of the head of household increased by 30 per cent. In Brandenburg alone, 80,000 children lived in a family whose head was unemployed, an increase of 54 per cent from 1991.[38]

A survey conducted in the Saxony-Anhalt in 1993 pointed to the link between women's unemployment risk and their status as mothers. At the time, 23 per cent of women with children who were married or lived in a partnership were unemployed. Of the female lone parents, 35 per cent were unemployed. Women without children also faced an unemployment risk, but at a lower level. At the time, just one in ten single women without children and one in six women living in a partnership or marriage but without children were out of work.[39] For 1992, Hölzler and Mächler recorded in their *Sozialbericht* that 17 per cent of women with children were unemployed compared to 11 per cent of women without children. Women with children under the age of three faced an even higher risk of unemployment, with 37 per cent out of work at the time.[40] Regional statistics for Brandenburg confirm this unemployment risk. Between 1991 and 1995, female unemployment had risen by about half; unemployment of single mothers, however, had soared by 142 per cent.[41]

In the social transformation of post-communist Germany, children have become an employment risk. This risk exacerbates the comparatively disadvantageous starting position of east German women in the market economy due to their concentration in certain branches and their career tracks, the limited use of their qualifications outside the GDR and their place at the lower end of the employment hierarchy. Moreover, the post-unification labour market displayed a bias in favour of men and against women from the outset. In the allocation of short-time working or specially funded work-creation employment, men took precedence over women and generally enjoyed better chances than women to re-enter the labour market after unemployment. In the post-communist transformation in Germany, women have been exposed to unemployment earlier and more severely than men. Nearly a decade after it first began to constitute a threat in the new Länder, unemployment has continued to rise, passing the 20 per cent mark in 1997. Throughout these years, at least 60 per cent of the unemployed have been women. Of a female labour force exceeding three million, close to one million are unemployed. Long-term unemployment has been a particular problem for women. Since 1991, at least 70 per cent of the long-term unemployed have been women.[42] The unemployment figures may even obfuscate a new 'silent reserve' of unemployed married women who do not appear in the statistics since they are not entitled to benefit on account of their husband's income. In Brandenburg, for instance, unemployment among married couples with children rose to 28,000 in 1993 but had fallen by 6,000 two years later. Given that unemployment has continued to increase generally and among women, the unexpected drop points to a 'silent reserve' of unrecorded unemployed rather than actual successes in the job market. Basing women's entitlement to benefit on husband's earnings may also mitigate against marriage, since single women – whether or not they live in a partnership – keep at least their entitlement to benefit in the case of unemployment and thus a slice of financial independence.

There are no signs that east German women are throwing in the towel and reinventing themselves in the role of housewife. In 1996, just one per cent of women in Saxony-Anhalt referred to themselves as housewives. The vast majority saw themselves as working women who were either in employment or looking for employment. In the GDR, women had valued the financial independence arising from their own earned income and prided themselves in contributing significantly – 40 per cent – to household incomes. While this contribution has now become less predictable, women's sense of self continues to focus on employment and financial independence while their personal strategies are designed to optimise their chances of obtaining them.[43]

Social transformation set in motion a growth and differentiation of incomes and replaced the shortage society of the GDR era with a western-style consumer society. In the 1940s and 1950s, the shift from post-war shortages to affluence raised living standards broadly enough to be credited with an 'elevator effect' (Beck). Although western Germans were better off in their affluent society than their parents or grandparents had been, social differences of income and status remained. In eastern Germany, social transformation displaced the state-imposed uniformity of incomes by differentiated earnings linked to achievement and status. Not everyone, however, was in a position to take part in it. Instead of an 'elevator effect', where everyone goes up together, some saw their financial situation improve rapidly while others were left behind. Generally speaking, households with only one income have been less well placed to benefit from income differentiation and income growth than households with two earned incomes. Unemployment and the income loss resulting from it further widened the gap (see Table 2).

TABLE 2

HOUSEHOLD INCOMES IN BRANDENBURG, 1991–95 (%)

Year	Under DM 1,000	DM 1,000– under DM 2,500	DM 2,500– under DM 4,000	DM 4,000 and over
(a) More Than One Income Earner				
1991	3	61	29	6
1995	1	20	44	34
(b) Only One Income Earner				
1991	41	58	–	–
1995	8	66	18	6

Source: Beiträge zur Statistik Brandenburgs 'Privathaushalte und Familien in den Jahren 1991–1995', Landesamt für Datenverarbeitung und Statistik H. 7 (Potsdam, 1996), p.10 (own calculations; percentages rounded and may not add up to 100).

In 1991, more than half the households with just one income were situated in the higher income bracket at the time, totalling between DM 1,000 and DM 2,500 per month. In 1995, only one in four one-income households remained in the higher income bracket, that is, had earnings over DM 2,500 while three-quarters fell below this level (see Table 2). Households with more than one income, by contrast, fared better in the social transformation. In 1991, 64 per cent of such households were located in the bottom half of the income ranges and just one-third in the higher ranges. Four years on, three-quarters of households with more than one income were placed in the upper half of the income range, earning DM 2,500 or more. One-third even earned over DM 4,000 per month.

Of the households with children, those with only one child fared worst. In one-third of such households, monthly income remained below DM 2,500 while 12 per cent had less than DM 1,000 at their disposal. Households with two or more children were financially better off. Just 15 per cent – compared to 32 per cent of one-child households – lived on incomes of less than DM 2,500. Not all one-child households had low incomes, but as a group they did less well. One in three (34 per cent) of households with one child belonged to the highest income group of DM 4,000, as did 40 per cent of the households with two or more children. One-child households are often single-parent households. According to Winkler,

75 per cent of single-parent households include just one child and tend to be low-income households.[44] A case study of Leipzig found in the mid-1990s that 40 per cent of recipients of a regular living allowance (*Sozialhilfe*) were single mothers and that their number among the poorest was on the increase.[45]

The years of 'normalisation' following the system transfer since 1990 have failed to remove unemployment as a social risk. Women continue to constitute two-thirds of the unemployed and women with children face a particularly high risk of labour market exclusion. At a time of income growth to catch up with western levels and income differentiation to break the state-administered wage uniformity that prevailed in the GDR, labour market exclusion prevents individuals from sharing in these developments. Even short-term unemployment is likely to reduce the earnings potential of individuals on re-entry to the labour market and pushes them to a lower rung on the earnings ladder. Unemployment itself – and non-employment generally – cuts those affected off from the income mobilisation around them. Given that access to earned income is the main source of personal income in eastern Germany, a relative decline in income at a time of income rises can result in poverty. Although individuals may succeed in re-entering the labour market and improving their personal circumstances, they are unlikely to close the gap. This is particularly true for women with children, that is, the majority of women in eastern Germany aged over 25. As the conflict between employment and family resurfaced with the transformation to a market economy, women were challenged to find their own, individualised, ways of resolving it. The privatisation of combining employment and family commitments has disadvantaged women generally and placed unfamiliar and often insurmountable obstacles in the way of women with children.

While the motivation of east German women remains undaunted – to be active in the labour market and also have children – those young enough to do so recast their biographies to manage the conflict imposed on them and find their own ways to engage in employment, motherhood, marriage and family. Common to all strategies has been the determination of east German women to retain a place in the labour market either in employment or as a registered unemployed and to escape the impoverishment which labour market exclusion may cause.

RESPONDING TO SOCIAL TRANSFORMATION

One of the first authors to highlight women's responses to the collapse of socialism and the social transformation that followed was Birgit Bütow in her 1990 study of women in Saxony. She found that 76 per cent were optimistic about their own future while 24 per cent felt largely pessimistic. Women whose place in the labour market has since turned out to be particularly uncertain harboured most doubts in the zero hour of post-communist development: women above the age of 45 (52 per cent), single mothers (52 per cent), women without recognised vocational qualifications (59 per cent) and unemployed women (46 per cent). University-educated women are an exception from this rule: they were most pessimistic about their personal future in 1990 but have since found it easier to establish a foothold in the transformed labour market and build a career.[46]

Before the full impact of social transformation on employment and income development or the blessings of a consumer society had become apparent, women were divided in their opinions how they themselves would be affected. Some relished the new challenges: 'So far, things have gone extremely well and the *Wende* brought nothing but advantages for me. More is demanded from me and I am surprised how much I can achieve and what I am capable of.'[47] Others saw that the certainties of old had gone for good and unemployment risks were an inevitable by-product of system transformation. A 24-year-old nursery nurse with one child under the age of three summed up the mix of risk and opportunity as follows: 'So far I am OK and have not fared badly; things are certainly better than under the old system. I am hoping that I will not lose my job; unemployment would make everything much more difficult.'[48] Some saw their own circumstances in a broader perspective and feared that social transformation would change women's situation generally. A 37-year-old skilled worker who had already lost her job and re-entered the labour market on a work-creation scheme linked women's unemployment with a tendency to exclude them as a group from the labour market and reinstate more traditional female roles. In the early days of unification, similar concerns were widely held: 'I am managing quite well in the new social system. The problem, as I see it, relates to women generally and the threat that they will be forced back to the hearth and into the home. If this were to happen, the living standards of my family would be reduced severely.'[49]

After unification, women who were single and childless, women who had recognised vocational qualifications or university degrees and women in medical and legal professions found it easier to adjust to the new working environment than women at the lower end of the qualifications hierarchy, unskilled or semi-skilled manual workers and women who had only completed partial or minimal training. Even in the GDR, women as a group had already developed a good deal of employment flexibility and mobility since it had normally been up to the woman to adapt her work schedule to accommodate family commitments. Thus women changed jobs to find more time to care for their children or tuned down their career orientation to combine employment and family roles. Frequently, east German women with children were employed below their formal qualifications and potential seniority to scale down the demands emanating from employment. Women also were less able to enrol in further qualification courses or engage in the political activism that was required for advancement at work. Thus, east German women had limited their commitment to employment in order to manage their day-to-day family duties. Their aim had not been career management but juggling roles in such a way as to create sufficient time for the family. At work, this adjustment manifested itself in numerous disadvantages, such as the lower wages and reduced access to senior positions mentioned earlier. Most women, however, were not career-oriented in a western sense but approached employment as a tenet of their lives that did not require special efforts or needed to open further opportunities. Men, by contrast, appear to have been more purposefully career-oriented and did not adjust their employment in line with family commitments.

After unification transformed the working environment, east German women could build on the flexibility they had already practised in the GDR era and their pragmatic determination to manage as best they could in adverse circumstances. New employment strategies were sorely needed. By 1991, one in three east Germans had changed jobs since the end of the GDR; of those in employment in the mid-1990s, four out of five had changed jobs or been out of work. Women, again, were more affected than men by employment insecurity. In the new Länder generally, job security for those in employment had begun to improve by 1995, but it had decreased for women in the age group 16 to 34.[50] More than ever, east German women were challenged to adjust and develop personal strategies of labour market management. In the GDR, they had applied personal strategies to reduce the potential conflict between employment and family roles at the expense of their career opportunities; in the transformed eastern Germany, the strategies of pragmatic adjustment to circumstances made women particularly resourceful in attempting to create new employment opportunities through education, retraining and by rethinking their family roles. It also made them more than ever sensitive about discrimination against them as women and, above all, as women with children.

It could be argued that women in the GDR did not share the sense of gender inequality that had emerged in western Germany. It would be misleading to claim that sexist attitudes at work did not exist, but they were not noticed since they did not exist officially.[51] The new women's movement view of patriarchy as an all-pervasive principle of the social order and of male behaviour in it was not shared in eastern Germany where women perceived their own place as on a par with that of men while evidence of gender inequality was either not known or not interpreted as such. While feminists in the west have viewed family duties as a potential impairment of their rights of self-determination, women in the east remained convinced that motherhood and – to a somewhat lesser degree – marriage constituted core parts of their lives together with employment. When east German women began to express feelings of dissatisfaction with their situation after the collapse of the GDR, they objected to the experience that their status as a woman prevented them from being treated fairly. In the past, their qualifications and achievement at work seemed to be gender-neutral. In the system transformation since 1990, no such neutrality was assured.

In 1996, a survey commissioned by the Federal Ministry for Families, Seniors, Women and Youth compared how men and women between the ages of 16 and 69 in the old and the new Länder viewed their personal situation. Respondents were invited to comment on the match between their circumstances at the time and their own expectations of fair rewards (see Table 3). In the old Länder, women under 50 were more likely than men to find their circumstances adequate, although discontent was somewhat higher among women over 50 than among men of this age group. In the new Länder, young women below the age of 34 were more positive about their own situation than their male peers. Women in the middle group of 35 to 49 were much more dissatisfied than east German men in that age group and,

TABLE 3

SATISFACTION WITH PERSONAL SITUATION BY AGE GROUP
AND GENDER, 1996 (%)

I have:	Total	16–34 Men	16–34 Women	35–49 Men	35–49 Women	50–69 Men	50–69 Women
(a) Old Länder							
More than I should have	7	14	8	6	4	5	2
about what I should have	65	60	68	60	67	69	68
less than I should have	25	23	23	29	24	25	27
(b) New Länder							
More than I should have	4	6	5	7	1	2	3
about what I should have	52	58	63	53	46	48	44
less than I should have	40	32	28	37	49	47	49

Note: The question was: If you think of your life just now, do you think you have, generally speaking, more than you should have, just about what you should have or less than you have have?

Source: Gleichberechtigung von Frauen und Männern. Wirklichkeit und Einstellung der Bevölkerung 1996, Bundesminister f. Familie, Senioren, Frauen und Jugend (Stuttgart: Kohlhammer, 1996), p.4.

together with east German women over 50, emerged as the most dissatisfied age group of all. Data collected in the mid-1990s by the Socio-Economic Panel on social transformation and attitude change confirmed the picture that east German women over the age of 35 were particularly dissatisfied with their personal circumstances and pessimistic about their long-term prospects in the labour market. Women aged 50 or over who were not in work doubted that they would ever find paid employment again (83 per cent) while women of this age group who were employed at the time of the study were even more certain (88 per cent) that they could never re-enter the labour market if they ever lost their job.[52]

Yet women in the new Länder have not resigned themselves to unemployment but strive to retain their rights of labour market participation and to optimise any chances of re-entry. A report on labour market development in Saxony-Anhalt revealed in 1997 that women who had lost their jobs tried harder than men to make a new start by gaining a new qualification or updating existing skills. At the time, 50 per cent more women than men had enrolled in retraining programmes. This even applied to women over the age of 50, whose chances of re-employment were low. While men in this age group usually interpreted unemployment as retirement, women tried to relaunch their careers in a different direction.[53] A similar activity bonus was apparent at the other end of the age spectrum. Young women were more active than young men in applying for apprenticeships and submitted more applications than men to find employment. Despite their more intense efforts to secure training and employment, young women in eastern Germany were less successful than young men in their actual transition from school to work. Here, west German inequalities seem to be replicated. Studies of the transition of girls and boys from school to apprenticeships and employment have noted since the early 1970s that young women's educational qualifications and higher grades were not matched with labour market chances. Here, young men remained advantaged despite their inferior performance at school.[54] At the lower end of the qualification spectrum, young west German women tended to respond to their poor prospects in the labour market by adjusting their initial expectations of combining employment and family and accepting a family-based role of housewife and mother. At the age of 14 or 15 this had not been their purpose in life; by the time they were in their late teens, the labour market obstacles and in particular the difficulties they encountered in gaining an apprenticeship and vocational qualifications turned the role of housewife and mother into one they accepted as an alternative to their original choice.[55] The development of family types and birth rates in west Germany confirms that women with lower qualifications tend to marry earlier, have more children and are more often not employed than their peers with higher educational and vocational or professional qualifications. For these women, however, successful labour market integration is often achieved by postponing family commitments and childbearing or avoiding them altogether.[56]

In contrast, women in the new Länder show no sign of accepting an alternative role of housewife regardless of their level of educational and employment qualifications and their discouraging experiences in the transformed labour market. The 1992 Shell study was among the first to observe gender differences and a distinctive motivation of young east German women to succeed:

> With regard to their personal plans in life, east German young women are the most ambitious. Some 19.6 per cent compared to 14.7 per cent of young men even declare to be very demanding and very ambitious … Girls and young women are ready to learn, mobile and flexible. They give their best, do not engage in violent resistance and adjust to new circumstances in terms of actively coping with them. The fact that despite these strengths they can expect to be disadvantaged is placing a considerable social strain on women as a group.[57]

Even young women who were only in their teens or younger when the GDR collapsed and whose adult life had yet to take shape retain the expectation of combining employment and a family of their own. Despite gender-specific obstacles that have made it more difficult for women to fulfil their employment motivation, their pragmatic adjustment takes the form of postponing family commitments until they feel secure in their employment situation. Being a housewife does not count as a valid role for a woman in eastern Germany.

INDIVIDUALISATION AND PERSONAL STRATEGIES

In the GDR era, women had to take a flexible approach to their employment in order to ensure that they could manage the combination of employment and family commitments expected of them. Their personal strategies of adjustment tended to reduce their employment load to match their personal agenda and were supported by the social system and the women's policies it had in place. The need for women to develop a flexibility that would allow them to combine employment and family did not expose them to western-style interrupted and unpredictable employment experiences. Yet, it would be wrong to conclude from the absence of piece-meal working lives in the GDR that 'the regime offered a seamless, fully organised biography' to all its citizens.[58] It did not for women. While the 'pressure of individualisation'[59] to which women were subjected was not comparable to that which commenced with the collapse of state socialism, east German women had already been challenged to show initiative, devise their own format of combining employment and family roles and respond flexibly to changing demands in their social environment. After unification, this experience in devising personal strategies prepared women for some of the challenges of individualisation despite the obstacles encountered by women with children and the unexpected impact of gender discrimination.

East German women built on their experience of devising personal strategies and pragmatically adjusting conflicting demands of employment and family in developing new strategies to cope with the impact of transformation since 1990. Recasting their biographies, they retained their motivation to have children of their own but pragmatically postponed its realisation to a later date. Outperforming men, they turned access to educational qualifications into their personal success story and have been more active than men in pursuing training and employment opportunities. While women's lower pay and generally lower occupational status in the GDR left them disadvantaged in the social market economy, their ability to respond flexibly to changing circumstances and adapt their personal strategies has been an asset. The young women who seek to secure their employment situation before having children have developed the career motivation which GDR women were unable to sustain and adjusted their situation in order to keep the option of a leadership or management role open for themselves.

In recasting the biography from what had been regarded as 'normal' in the GDR, women intend to create chances and optimise their labour market opportunities. Although less content than men with their actual circumstances, east German women transform their discontent into activity. Far from sitting resigned, hands folded in their laps, they are constantly searching for openings to enter the labour market, find a new route or qualification and a new way of gaining acceptance. They are searching for solutions, compromises and concessions that are suitable to their own personal circumstances. They have managed to handle the pressures of individualisation, although their resourcefulness is by no means certain to lead to success.

Mrs K, whom I interviewed in Leipzig in 1993 when she was in her mid-40s, is a good example of the willingness of east German women to adapt and persist in their search for employment opportunities. During the GDR era, she had been employed in the university sector as a non-academic member of staff and lost her job in the course of university reorganisation. As soon as she knew that unemployment was inevitable, she founded a one-person business, a pet and seed shop run from the garage of her home. At the same time, she applied for and obtained new, temporary employment through a work-creation scheme. At the time of the interview, this employment had come to an end and she was in the process of trying for a follow-on – a two-year affiliation to a research project. Despite her full-time employment through the work-creation programme, Mrs K had kept her own little business going, opening in the evenings and at weekends. Not that she could have lived on the proceeds, but it constituted a defence against the loss of self and purpose which Mrs K associated with unemployment.[60]

With differences in the actual biographical detail, there are innumerable Mrs Ks in the new Länder. They have in common the determination to respond to the new uncertainties in their social environment by developing new skills and changing the way in which they have lived so far:

> It is to be hoped that women will fight the long-term unemployment imposed on them and the unwanted role of housewife. The gulf between the life women wish to lead and the life they can actually lead is much larger in the new Länder than in the old. On the one hand, it came totally out of the blue and without preparation; on the other hand, women have been losing positions and career prospects they had already secured as a result of unemployment which has been worse than anything in the 1920 or the 1950s. Without women's contribution to household income, moreover, material hardship and even poverty seem inevitable.[61]

Attitudes underline the distinctiveness of east German women. They are more confident than men in their own abilities to shape their circumstances instead of looking towards the state to do it for them. Table 4 suggests that west Germans generally are more inclined than east Germans to trust the individual (70 per cent) while east Germans are torn between the effectiveness of the individual (50 per cent) and the obligation of the state (45 per cent) to secure equal treatment in society. In eastern Germany, more women than men (53 per cent compared with 47 per cent) accorded the individual the key role in matters of equality. This could mean that women distrust the state or lost the confidence in the state they may once have had; it could, however, also mean that women in the new Länder have confidence in their own abilities to order their own lives and achieve equality of opportunity and treatment as it suits them, not as commanded by the state.

This confidence in the strength of the individual builds on east German women's experiences in ordering their own lives by adjusting the conflict between employment and family duties to suit their own circumstances. A survey of attitudes in eastern Germany which was conducted in 1990 before unemployment had dismantled the working landscape while the full impact of system transformation had yet to take effect, suggested that east German women had an individualisation bonus compared to men. Asked what they

Putting Equal Opportunities into practice is a matter for	Total	Women	Men
(a) Old Länder			
The state	26	28	25
The individual	70	68	72
Don't know	4	4	4
(b) New Länder			
The state	45	41	43
The individual	50	53	47
Don't know	6	6	5

Note: The question was: 'Putting equal opportunities into practice, is this predominantly a matter for the state or for the individual?'

Source: *Gleichberechtigung von Frauen und Männern*, p.73.

found particularly satisfying in their employment, more women (42 per cent) than men (37 per cent) valued their scope to work independently. Comparing across the former state border, east German women were as likely as west German men to put their scope for independence at work at a premium.[62]

OUTLOOK

East German women are determined to reorganise their personal lives between employment, family and children in such a way that combining the various realms will be possible despite the post-unification obstacles and gender barriers. These recast biographies are evidence of their willingness to respond flexibly and pragmatically to difficult and often unfavourable circumstances. East German women's determination to retain their employment motivation and also fulfil their wish to have a family has lost nothing of its intensity.

By resisting pressures and unspoken assumptions that women should step back from the labour market and accept a traditional role as housewives, east German women have formulated and made visible a distinctive, east-specific view of women's role. They highlighted their own unequal and discriminatory treatment in the transformed labour market of the new Länder. They also highlighted that the civil right of equal treatment in society continues to elude women, and in particular women with children.

NOTES

1. H. Wiesenthal, 'Einleitung: Grundlinien der Transformation in Ostdeutschland', in H. Wiesenthal (ed.), *Einheit als Interessenpolitik: Studien zur sektoralen Transformation* (Frankfurt/Main: Campus, 1995), pp.6 ff.; for the most comprehensive analysis, see Kommission für die Erforschung des sozialen und politischen Wandels in den neuen Bundesländern (ed.), *Berichte zum sozialen und politischen Wandel in Ostdeutschland*, 6 vols. (Opladen: Leske & Budrich, 1996).

2. A. Segert and I. Zierke, *Sozialstruktur und Milieuerfahrung. Aspekte des alltagskulturellen Wandels in Ostdeutschland* (Opladen: Westdeutscher Verlag, 1997), p.48.

3. H.-M. Nickel, 'Der Transformationprozess in Ost und Westdeutschland und seine Folgen für das Geschlechterverhältnis', *Aus Politik und Zeitgeschichte*, B51 (1997). Also C. Sombrowsky (ed.), *Zerbrochene Karrieren. Ostdeutsche Frauen (und Männer) zwischen Anpassung und Widerstand* (Halle: Land Sachsen Anhalt Leitstelle für Frauen, n.d.), pp.102ff.

4. B. Bertram, K. vel Job and W. Friedrich, *Adam und Eva heute* (Leipzig: Verlag für die Frau, 1988), pp.99–104.

5. E. Kolinsky, *Women in Contemporary Germany* (Oxford: Berg, 1993), ch.7.

6. E. Kolinsky, 'Women after *Muttipolitik*', in E. Kolinsky (ed.), *Between Hope and Fear. Everyday Life in Post-Unification East Germany* (Edinburgh: Edinburgh University Press, 1995), pp.188–91.

7. Details in E. Kolinsky, 'Recasting Biographies', in E. Kolinsky (ed.), *Social Transformation and the Family in Post-Communist Germany* (London and Basingstoke: Macmillan, 1998), pp.128–32.

8. Nickel, 'Der Transformationsprozess in Ost- und Westdeutschland', pp.24 ff. Also 'Can the Future (Still) Be Shaped? Gender Difference(s) at Work and by Sector', paper presented at the ESRC research workshop *Social Transformation and the Family* at the University of Potsdam, 20–22 Feb. 1998.

9. *Gleichberechtigung von Frauen und Männern. Wirklichkeit und Einstellungen der Bevölkerung*, ed. Bundesminister für Familien, Senioren, Frauen und Jugend (Stuttgart: Kohlhammer, 1996), p.19.

10. G. Winkler, *Frauenbericht '90* (Berlin: Die Wirtschaft, 1990), p.141; also Stadt Leipzig, Amt für Wahlen und Statistik, *Statistischer Quartalsbericht*, 3 (1997), p.20.

11. Frau Lehmann, born 1954, Technical College qualifications as an economist, two children, divorced; quoted from L. Böckmann, 'Berufsverlauf und weiblicher Lebenszusammenhang', *Zeitschrift f. Frauenforschung*, 4 (1993), p.55.

12. *Gleichberechtigung von Frauen und Männern*, p.25.

13. Ibid., p.27.

14. Sombrowsky (ed.), *Zerbrochene Karrieren*, p.97.

15. B. Nauck, 'Lebensbedingungen von Kindern in Einkind-, Mehrkind- und Vielkindfamilien', in B. Nauck and H. Bertram (eds.), *Kinder in Deutschland*, DJI Familien Survey 5 (Opladen: Leske & Budrich, 1995), p.164.

16. Frau Schütz, born 1950, A-level, diploma, working as a legal consultant, single. Quoted from Böckmann, 'Berufsverlauf und weiblicher lebenszusammenhang', p.59.

17. *Frauen im Land Brandenburg. Daten und Analysen*, ed. Landesamt für Datenverarbeitung und Statistik, Land Brandenburg, no.1 (Potsdam, Feb. 1997), p.10.

18. Kolinsky, *Recasting Biographies*, p.134.

19. M. Schwan, 'Kinder kosten auch Geld', *Zeitschrift f. Frauenforschung* (1997), pp.124–5.

20. *Datenreport 1997*, ed. Statistisches Bundesamt (Bonn: Bundeszentrale für politische Bildung, 1997), p.477.

21. W. Hanesch, *Armut in Deutschland* (Reinbek: Rowohlt, 1994), pp.172ff.

22. *Datenreport 1997*, p.474.

23. *Statistisches Jahrbuch 1996 Mecklenburg-Vorpommern*, ed. Statistisches Landesamt Mecklenburg Vorpommern (Schwerin, 1996), p.341.

24. Ibid., p.46.

25. *Land Brandenburg. Statistisches Jahrbuch 1995*, p.32.

124 RECASTING EAST GERMANY

26. *Statistisches Jahrbuch 1995 Mecklenburg Vorpommern*, p.40.
27. *Frauen im Brandenburg*, p.13.
28. *Statistisches Jahrbuch des Landes Sachsen Anhalt 1996*, part I, Halle 1996, p.62.
29. *Frauen im Land Brandenburg*, p.17.
30. M. Dennis, 'Family Policy and Family Function in the German Democratic Republic', in Kolinsky (ed.), *Social Transformation and the Family*, pp.45ff.
31. *Gleichberechtigung von Frauen und Männern*, p.15.
32. Bertram *et al. Adam und Eva heute*, pp.142ff.
33. Segert and Zemke, *Sozialstruktur und Milieuerfahrungen*, p.145.
34. Beiträge zur Statistik Brandenburgs. *Privathaushalte und Familien in den Jahren 1991–1995*. Landesamt für Datenverarbeitung und Statistik H. 7 (Potsdam, 1996), p.6.
35. Ibid., p.7.
36. Ibid., p.22.
37. Ibid., p.9.
38. Ibid., p.22.
39. *Die Beschäftigungsentwicklung in Ostdeutschland* (Madgeburg: Amt f. Gleichstellungsfragen, n.d.), p.55.
40. I. Hölzler and H. Mächler, *Sozialbericht 1992. Daten und Fakten zur sozialen Lage in Sachsen-Anhalt* (University of Magdeburg: Institute for Sociology, 1993), pp.90–91.
41. *Privathaushalte und Familien*, p.27.
42. Details in U. Engelen-Kefer *et al.*, *Beschäftigungspolitik* (Cologne: Bund Verlag, 1995), p.324; also E. Kolinsky, 'Germany Transformed', in Kolinsky (ed.), *Between Hope and Fear*.
43. Ministerium für Arbeit, Soziales und Gesundheit des Landes Sachsen-Anhalt, *Arbeitsmarkt-Monitor* (Jan. 1996), Table B-05.
44. Hölzer and Mächler, *Sozialbericht 1992*, p.238.
45. E. Kolinsky, 'Women after *Muttipolitik*', in Kolinsky (ed.), *Between Hope and Fear*, p.192.
46. B. Bütow, *Frauen in Sachsen. Zwischen Hoffnung und Betroffenheit* (Leipzig: Rosa Luxemburg Verein, 1990), p.9.
47. The respondent was aged 22, childless, employed full-time as a secretary and had completed an apprenticeship. Bütow, *Frauen in Sachsen*, p.41.
48. Ibid., p.41.
49. Ibid.
50. *Datenreport 1997*, p.496.
51. *Zerbrochene Karrieren*, p.277; also S. Metz-Göckel, U. Müller and H.M. Nickel, 'Geteilte Welten. Geschlechterverhältnis und Geschlechterpolarisierung in West und Ost', in Jugendwerk der Deutschen Shell (ed.), *Jugend '92. Lebenslagen, Orientierungen und Entwicklungsperspektiven im vereinigten Deutschland* (Opladen: Leske & Budrich, 1992), p.347.
52. *Datenreport 1997*, p.493.
53. K. Otto, *Frauen zwischen Familie, Beruf und Sozialpolitik am Beispiel Sachsen-Anhalt* (Diplomarbeit, Fachhochschule Magdeburg, 1997, unpublished), p.18. The main findings were published by the Gleichstellungsbeauftragte, Sachsen-Anhalt in a discussion paper, *Die Beschäftigungssituation in Ostdeutschland seit der Wende* (Halle, n.d.).
54. See Kolinsky, *Women in Contemporary Germany*, ch. 4.
55. A. Seidenspinner *et al.*, *Mädchen '82* (Munich: Deutsches Institut für Jugendforschung (DJI)), 1983).
56. C. Dannenbeck, 'Einstellungen zur Vereinbarkeit von Familie und Beruf', in H. Bertram (ed.), *Die Familie in den neuen Bundesländern. Stabilität und Wandel in der gesellschaftlichen Umbruchsituation*, DJI Familien Survey 2 (Opladen: Leske & Budrich, 1992), pp.239ff.
57. Metz-Göckel *et al.*, 'Geteilte Welten', p.341.
58. H. Betram, 'Der soziale und politische Wandel als Forschungsaufgabe des Deutschen Jugendinstituts', in *DJI Jahresbericht* (Munich: DJI, 1991), p.176.
59. K. Schule Buschoff, 'Der Konflikt Familie und Erwerbsarbeit', *Zeitschrift f. Frauenforschung*, 1–2 (1996), p.122.

60. Interview with Mrs K in Leipzig, 28 March 1993.
61. B. Bertram, quoted in *Zerbrochene Karrieren,* pp.203–4.
62. R. Habich *et al,* '"Ein unbekanntes Land". Objektive Lebensbedingungen und subjektives Wohlbefinden in Ostdeutschland', *Aus Politik und Zeitgeschichte,* B32 (1991), p.30.

Education Transformed? The East German School System since the *Wende*

ROSALIND M.O. PRITCHARD

After unification, selective systems of secondary education were established in the new Länder. While the transformed system succeeded in widening access to university entrance qualifications compared with the restrictive practice in the GDR, it failed to deliver quality education. Performance in key subjects has decreased since unification as the combination of migration losses and a sharply reduced birth rate in east Germany made the transformed education system over-differentiated and unable to function. The paper argues that declining student numbers led to a deterioration of provisions effectively curtailing educational choice in rural areas and for those now trapped at the lower end of the new divide. While east Germans generally and east German employers specifically do not recognise the leaving certificates of Hauptschule *as meaningful qualifications, they value apprenticeships and the vocational qualifications they offer. A shortage of training places in east Germany is exacerbated by demand from young people with grammar school education while young people without apprenticeships have been particularly prone to turn to violence.*

FLAWS IN THE *STATUS QUO*

Education was the German Democratic Republic's major agent of political socialisation into Marxism-Leninism, and its pre-eminence in national life was reinforced by the fact that Margot Honecker, wife of the First Secretary of the SED, was its Minister from 1963 to 1989. Due to particular historical factors, educational development in the GDR displayed a steady, consistent, forward movement which evinced the fewest breaks of any country in east-central Europe.[1] The fact that after 1945 the territory of the Soviet Zone was occupied by one power rather than three left less room for conflicts to develop.[2] The GDR lost many of its dissidents to the west, and did not experience insurgent movements of the magnitude which took place in some other Iron Curtain countries.[3] As a result, it was divested of large swathes of the middle classes which played a powerful role in countries like

Rosalind Pritchard, University of Ulster, Coleraine.

Czechoslovakia, Poland and Hungary; its socialist regime experienced continuous growth, and its education system was not subject to abrupt changes and discontinuities. Disagreement on matters of principle was not tolerated, and since the broad parameters were so firmly set, substantive matters – particularly curriculum content – received enormous attention.

A covert, embryonic, reform movement did, however, exist prior to the *Wende* and resulted in a submission of 403 communications to the Ninth Education Congress of the GDR[4] just before the fall of the state. Most of these letters and policy proposals emanated from groups associated with the Lutheran Church and were hushed up, some even finding their way into Stasi files. After the *Wende*, easterners were suddenly freed from ideological and political constraints and felt free to utter their real opinions and aspirations in public. The short period from October 1989 to September 1990 was one of great creativity when all things seemed possible in the realm of education. An intense and passionate debate about educational issues took place, stimulated and led by grassroots groups like *Volksiniative Bildung* and *Bürgeriniative Bildungsreform Karl-Marx-Stadt*. By 31 December 1989, the Ministry of Education had received over 8,000 communications from individuals and groups all wanting to express their ideas. A selection of their communications was analysed in the *Enquête Kommission zukünftige Bildungspolitik – Bildung 2000*[5] for the 11th session of the Bundestag and conveys east Germans' perception of their own education system and its associated problems.

Despite the GDR's official commitment to equality, the theme of social justice had become a dominant concern.[6] The GDR state's policy of positive discrimination in favour of workers and peasants was intended to abolish 'bourgeois' educational privileges and, until the 1960s, this was successful in broadening the class basis of educational opportunity. In 1955, 55 per cent of students were from genuine worker and peasant families, but by the 1970s and 1980s this figure had dropped to about 28 per cent.[7] Yet study was not financially lucrative, especially for young people: by age 30, university graduates were being paid only 61–74 per cent of skilled workers' income. Naturally, this tended to make higher education unattractive to the workers but it had the function of strengthening the self-reproduction of the intelligentsia as a class. Party apparatchiks, despite their high positions, defined themselves officially as 'working class' and were often able to ensure that their children were favoured in the education system. Misleading modes of categorising social class origins covered up the politically unwelcome fact that a large percentage of students came from families where one or both parents had a higher education qualification. In 1990, the percentage of such students in the new Länder was twice as large as in the old Länder. Students who themselves had a vocational qualification (about one-third of new entrants) were classified as 'workers' even though they were children of doctors, engineers and academics. Sixty-two per cent of students labelled 'workers' had parents with tertiary educational qualifications, as had 19 per cent of those officially called 'production workers'.[8]

The population of the former GDR was in fact well educated and well qualified. Weishaupt and Zedler[9] quote figures showing that whereas in 1992 19.5 per cent of west Germans had no formal qualification, this was the case for only 7.3 per cent of east Germans. However, access to higher education was very restricted, and the biggest hurdle in the selection process came at school, not, as one might suppose, after the *Abitur*, but after the eighth year when college-preparatory classes (*Erweiterte Oberschule* (EOS)) began (from 1983/84 onwards this changed to after the tenth year). The admissions quota for the EOS was usually about 16 per cent – about three pupils per class – and the wastage rate allowed was small: all but 10–20 per cent were expected to proceed to higher education.[10] The academic filter for higher education thus occurred very early in the average child's life, and political considerations played a large role in this process. Negative discrimination prevailed against those – like the children of clergymen – who dissented from the party's ideology. To their credit, GDR schools excelled at maximising the achievements of average and less able students and for this purpose they had a whole series of stratagems such as peer tutoring, home visits and voluntary out-of-school lessons by dedicated teachers. There was, however, a widespread perception that the most able pupils were not being given a fair deal, and were disadvantaged in the undifferentiated, all-ability schools of the GDR (*Einheitsschulen*). After the *Wende*, the reform demands of the east Germans therefore centred around calls for increased access to higher education, a depoliticisation of selection procedures, and a concern to cultivate the talents of bright children as fully as possible.

STRUCTURAL FEATURES OF THE TRANSFORMATION

The introduction of the west German legal framework heralded an end to the heroic period from October 1989 to September 1990 when 'a thousand flowers bloomed'. Articles 37 and 38 of the Unification Treaty dealing with schools, higher education and research instigated a broad, rapid and deep restructuring of the new Länder education system so as to align it with that of the old Länder. In this transformation, the east Germans were given what many of them had been demanding: namely a differentiated post-primary system, with grammar schools for the upper range of the pupil ability spectrum. Strictly speaking, only school types specified in the 1964

Hamburg Agreement[11] were allowed, the main types being *Grundschule, Hauptschule, Realschule* and *Gymnasium*. Of these, the only secondary school type which is not allowed a selection procedure for admission is the *Hauptschule*, which thus counts as the least academic. In the 1960s, experiments began with comprehensive schools (*Gesamtschulen*), which were intended as a corrective to the rigid tracking system of secondary education and as a response to the demands of a fast-changing society.[12] They were for a time popular, especially in the social-democratic Länder such as Berlin, Hamburg and Hesse, but became highly politicised in the mid-1970s and were not introduced on a Länder-wide basis. However, in the 1980s they were recognised as a valid school form for the whole Federal Republic by the *Kultusministerkonferenz*.[13]

Notwithstanding the Hamburg Agreement, Saxony, Saxony-Anhalt and Thuringia all succeeded in producing hybrid school types which were approved by the *Kultusministerkonferenz* in its decision of 25/26 June 1992 on condition that they enabled pupils to take the leaving certificates of the established *Haupt-* or *Realschule* tracks (and to transfer to *Gymnasium* if sufficiently able). A simplified table of the new school structures is shown in Table 1, with the hybrid school types in italic (day-care institutions, special education and the vocational tracks are excluded). In some Länder, a cycle of guidance and orientation may take place in the fifth and sixth years, in which case the real process of differentiation occurs from the seventh year onwards.

AN INCLEMENT EDUCATION ECOLOGY

The successful functioning of these structures is now jeopardised by certain adverse developments in the socio-economic framework of the new Länder within which the education sector exists. The most notable are (a) the difficulties of the east German economy, (b) the growth of unemployment and (c) the fall in the number of live births.

(a) Regarding the east German economy, Hughes Hallett and Ma estimated that it would take at least 20 years and might take up to half a century to catch up with the west and achieve complete integration without a *Mezzogiorno* problem.[14] In their view, eastern demands for wage parity and continued low productivity constitute the main obstacles to closing the gap. Moreover, state subsidies, although understandable for moderating the social impact of transformation in the east, may make the goal of self-sustaining economic growth in east Germany more difficult to attain. Table 2 records these projections of economic convergence applying the International Monetary Fund's economic model (MULTIMOD) to the German situation.

TABLE 1

SECONDARY EDUCATION STRUCTURES IN THE NEW BUNDESLÄNDER
(EXCLUDING POST-COMPULSORY AND VOCATIONAL EDUCATION)

	No. of years to *Abitur*	Names of school types
East Berlin	13	Hauptschule Realschule Gesamtschule Gymnasium
Brandenburg	13	Gesamtschule Realschule Gymnasium
Mecklenburg-Vorpommern	12	Hauptschule Realschule Gesamtschule Gymnasium
Saxony	12	Mittelschule Gymnasium
Saxony-Anhalt	12	Sekundarschule Gymnasium
Thuringia	12	Regelschule Gymnasium

Source: Synopse der Schulgesetze der neuen Länder und Berlins (erweiterte und aktualisierte Fassung, Bonn: Bundesministerium für Bildung, Wissenschaft, Forschung und Technologie), March 1994.

TABLE 2

CLOSING THE EAST–WEST ECONOMIC GAP IN GERMANY

Projected productivity growth in east Germany (%)	No. of years required to reach west German levels of economic performance
9.1	20
6.7	30
5.5	49

Source: A. Hughes Hallett and Y. Ma, 'East Germany, West Germany and their Mezzogiorno', *Economic Journal*, 103 (1993), p.417.

(b) Unemployment, the second of the adverse consequences of transformation to impact on education in east Germany, affected an estimated 27 per cent of the workforce in 1993, which then numbered 8.8 million. As shown elsewhere in this volume (Flockton), migration losses, retirements and early retirements have since reduced the potential labour force by about one-quarter. Not only has unemployment not abated in the interim; it would be significantly higher but for the moderating effect of special labour market programmes. Throughout the post-communist transformation in east Germany, women have borne the brunt of unemployment.[15]

(c) An unexpected consequence of transformation with long-term repercussions in the education sector has been the decline of the birth rate by about 60 per cent since 1990. Although the decline seems to have been halted in 1996, the number of births remains low. Given the much-reduced cohort of pre-school children, demand for child-care and provision of places also decreased while the number of children aged six and ready to enter primary schools is much lower today than in the GDR and in the early years of post-communist development. The continued small size of age cohorts born since 1991 will gradually work its way through to secondary and university level and curtail the demand for places from young east Germans.[16] It has been estimated that by the year 2003 school rolls will have decreased by 60 per cent, reaching a trough for secondary schools generally in 2007 and for grammar schools and A-level studies in 2010.[17]

These factors have changed the entire ecology of education in east Germany, with profound consequences for teachers, families and pupils in both general and vocational education. The fact that so few children are available for school recruitment constitutes a planner's nightmare and shows up the short-sightedness of introducing a highly differentiated post-primary system in thinly populated regions. The new Länder as a territory are less densely settled than the old Länder, and in Thuringia, for example, the school network is already so wide-meshed that almost half of the officially designated communities (*Gemeinden*) have no school at all (461 out of 1033).[18] Strangely, Mecklenburg-Vorpommern with its rural character and sparse population introduced a particularly highly differentiated school structure amongst the new Länder, incorporating *Hauptschule*, *Realschule*, *Gymnasium* and *Gesamtschule*. The last-named, the 'comprehensive school', can only be formed on the basis of the tripartite system, so this school type is not 'comprehensive' in the sense that the Swedes or the English would understand the term: it does not recruit over the whole ability spectrum and is not a neighbourhood school like the GDR's *Einheitsschule* was. Buhren and Rösner state that the 'comprehensive' is thought of as a 'substitute school' in Germany and that this sets limits to its development, putting it at the mercy of lawmakers and school providers.[19] The reconstruction of the GDR school system may have been, they believe, the last big chance to reform the west German system in keeping with European standards (the implication is that the chance was 'blown'). The researchers of the Max-Planck-Institut argue that a two-stream *Gesamtschule* could well serve as 'the school of choice' in areas of low population and in time of demographic downturn.[20] An important opportunity may have been missed in making it marginal in Mecklenburg-Vorpommern, and east Germany generally.

The *Hauptschule* was already unpopular in west Germany at the point when it was set up in the new Länder; although the term means 'main school', it is the case that in all old Länder it has fewer pupils than the more advanced *Realschule* and *Gymnasium* put together.[21] In the west, it is often regarded as a sink school for *Gastarbeiter* and the least gifted German pupils; it is plagued with high absentee rates and discipline problems. Girls, whose good work ethos usually exercises a steadying effect on male peers, are in the minority at the *Hauptschule*. Regionally, country children are more likely than town children to attend such institutions. The *Hauptschule* is subject to a role conflict which renders clearly defined development difficult. If it strives for a special profile, as in some south German Länder, it risks isolation, whereas if it tries to compete with other school types by becoming more differentiated and 'theory-oriented', it loses distinctiveness.[22]

In the new Länder, the *Hauptschule* has an even lower proportion of pupils than in the old Länder. In 1990/91, 34.2 per cent of form 7–9 pupils in the old Länder atttended *Hauptschule*, whereas this was true of only ten per cent in Sachsen-Anhalt and Thuringia, and 13.2 per cent in Mecklenburg-Vorpommern.[23] Here, the *Hauptschulen* cannot exist independently, and all but two are accommodated in the same buildings as *Grundschulen* (32 schools) or *Realschulen* (274 schools); in the long term, this school type cannot survive.[24] According to present trends, after the year 2005 in many regions of east Germany *all* secondary pupils will be able to find a place in a *Gymnasium*, so the prospects for the *Hauptschule* look bleak, and serious questions may arise about the 'product quality' of *Gymnasium* leaving certificates.[25] At present, the *Realschule* leaving certificates are seen as the equivalent of the ten-year *Polytechnische Oberschule* certificate in the former GDR. By comparison, *Hauptschule* certificates are unattractive to employers, and some of the hybrid school types have already divested themselves of their *Hauptschule* track altogether.[26]

MERGERS, CLOSURES AND THEIR EFFECTS

In parts of the new Länder, it will be necessary to merge or close entire schools. In an effort to keep schools alive, class mergers are being actively considered and implemented. Indeed, Baumbach, Holldack and Klemm anticipate that about 20 per cent of primary schools in Mecklenburg-Vorpommern will have to be closed if the principle of one class for each age cohort is retained.[27] The rationale for multi-age classes is sometimes explicitly based on the so-called Jena Plan derived from the work of the educationalist Peter Petersen,[28] and also explored by Fickermann.[29] Experience in the Netherlands is being used to guide planners' coping strategies. It is an irony that whereas the former GDR was proud of having 90 per cent of its pupils educated in their own age groups,[30] there is now a need to reverse this trend by introducing multi-age classes. Moreover, for such classes to succeed, an ethos of mutual help is needed of precisely the sort which was deliberately cultivated in the GDR. Marotzki and Schwiering emphasise how debilitating it is for communities to lose their schools, and they highlight the need for teachers to use a rich repertoire of methodology to retain small schools without detriment to the quality of education offered in them.[31] Parents are, they argue, more influenced in their school choice by qualitative factors like the reputation of the school than by the actual breadth of its curricular offering.

Because the number of possible recruits is so limited, schools can find themselves in competition with each other, and many teachers live in constant fear of losing their jobs through no fault of their own. Each institution can ill afford to lose pupils, and so is cautious about transferring them to other school types. It is rare for pupils to transfer 'down' from grammar school even if they are over-challenged there and success seems doubtful. In Thuringia, in 1992/93 only 2.5 per cent of pupils left the *Gymnasium* for a lower school type (*Regelschule*).[32] Similarly, transfer 'up' is modest: Weishaupt and Zedler calculate that in 1992 about five per cent of fifth year *Regelschule* pupils moved into the sixth year of a *Gymnasium*, and after the sixth year another 6.7 per cent moved into the seventh year of a *Gymnasium*.[33] The fact that teachers' jobs are linked to pupil recruitment makes them reluctant to send pupils elsewhere.[34] The non-*Gymnasien* are now deprived of the brightest pupils who in GDR days helped to lift the level of the others, and the integration of those who have come 'down' from other school types is a pedagogical challenge. The problem in the *Gymnasien* is that they are much more heterogeneous than the EOS ever was, and many teachers are rather disappointed in the pupils compared with the old EOS days.[35]

The extent of grammar school provision varies regionally, and in

Mecklenburg-Vorpommern and Thuringia they tend to be concentrated in urban rather than rural areas.[36] Startling disparities in the rate of transfer to *Gymnasien* can lead to regional inequality: in Thuringia, it varies between ten per cent and 60 per cent, and even within one urban area, Erfurt, the capital of Thuringia, the transfer quota varies between 19 per cent and 67 per cent.[37] In Saxony, access to grammar schools can vary between five per cent and 50 per cent.[38] Gender disparities also exist, since on average 60 per cent of grammar school pupils are girls.[39] Obviously, this means that boys are in the majority in 'lower' school types: Melzer and Stenke state that the percentage of boys in Saxony's *Mittelschulen* is 55 per cent, in special education classes 65 per cent, and in the *Gymnasien* 40 per cent; boys in Saxony's *Mittelschulen* often appear unmotivated and can be difficult to deal with.[40]

ACADEMIC ACHIEVEMENT AND THE QUALITY OF SCHOOL LIFE

After the *Wende*, easterners had called for the *Gymnasium* but had given insufficient thought to the role of non-selective school types, and were insufficiently aware of the educational merits of their existing system. A longitudinal study of pupils' achievement in east and west Germany begun shortly after the *Wende* applied measures of achievement independent of the schools' marks; its methodology therefore carries a high degree of credibility.[41] It showed that easterners' performance in the seventh year was superior in German, mathematics and biology. East German girls scored higher than west German girls in maths and physics. This study came to the important conclusion that *no* evidence could be found that the undifferentiated school system in the GDR had damaged the performance of the more able pupils. A comparative study of teaching in maths and natural sciences found that the ten highest placed countries were east European, and that Germany was somewhere near the middle of the league table, similar in quality to England and the USA.[42] The same study demonstrated that the younger east German cohort who had not been been educated in the *Polytechnische Oberschule* had almost completely lost the former GDR lead.[43] *Hauptschule* pupils in Germany as a whole scored very badly: only Iran, Kuwait and South Africa were ranked lower. *Gymnasium* pupils, by contrast, scored well.

The issue of the divided school system is a very sensitive one, and research findings differ as to the quality of life and teaching on offer. Scholars at the Max-Planck-Institut point out that the *Gymnasium* is absorbing all the best pupils.[44] Yet in a substantial empirical study by Kanders a much smaller percentage of *Gymnasium* than of *Hauptschule* pupils perceived their teachers as very helpful (35 per cent *Gymnasium*; 50 per cent *Hauptschule*).[45] Twenty-four per cent of *Hauptschule* pupils, but only 15 per cent of *Gymnasium* pupils found their teachers quite good at explaining difficult subject content. *Gymnasium* pupils trusted their teachers least of all school types: a majority of pupils in both the old and the new Länder believed that it was important to have confidence in teachers (59 per cent), but only eight per cent in the new Länder and 11 per cent in the old Länder actually had such confidence. Only one-fifth of pupils believed that teachers cared about their well being, and more westerners than easterners (59 per cent/50 per cent) thought that this was important. When asked to judge how much trouble they went to over the pupils, 68 per cent of west German teachers said 'a lot' compared with only 55 per cent of east German teachers.[46] It is difficult to explain why this state of affairs should have arisen but it is possible that chronic insecurity in the east may cause some east German teachers to derogate from the high standards of dedication to pupil care and welfare which were expected in the GDR. By contrast, Böttcher found in a study of *Regelschulen* and *Gymnasien* in Thuringia, that teachers in both school types were strongly achievement-oriented, and that they went to considerable lengths to establish an attractive way of life in their schools.[47] In one of the sampled schools, concern for the less able resulted in the best teachers being assigned to the *Hauptschule* track.[48] So, clearly, something of the former east German spirit survives in some schools. However, it would be strange if the pupils at the bottom of the 'heap' did not become demoralised, as parents and teachers appear to have wanted an inner renewal, not a change of school structure.

Allocation to school type in a hierarchical or differentiated structure impacts on children's self-image.[49] The 1994 study suggested that non-grammar school pupils were much more negative in their attitudes to school than pupils in other school types, either east or west. In the new Länder they also had a negative self-evaluation, yet in comparison with their counterparts in the old Länder, they manifested a higher level of academic attainment.[50] Rosenthal and Jacobson claim that a self-fulfilling prophecy operates in education and that pupils' perceptions of teachers' expectations influence the formers' measured attainment levels.[51] Pupils who have been consigned to 'lower' school types tend to lose confidence in themselves and eventually produce lower achievements. Teachers in such schools, in order to combat pupils' incipient hostility, alienation, despair or low self-esteem, are driven to make a greater effort with them, whereas teachers in the 'higher' school types can usually count on their pupils' natural ability: this may lead to complacency and lack of effort from those in charge of the educational process. Well-authenticated experience from abroad suggests that a differentiated school system tends to polarise achievement. In the

United Kingdom, for example, Northern Ireland still has grammar and secondary schools with selection at age 11; until recently, it produced both the best and the worst results in public examinations of any region of the UK.[52] The findings relating to east Germany suggest that concern about educational deficit on the part of the most able east German pupils may have been unjustified. Even if it were justified, the redress has now been over-compensated with the result that the least able are now at a disadvantage compared to GDR times.

PUBLIC REACTION TO THE TRANSFORMATION OF EDUCATION

The Institute for Research in School Development regularly conducts surveys into attitudes towards schools, and in 1991, 1993 and 1995 has included east Germany.[53] Since 1991, east Germans have been asked whether they were satisfied with the restructuring of education in their region, and if not, which option (a), (b) or (c) they would have preferred:

(a)   the GDR system retained unchanged;
(b)   change in both the external school structure and the internal curriculum;
(c)   the external school structure of the GDR to be retained but divested of its party-political ideological pedagogy. *Polytechnische Oberschule* for all children, then *Erweiterte Oberschule* or an apprenticeship, vocational education with *Abitur* – all these should have been retained.

In 1995, as in 1993, just one-fifth of all respondents chose option (b) – which was what had *actually* happened. The higher the school qualification of the respondents, the stronger the tendency to go for this option. Thus *Gymnasium* parents were much more satisfied with educational provision than *Hauptschule* parents. By far the favourite was option (c), chosen by 58 per cent of parents. In 1995, one-quarter even chose option (a), whereas in 1991 only five per cent had done so. The proportion wishing 'no change' from the GDR has, therefore, risen sharply since easterners experienced the reality of restructuring at first hand. Seventy-three per cent endorsed the concept of common education for all children up to age 16 (form 10), up from 57 per cent in 1991, and working class parents were keener on a unified post-primary sector than middle class parents. The easterners emphasised the values of social justice, achievement and discipline to a greater extent than the westerners. They seemed dissatisfied with the way in which their new school structure was developing.[54] However, it must not be forgotten that at the time of the *Wende* there was considerable popular pressure to establish grammar schools, and if this had not happened, the percentage of private schools would certainly have increased, thereby constituting a danger of balkanising the system.

Despite all negativity, the reform *has* been successful in one important respect: the number of young people in east Germany qualified to enter higher education has greatly increased: at almost 35 per cent in 1995 it was exactly the same percentage of the age cohort as in the old Länder, and double the 16 per cent level of 1990.[55] This is a considerable achievement. However, the proportion of those who subsequently move into higher education is subject to fluctuations and discontinuities. In some respects the class composition of higher education has not really changed substantially. It is interesting to note that in 1993 the proportion of new university entrants from working class backgrounds in the new Länder (8.1 per cent) was only slightly over half that in the old Länder (15.1 per cent).[56] Students from working class homes are thus still under-represented in higher education. The take-up rate for higher education in the new Länder is much lower than the matriculation rate and lower than in the old Länder. In 1995, 19.1 per cent of potential candidates in east Germany and 27.3 per cent in the west actually enrolled for university studies.[57] Since GDR times, demand for the *Gymnasium* has increased (especially as its leaving certificate, *Abitur*, can now be used to obtain an apprenticeship), whereas demand for higher education has decreased. This unwillingness to enter higher education can be attributed in large measure to the chronic insecurity pervading east German social and economic life. As a legacy of the GDR, there is also a residual attachment to vocational education which makes many want to enter employment as soon as possible; this may be a hangover from the GDR's restrictions on entry to the selective secondary track (*Erweiterte Oberschule*) and an upward evaluation of apprenticeships.[58]

East Germans hoped that the new structures after unification would help to correct the imbalances and injustices which had arisen in the GDR system. Ironically, however, problems of social justice did not disappear – they just turned into different sorts of equity problems pertaining to choice of school type, region and gender. The existence of comprehensive schools (*Einheitsschulen*) in their purest form combined with GDR teachers' special attention to the less able pupils had tended to minimise the attainment differentials between individuals and contributed to a more homogeneous society. The fact that education did not attract high economic rewards intensified this homogeneity. What ran counter to 'equality' was the dominance of party and ideology. After the *Wende*, the new school structure and the fact that some school types, but not others, had the right to be selective tended to polarise secondary schools in terms of quality of pupil intake and public esteem – with concomitant pedagogical problems. Combined with inequalities arising from parental unemployment and the introduction of the market economy, the effect of the differentiated school system is to increase the cultural capital of some families and decrease that of others. The onus for achievement is shifted away from teachers and moved towards pupils and their families within a stratified secondary system. It is hard for children to move to a higher stratum once they have been placed on a particular level. 'Equality of opportunity' can mean in practice the opportunity to turn out 'unequal'.

Bourdieu and Passeron point to the function of education in reproducing class relations and ensuring the hereditary transmission of cultural capital.[59] This eventually happened in the GDR, despite initial efforts to the contrary, and the trend is likely to continue in the new Länder. One difference, however, is that the state will make no effort to penalise the 'intelligentsia' by controlling their salaries downwards. The transformation of education in the GDR represents a kind of natural experiment in which society has passed from a valuation of social unity to one of diversity, and in which the power of families to influence life chances differentially has been strengthened in comparison to what went before.

VOCATIONAL EDUCATION: PRE-*WENDE* CRITICISMS IN EAST AND WEST

Normally the vocational education system would be expected to absorb those *non*-grammar school youngsters who are not in the top academic flight. It can offer them a satisfying training, a steady way of life, and harness their skills for the good of society. A good vocational education system can contribute greatly to the stability and cohesion of society. West Germany's dual system has traditionally been the envy of other countries, but by 1989, when it was transferred to the east, it was beginning to show signs of internal stress.[60] Some of the official job designations and parts of the training curriculum were obsolescent, and the authorities were slow at replacing them with more relevant job concepts taking account of the latest technology. There were regional, sectional and gender disparities. Vocational schools were under-resourced compared with the powerful training centres operated by the Chambers of Commerce. Some argued that trainees were overpaid; the gap between their wages and the payment for those who had qualified was too narrow, and this wage-induced complacency had an adverse effect on their motivation to complete their training courses successfully. Employers were not always willing to offer training opportunities. The free-standing *Überbetriebliche Ausbildungs-stätten* were becoming so dominant that some expert observers openly regarded the system as no longer 'dual' at all, but pluralistic.[61]

Notwithstanding these problems, the west German dual system was exported to east Germany after the *Wende*. Naturally, the two systems had common roots in the days before Germany had been divided. After partition, the GDR went for a more unified structure based on the *Betriebsberufsschule*, in which theory and practice were ideologically seen as a unity and deliberately mediated in the same location rather than being legally split between the commercial and the school sector.[62] Most GDR training took place in large state-owned *Kombinate*, whereas in the Federal Republic only 11 per cent of trainees qualified in a firm with more than 500 employees.[63] Towards the end of the 1980s, training in large *Kombinate* began to change somewhat in favour of training in vocational institutions taking about 200 apprentices. Young east Germans had already undergone a significant process of anticipatory socialisation for the world of work through their school curriculum in which they were exposed to *Polytechnischer Unterricht* intended to give them experience of the process of production. Easterners expected their young people to grow up more quickly than was the case in the west, and were less indulgent towards protracted periods of education and training. The expectation was that they should qualify reasonably rapidly, and begin making an active contribution to society. The preliminary work done in school made it possible for east German youth to get through their apprenticeships expeditiously. Useful bridges existed between general and vocational education. One of the more attractive was vocational education with *Abitur* (*Berufsbildung mit Abitur*) which could be done at school and which maximised options in either tertiary education or employment.

Of course, the east German system, like that in the west, was imperfect and exhibited cracks and strains at the time of the *Wende*. Apprentices were sometimes 'eased' through their courses and officially 'passed' even if less than competent; to do otherwise would have caused trouble, and put the central plan out of kilter. Employers had little choice as to which trainees they had to accommodate, and the apprentices too were 'guided' sometimes remorsely and with insufficient regard to their true preferences. Because of the GDR's ideological commitment to manufacturing industry, there was not enough emphasis on modern computer technology and related trades. Like the west, the GDR was sluggish in updating its roster of recognised occupations. Moreover, even though the workforce was, broadly speaking, well trained, the infrastructure creaked so badly that it could not provide sophisticated job outlets for some of the best qualified young workers. This resulted in disaffection and low morale.

STRUCTURAL TRANSFORMATION

From 13 August 1990 onwards, the West German Vocational Training Law (*Berufsbildungsgesetz*) was applied to east Germany, and by the end of

October 1990 about 80 per cent of apprentices were already being trained
according to the new regulations. The remainder were trained according to
GDR rules for a transitional period. Former GDR state-recognised training
courses were discontinued, and the west German list substituted. Firms
training for the first time and those training for newly recognised jobs had
an especially rocky ride during the transitional period, and the trainers
themselves had to undertake courses in order to be allowed to accept
apprentices. The training period was now longer than before, three to three
and a half years as opposed to two in the GDR. Vocational training with
Abitur was discontinued – a decision largely due to the resistance of the
Chambers of Commerce and regretted in retrospect by many. A sum of DM
703 million was allocated to the NBL for vocational training in 1991. The
vocational schools were transferred to new providers under the control of
the Land, while the *Kombinate* were broken up, and the firm-based training
structures transferred to the control of the *Bund*, as had long been the case
in the Federal Republic. At first, many participants were unsure about the
new training regulations and advice structures; mistakes were made in the
recast regime,[64] even by trainers who had been very well prepared for their
tasks in the former GDR.[65]

YOUNGSTERS STRUGGLE TO FIND TRAINING PLACES

The west German dual system had rested on secure economic foundations;
in fact the year 1988/89, prior to unification, had been the most successful
one ever since statistical records began: the supply of training places had
outstripped demand by 11 per cent.[66] This was to change after unification.

Young east Germans began to pay the price of their divided and selective
school system. *Hauptschüler* found their leaving certificates unattractive to
employers, who tended mentally to equate it with the GDR arrangements
for the least able pupils leaving school after the eighth year.[67] Success
differed considerably according to school type, and young people found that
general education was more effective than vocational education in keeping
their options open. The full-time vocational school was less valuable than
the *Realschule* when it came to finding an apprenticeship. In autumn 1997,
about 34 per cent of *Realschule* pupils had a trainee place (37 per cent male,
30 per cent female) whereas this was the case for only 20 per cent of the
full-time vocational school pupils.[68] Yet a residual confidence in the value
of work and of training remained: 60 per cent of secondary school pupils in
the new Länder as opposed to only 52 per cent in the old would recommend
a young person to take up an apprenticeship rather than continue studying
after the age of 16 (the end of compulsory education) and even after
completion of *Abitur*.[69] These data suggest that belief in artisan-type work

remained strong in east Germany, despite difficulties in securing it.

Whereas in the old days prior to the *Wende* the typical experience would have been that a group or community of several young people were placed in the same large firm and could give each other companionship and mutual support, the more usual situation now was one of isolation in a small to medium-sized enterprise. By 1993, such companies were training 37 per cent of apprentices, having formerly trained only nine per cent.[70] Young people had to undertake the unfamiliar task of striving hard to find an apprenticeship which formerly would have been allocated to them by officialdom. The GDR mechanisms for matching trainees to the planned needs of the economy had disappeared. The bigger the business, the less satisfied the trainees were with their career choice – perhaps because the chances of being taken on permanently were lower in such firms, many of them, in fact, remnants of former *Kombinate* and without a secure future.[71]

More seriously still, the poor economic situation soon led to real problems in finding an apprenticeship at all. It took about two years after the introduction of the west German training structures for this problem to appear in its full gravity. At the end of September 1991, there were only 2,421 unplaced applicants and there were 6,608 training places for them to choose from.[72] Within two years of the *Wende*, the number of apprenticeships had reduced by one-third, and by late 1994 demand outstripped supply by 2:1.[73] As a result of economic stringency, many employers had become unwilling to train. The authorities responded by deploying public funds on a massive scale in order to break through this reluctance, give young people a chance in life and maintain the skills base of German industry. By 1995, 65 per cent of new indentures in east Germany were financed with public money.[74] According to the most recent Annual Vocational Education Report,[75] in September 1997 99,300 out of 125,700 new training contracts were partially or fully state-financed, which represents 79 per cent of the total.

This money came from various donors and was used in various ways. The European community was an important source of funds, and from 1991 to 1993 granted DM 6.2 billion. The EC Social Fund contributed DM 1.85 billion to help solve structural problems, create new permanent jobs and combat long-term unemployment. A further DM 226 million flowed from the EC Regional Fund.[76] Employers were given government grants as an inducement to accept trainees, the amount varying between DM 700 and DM 10,000 per place. A number of free-standing training centres (*Außerbetriebliche Ausbildungsstätten*) were established in which apprentices were involved in both theoretical and practical studies. Strictly speaking, these training centres are incompatible with the model of the dual system, and indeed the authorities would prefer the traditional pattern in which the employers make their full and proper contribution. The centres are regarded in some quarters as symptomatic of the break-up of the Dual System. Those who are trained in them are significantly less satisfied than those working in a genuine duality of school and firm, and because they do not have access to an industrial network, are less likely to obtain work when they have qualified.

FEMALES AND VOCATIONAL EDUCATION

In the vocational education system of the new Länder, young women face special difficulties, and display a special profile. They very much want to work. Beer-Kern showed that women were less prepared than their male counterparts to give up work temporarily for family reasons (28 per cent/31 per cent), and could less imagine doing without work altogether (13 per cent/19 per cent).[77] In pursuit of work, they have displayed flexible attitudes which should be conducive to success. The reality is, however, that women have encountered far more difficulty than men in securing an apprenticeship of their choice and in entering the labour market. In general, young east Germans are twice as ready as youngsters in the west to change their place of residence in order to obtain an apprenticeship (52 per cent/23 per cent). Within the new Länder, females are more prepared to move than males (54 per cent/50 per cent).[78] Unfortunately, they are less able than males to access informal networks and are obliged to rely on the *Arbeitsamt* (job centre) and on official channels for placement opportunities; informal networks are, however, more effective in procuring patronage, placements and even employment for young people. Sixty-six per cent of women against 48 per cent of men in east Germany have obtained the address of their training institution from an official source. Far fewer females than males are trained in-plant (54 per cent/76 per cent), and this has an adverse effect on their future employment prospects.[79] The women have to make almost twice as many applications for apprenticeships as men and persevere longer. Beer-Kern and colleagues show that 28 per cent of the males compared with 15 per cent of the females had already abandoned their search. In general, those seeking an apprenticeship in east Germany were more willing than in west Germany to give positive consideration to a wide range of options,[80] but east German women appear to focus on a narrow range of jobs: typically hairdressing, insurance, the retail trade, banks, administration, office work and various paramedical occupations.[81]

Despite these problems, most young people in apprenticeships enjoyed them, and were positive about their future.[82] It is those failing to obtain apprenticeships or employment who give cause for concern, especially as the general school system tends to stratify and label people in ways difficult to transcend, and leaving certificates from 'lower' schools often have a low surrender value. For the moment, unemployment seems structurally determined and is likely to contribute to social inequality; a divided and selective school system does little to break this vicious circle and may even reinforce it. The Ninth Youth Report discerned a powerful cocktail of 'growing distance between individuals and political institutions, the experience of political or social exclusion, abstinence from participation co-existing with simultaneous dispositions to expressive, identity-related action'.[83] In view of this conflict-laden situation, it concluded, 'manifestations of political alienation are not surprising', and it considered violence a predictable reaction to feelings of marginalisation among east Germany's youth. In the mid-1990s the proportion of youth willing to condone and undertake acts of violence was larger in east than in west Germany. Since then it has increased further.[84]

CONCLUSION

Taken in combination, widespread unemployment, financial hardship and the decline in the birthrate have had a profound and deleterious influence on the transformation of general and vocational education. There can be no doubt that in the haste to bring the two education systems together, western institutional structures with known shortcomings were exported to the east, and their negative features subsequently magnified by the inclement east German education ecology. Certainly, the conditions have been created for the most able to do well and for more young people to enter higher education, but a pre-conditioning from former times leads east Germans to value working life in a way which can lead them to prefer employment to higher education, given the choice. Thus, despite the increased proportion of young people qualified to enter universities, the take-up rate remains disappointing. The concern which in GDR times was (rightly or wrongly) expressed about the education of the most able must now be transferred to the least able, particularly as the safety net of apprenticeship is no longer as reliable as it once was.

NOTES

1. J. Connelly, 'Humboldt Coopted: East German Universities, 1945–1989', in M.G. Ash (ed.), *German Universities Past and Future: Crisis or Renewal?* (Oxford and Providence, RI: Berghahn, 1997).
2. T. Ramm, 'Die Bildungsverfassungen', in O. Anweiler *et al.* (eds.), *Vergleich von Bildung und Erziehung in der Bundesrepublik Deutschland und in der Deutschen Demokratischen Republik* (Cologne: Verlag Wissenschaft und Politik, 1990), pp.34–56.

3. C. Joppke, 'Why Leipzig? "Exit" and "Voice" in the East German Revolution', *German Politics*, Vol.2, No.3 (1993), pp.392–414.

4. M. Honecker, *Unser sozialistisches Bildungssystem – Wandlungen, Erfolge, neue Horizonte. IX. Pädagogischer Kongreß der DDR. 13. bis 15. Juni 1989* (Berlin: Dietz, 1989).

5. J. Hofmann *et al.* (eds.), *Diskussionspapiere der Enquête-Kommission 'Zukünftige Bildungspolitik-Bildung 2000' des 11. Deutschen Bundestages: Inhaltsanalytische Untersuchung von im Zeitraum Oktober 1989 bis März 1990 außerhalb institutionalisierter Strukturen entstandenen bildungskonzeptionellen Vorstellungen* (Bonn: Vorsitzender des Ausschusses für Bildung und Wissenschaft des Deutschen Bundestages, Bundeshaus, 1991).

6. Ibid., p.42.

7. G. Buck-Bechler, H.-D. Schaefer and C.-H. Wagemann (eds.), *Hochschulen in den neuen Ländern der Bundesrepublik Deutschland* (Weinheim: Beltz/Deutscher Studien Verlag, 1997).

8. Ibid.

9. H. Weishaupt and P. Zedler, 'Aspekte der aktuellen Schulentwicklung in den neuen Ländern', in H.-G. Rolff *et al.* (eds.), *Jahrbuch der Schulentwicklung Band 8: Daten, Beispiele und Perspektiven* (Weinheim und München: Juventa, Institut für Schulentwicklungsforschung, 1994), pp.395–429.

10. Buck-Bechler *et al.* (eds.), *Hochschulen*, p.171.

11. E. Jobst, *Das neue deutsche Recht für Schule, Berufsausbildung und Hochschule* (Bad Honnef: K.H. Bock, 1991).

12. Max Planck Institut für Bildungsforschung (MPI), *Das Bildungswesen in der Bundesrepublik: Strukturen und Entwicklungen im Überblick* (Reinbek bei Hamburg: Rowohlt, 1994).

13. C. Führ, *Zum Bildungswesen in den neuen Ländern der Bundesrepublik Deutschland* (Bonn: Inter Nationes, 1992).

14. A.J. Hughes Hallett and Y. Ma, 'East Germany, West Germany, and their Mezzogiorno: A Parable for European Economic Integration', *Economic Journal*, 103 (1993), pp.416–28.

15. Details in Weishaupt and Zedler, 'Aspekte der aktuellen Schulentwicklung in den neuen Ländern'; see also the chapters by Mike Dennis and Eva Kolinsky ('Women, Work and Family') in this volume.

16. *Grund- und Strukturdaten 1995–96* (Bonn: Bundesministerium für Bildung, Wissenschaft, Forschung und Technologie, 1995).

17. D. Fickermann, H. Weishaupt and P. Zedler, 'Kleine Grundschulen in Deutschland: Rückblick und Ausblick', in D. Fickermann, H. Weishaupt and P. Zedler (eds.), *Kleine Grundschulen in Europa: Berichte aus elf europäischen Ländern* (Weinheim: Beltz, 1998), p.23.

18. G. Köhler, M. Kuthe and P. Zedler, 'Schulstruktur im Wandel: Veränderungen des Schul- und Unterrichtsangebots in den neuen Bundesländern am Beispiel Thüringens', *Zeitschrift für Pädagogik, Beiheft 37, Kindheit, Jugend und Bildungsarbeit im Wandel* (Weinheim: Beltz, 1997), p.148.

19. C.G. Buhren and E. Rösner, 'Gesamtschule – eine Zwischenbilanz', in H.-G. Rolff *et al.* (eds.), *Jahrbuch der Schulentwicklung Band 9: Daten, Beispiele und Perspektiven* (Weinheim und München: Juventa Institut für Schulentwicklungsforschung, 1996), p.305.

20. Max Planck Institut, *Das Bildungswesen in der Bundesrepublik*, p.539.

21. Ibid., p.435.

22. Ibid., p.430.

23. Weishaupt and Zedler, 'Aspekte der aktuellen Schulentwicklung in den neuen Ländern', p.398.

24. H. Weishaupt, 'Folgen der demographischen Veränderung für die Schulentwicklung', in H.-H. Krüger and J.C. Olbertz (eds.), *Bildung zwischen Staat und Markt* (Opladen: Leske und Budrich, 1997), p.613.

25. Köhler *et al.*, 'Schulstruktur im Wandel', p.158.

26. G. Elsner and H. Rademacher, 'Soziale Differenzierung als neue Herausforderung für die Schule. Erfahrungen aus einem Modellversuch zur Schulsozialarbeit in Sachsen', *Zeitschrift für Pädagogik, Beiheft 37, Kindheit, Jugend und Bildungsarbeit im Wandel* (Weinheim:

Beltz, 1997), p.187.

27. J. Baumbach, E. Holldack and K. Klemm, 'Demographische Perspektiven, regionale Schulentwicklung und schulrechtliche Rahmenbedingungen in Mecklenburg-Vorpommern' (Berlin, Essen: Gutachten im Auftrag der Hans-Böckler-Stiftung, 1994).

28. T. Dietrich, *Die Pädagogik Peter Petersens: Der Jena-Plan Beispiel einer humanen Schule* (Bad Heilbrunn: Klinkhardt, 1995).

29. Fickermann *et al.*, *Kleine Grundschulen in Europa*.

30. Max Planck Institut, *Das Bildungswesen in der Bundesrepublik*, p.426.

31. W. Marotski and K. Schwiering, 'Aspekte regionaler Schulentwicklung: Schulproblematik und Ruf der Schule', *Zeitschrift für Pädagogik, Beiheft 37, Kindheit, Jugend und Bildungsarbeit im Wandel* (Weinheim: Beltz, 1997), pp.277–91.

32. Max Planck Institut, *Das Bildungswesen in der Bundesrepublik*, p.405.

33. Weishaupt and Zedler, 'Aspekte der aktuellen Schulentwicklung in den neuen Ländern', p.401.

34. H.N. Weiler, H.A. Mintrop and E. Fuhrmann, *Educational Change and Social Transformation* (London: Falmer, 1996).

35. I. Böttcher, M. Plath and H. Weishaupt, 'Schulstruktur und Schulgestaltung; Die innere Entwicklung von Regelschulen und Gymnasien – ein Vergleich', *Zeitschrift für Pädagogik, Beiheft 37, Kindheit, Jugend und Bildungsarbeit im Wandel* (Weinheim: Beltz, 1997), pp.161–82.

36. Weishaupt and Zedler, 'Aspekte der aktuellen Schulentwicklung in den neuen Ländern'.

37. M. Kuthe and E. Schwerd, 'Das Forschungsprojekt "Schulstrukturwandel in Thüringen"', in H. Weishaupt and P. Zedler (eds), *Schulstrukturwandel in Thüringen: Ergebnisse einer Befragung von Schulen, Eltern und Lehrern in der Stadt Erfurt* (Erfurt: Pädagogische Hochschule, 1993), p.39.

38. W. Melzer and D. Stenke, 'Schulentwicklung und Schulforschung in den ostdeutschen Bundesländern', in H.-G. Rolff *et al.* (eds.), *Jahrbuch der Schulentwicklung Band 9: Daten, Beispiele und Perspektiven* (Weinheim und München: Juventa, Institut für Schulentwicklungsforschung, 1996), pp.307–38.

39. Buck-Bechler *et al.* (eds.), *Hochschulen*, p.274.

40. Melzer and Stenke, 'Schulentwicklung und Schulforschung in den ostdeutschen Bundesländern', p.324.

41. Bildungsverläufe und psychosoziale Entwicklung im Jugendalter (BIJU), 'Zwischenbilanz für die Schulen, 1994'; 'Bericht für die Schulen, 1996' (Berlin: Max-Planck-Institut für Bildungsforschung, 1994 and 1996).

42. J. Baumert *et al.*, *TIMSS – Mathematisch-naturwissenschaftlicher Unterricht im internationalen Vergleich: Deskriptive Befunde* (Opladen: Leske und Budrich, 1997).

43. Ibid., p.119.

44. Max Planck Institut, *Das Bildungswesen in der Bundesrepublik*, p.512.

45. M. Kanders, E. Rösner and H.-G. Rolff, 'Das Bild der Schule aus der Sicht von Schülern und Lehrern – Ergebnisse zweier IFS-Repräsentativbefragungen', in Rolff *et al.* (eds) *Jahrbuch der Schulentwicklung Band 9*, pp.57–114.

46. Ibid., p.76.

47. Böttcher *et al.*, 'Schulstruktur und Schulgestaltung', p.161

48. Ibid., p.172.

49. Ibid., p.162.

50. *Bildungsverläufe*, 1996.

51. R. Rosenthal and L. Jacobson, *Pygmalion in the Classroom: Teacher Expectation and Pupils' Intellectual Development* (New York and London: Holt, Rinehart and Winston, 1968).

52. Government Statistical Service (ed.), *Regional Trends 23* (London: HMSO, 1988, 1990, 1991) (3 separate volumes).

53. H.-G. Rolff *et al.* (eds.), *Jahrbuch der Schulentwicklung Band 7: Daten, Beispiele und Perspektiven* (Weinheim und München: Juventa, Institut für Schulentwicklungsforschung, 1992); Rolff *et al.* (eds.), *Jahrbuch der Schulentwicklung Band 8*; Rolff *et al.* (eds.), *Jahrbuch der Schulentwicklung Band 9*.

54. Rolff *et al.* (eds.), *Jahrbuch der Schulentwicklung Band 9*, pp.51–4.
55. Buck-Bechler *et al.* (eds.), *Hochschulen*, p.229.
56. Ibid., p.256.
57. Ibid., p.239.
58. E. Wild, 'Bedingungen der Schullaufbahn ost- und westdeutscher Jugendlicher am Ende der Sekundarstufe 1', *Zeitschrift für Pädagogik, Beiheft 37, Kindheit, Jugend und Bildungsarbeit im Wandel* (Weinheim: Beltz, 1997), pp.229–54.
59. P. Bourdieu and J.-C. Passeron, *Reproduction in Education, Society and Culture* (London and Beverly Hills, CA: Sage, 1977).
60. R.M.O. Pritchard, 'The German Dual System: Educational Utopia?', *Comparative Education*, Vol.28, No.1 (1992), pp.131–43; R.M.O. Pritchard, *Reconstructing Education: East German Schools and Universities After the Fall of the Wall* (Oxford and Providence, RI: Berghahn, 1999).
61. A. Kell, 'Rahmenbedingungen der Berufsbildung', in R. Arnold and A. Lipsmeier (eds.), *Handbuch der Berufsbildung* (Opladen: Leske and Budrich, 1995), pp.369–97.
62. W. Hörner, *Bildung und Wissenschaft in der DDR: Ausgangslage und Reform bis Mitte 1990* (Bonn: Bundesminister für Bildung und Wissenschaft, 1990).
63. Max Planck Institut, *Das Bildungswesen in der Bundesrepublik*, p.581.
64. *Berufsbildungsbericht, 1991* (Bonn: Bundesminister für Bildung und Wissenschaft, 1991).
65. I. Kroymann and S.O. Lübke, *Berufliche Bildung in den neuen Bundesländern* (Cologne: Bund-Verlag, 1992), p.35.
66. *Berufsbildungsbericht, 1991*, p.1.
67. B. Autsch, 'Ausgangsbedingungen bei der Umstellung des DDR-Berufsbildungssystems aus der Sicht rechtlicher und organisatorischer Rahmenbedingungen', in U. Degen, G. Walden and K. Berger (eds.), *Berufsausbildung in den neuen Bundesländern: Daten, Analysen, Perspektiven* (Bundesinstitut für Berufsbildung: Der Generalsekretär, 1995), pp.26–7.
68. *Berufsbildungsbericht, 1998*, p.24.
69. Kanders *et al.*, 'Das Bild der Schule aus der Sicht von Schülern und Lehrern', p.109.
70. K. Schober, 'Von der Lehrstellenbilanz zum Lehrstellenmarkt – Auswirkungen der "Wende" auf das Ausbildungsverhalten von Jugendlichen und Betrieben und auf die Strukturen beruflicher Erstausbildung', in R. Jansen (ed.), *Arbeitsmarkt und Berufsbildung in den neuen Bundesländern* (Bielefeld: Bertelsmann, 1995), pp.33–68.
71. D. Beer-Kern, M. Granato and K. Schweikert, *In der Mitte der Ausbildung: Auszubildende in den neuen Bundesländern* (Berlin and Bonn: Bundesinstitut für Berufsbildung, 1995).
72. Bund-Länder-Kommission für Bildungsplanung und Forschungsförderung, *Entwicklung des Bildungsplanung in den neuen Ländern* (Bonn: BLK, 1993).
73. Schober, 'Von der Lehrstellenbilanz zum Lehrstellenmarkt', pp.39–40.
74. *Berufsbildungsbericht* (1996).
75. *Berufsbildungsbericht* (1998).
76. Bund-Länder-Kommission, *Entwicklung der Bildungsplanung in den neuen Ländern*.
77. D. Beer-Kern, 'Auszubildende und unversorgte Jugendliche – Ausbildungssituation und Fremdenfeindlichkeit', in R. Jansen (ed.), *Arbeitsmarkt und Berufsbildung in den neuen Bundesländern* (Bielefeld: Bertelsmann, 1995), pp.145–68.
78. *Berufsbildungsbericht* (1998), p.24.
79. Beer-Kern, 'Auszubildende und unversorgte Jugendliche', pp.150 and 153.
80. *Berufsbildungsbericht* (1998), p.24.
81. Beer-Kern, 'Auszubildende und unversorgte Jugendliche', p.152.
82. Beer-Kern *et al.*, *In der Mitte der Ausbildung*.
83. Bundesministerium für Familie, Senioren, Frauen und Jugend, *Neunter Jugendbericht: Bericht über die Situation der Kinder und Jugendlichen und die Entwicklung der Jugendhilfe in den neuen Bundesländern* (Bonn: BFSFJ, 1994), p.189.
84. Ibid., p.192.

Political Participation of Young People in East Germany

HANS OSWALD AND CHRISTINE SCHMID

The paper presents key findings of a three-year longitudinal study of political participation. Drawing on the distinction between conventional and unconventional political participation, the study focused on grammar school students in the Land Brandenburg between the ages of 16 and 18 in order to determine how political behaviour develops and which forms of political participation prevail. While political interest among young east Germans remains comparatively low, it increased over time and respondents in the older age groups were more likely to opt for conventional forms of participation (voting) than younger ones. Friends and parents played a key part in political socialisation. The inclination to use violence was closely linked to clique membership but pertained only to a minority of young people. The study also found interesting gender differences concerning policy issues and patterns of political participation.

POLITICAL PARTICIPATION AND YOUNG PEOPLE

Political participation is a central principle of liberal democratic systems. It is an indispensable part of the citizen's role, and the readiness to participate or not to participate, or to participate in some respects and not in others, is an important part of the political identity of citizens. From the point of view of the government and other democratic institutions, participation is a mechanism to produce legitimacy for single political decisions as well as for the political system as a whole. Therefore, schools, political parties and other organisations are given the responsibility to promote positive attitudes in young people towards political participation. The readiness to participate or to renounce participation emerges during the process of political socialisation in childhood and adolescence. Parents, peers and teachers are the most important agents in influencing the readiness of young people to participate and to develop a participating political identity.

As a means of producing legitimacy for the new German democracy political participation is especially important in the new states of Germany.

Hans Oswald and Christine Schmid, University of Potsdam.

The population raised in the former GDR feels somewhat distant from the western democratic system. On the one hand, a majority of adults accepts and acknowledges basic democratic rights and principles in east Germany as a similar majority does in west Germany.[1] On the other hand, more adults in the new Länder than in west Germany are sceptical about the realisation of democracy in the new German Republic. This scepticism is closely related to concrete experience of the economic turmoil associated with the *Wende*.[2] Meulemann summarises several studies in the following way: 'The idea of socialism works as a yardstick for the evaluation of actual democracy much more in the east than in the west.'[3] Because participation is one of the legitimating mechanisms of the democratic political system,[4] it can be hypothesised that the more citizens in the east participate politically, the more they will change their sceptical attitude and accept the new democratic institutions and decision-making processes of the democratically elected governments and parliaments. Up to now, the best information source about the political attitudes of east German adolescents in the new states of Germany as compared to the old states is the study by Hoffmann-Lange with data from 1992.[5]

Participation begins with showing political interest. One can justify the study of political interest under the heading of participation, for the reason that many forms of participation including voting in general elections are closely related to political interest.[6] After an enormous increase in political interest in east Germany during the *Wende* and the unification process,[7] that of adults and adolescents has decreased since 1992 and has since been lower than in the west.[8] One of the stable findings in political socialisation research is the relationship between political interest and political knowledge and readiness to participate politically.[9] In addition, the degree of consistency in political attitudes is related to the degree of political interest.[10]

Compared with other domains of life, the significance of the political sphere is rather small for both adults and young people. However, political interest has increased in the second half of this century in west Germany,[11] as well as in countries like the United Kingdom, France and the United States.[12] One of the reasons for the increase in political interest is the increase in formal education, education being one of the best predictors of political interest. Pupils in the more academic streams were more interested than pupils in the less academic streams in different countries.[13] In east Germany, the relationship between education and political interest is even stronger than in west Germany. In general, females are less interested in politics than males in both parts of Germany as well as in other countries.[14] However, the difference between males and females has decreased since the 1950s in western Germany[15] and the interest of girls in specific topics like peace and ecology seems to be higher than that of boys in the new Länder of Germany.[16]

Another form of participation is related to interest, and that is the search for information in the mass media and in political discussions with parents, peers and teachers. The information sources most frequently used by adolescents are the news broadcasts on TV followed by those on radio. Newspapers are less important. This reliance on the medium of TV rather than print media is often criticised. In the tradition of Lazarsfeld and Merton's hypothesis of the 'narcotic dysfunction' of the mass media,[17] scholars write about the escape function of heavy TV viewing. Some studies in Germany show a negative correlation between heavy TV viewing and readiness to participate politically.[18] However, this negative view of the effects of the mass media can be contested. It seems that seeking information from TV has positive effects on the emergence of political identity in adolescence.[19]

Several parent–child studies of political socialisation show the importance of parents. These studies found correlations between political attitudes of parents and their offspring in different countries, including Germany.[20] Political opinions are at least partly formed by parents. The influence of parents seems to be greater if father and mother have the same opinion.[21] Some results from the USA show a greater importance of mothers (especially mothers in high professional positions) than of fathers.[22] Agreement between parents and their children increases when parents are interested in politics and discuss political problems with their children. The influence of peers in the process of political opinion formation seems to be smaller than the influence of parents. Some authors discuss the possibility that parents are politically influenced by their children, but little research has been done in this field.

Teachers should be influential by means of lessons on political topics. In the GDR, political indoctrination was paramount but civic education on the basis of Marxism-Leninism had already lost its influence during the 1980s.[23] In the new Länder, civic education in the west German sense was introduced in all types of schools and teachers were trained in special courses at the universities by political scientists. Until now, little has been known about the instruction practices of newly trained teachers and about the political influence of teachers teaching other subjects. Another study by Oswald has speculated about the influence of communist-trained teachers in the new Länder:

> It can be assumed that the political instruction by these teachers is confined to making the political institutions known and to teaching the general principles of democracy. Their attitudes towards the

reality of democracy in the unified Germany may be just as critical as that of the majority of the eastern adult population and it can be suspected that many teachers communicate their sceptical attitudes to the students.[24]

The 1960s student unrest in Western democracies produced a participatory shift from institutionalised participation in political parties and elections to unconventional political participation like demonstrations, boycotts, citizens' initiative groups (*Bürgerinitiative*), which have been called protest behaviour. Some political scientists spoke of a 'participatory revolution'.[25] The direct, non-institutionalised, non-electoral modes of political involvement of citizens in the late 1960s and early 1970s changed the character of Western democracies. One of the most important research endeavours in this realm was the seminal work 'Political Action' in eight countries by Barnes and Kaase in 1979[26] and its follow-up in west Germany, the Netherlands and the United States.[27] Numerous studies, including this one by the present authors, have used adaptations of the scales utilised in this research about legal and illegal unconventional protest forms.

The results so far show that participation in elections is still the main mode of participation, but this conventional behaviour had been supplemented by several forms of unconventional participation. Among them, civil disobedience behaviour 'was limited to a small part of the citizenry'.[28] Three socio-structural correlates were found in this research over time. Firstly, legal and illegal forms of unconventional participation are strongly related to the level of education, the higher educated being more ready to participate than the lower educated. Secondly, 'unconventional involvement, rather than conventional participation, has been and remains clearly and inversely related to age', the younger age cohorts being more ready to participate unconventionally than the older.[29] However, two reservations have to be made. The age effect occurred when age cohorts below 20 and above 20 were compared, whereas the longitudinal comparison of younger pupils showed a steady increase in the readiness to participate between grade eight and grade ten in east and west Berlin.[30] Another reservation refers to the difference between readiness to act and action: 'The impact of age is reduced the most, the closer one moves (from attitude) to action.'[31] In addition to age effects, there are slight cohort (generation) effects in the United States and period (historic) effects in west Germany and in the USA. Thirdly, the impact of gender is small compared with the impact of education and age. The gender difference in unconventional compared to conventional political participation is smaller.[32]

In the remainder of this chapter, results are presented from the authors' three-year longitudinal study of political participation by adolescents in one of the new German Länder. The adolescents were attending the *Gymnasium*, the most academic of the school types in the German system of secondary education. In Germany, pupils who wish to attend university have to complete 13 years of schooling in order to obtain the highest school certificate, known as the *'Abitur'*. The study focuses on this type of school, because the pupils will occupy the higher ranks in society. Many of them may become opinion leaders, some of them may become directly involved in politics. Therefore, the development of their readiness to participate during adolescence is of special significance for the establishment of a working democracy in east Germany. It should be noted that the results presented in this chapter are restricted to this upper stratum of the adolescent population.

After a brief outline of the research design, data is presented on changes in attitudes to participation over the three-year period. Here, it is hypothesised that political interest, discussions about politics, and the readiness to participate increase with age. Second, data is presented about the influence of parents and peers on the adolescent's readiness to participate politically, testing the hypothesis that parents and peers exert influence.

THE EMPIRICAL STUDY INTO THE DEVELOPMENT OF POLITICAL PARTICIPATION AMONG ADOLESCENTS IN BRANDENBURG

The analysis in this chapter is based on a longitudinal investigation in Brandenburg, one of the new Länder.[33] The subjects are pupils from 18 randomly selected schools. Data was collected in three waves from 1996 to 1998. The sample in the first wave of data collection was representative of all pupils in Brandenburg attending the tenth grade of the *Gymnasium* in 1996. Because all tenth-grade pupils in the selected schools were included in the study, the sample contains many dyads of best friends who are identifiable. The questionnaires were filled out in the classroom during one regular lesson (45 minutes). All pupils were given two questionnaires for their parents, which were filled out at home and were posted to us at a later date. The same pupils were interviewed again at grade 11 and 12 in 1997 and 1998 respectively. The same procedure for the inclusion of parents and friends was used at all three points in time.

Most of the following information about the development of political participation is based on a data set containing 638 adolescents for whom we have answers for each of the three years. Of the respondents, 224 were males and 414 were females. The over-representation of females is due to the over-representation of girls in the highest academic school type in

Germany as well as to the greater readiness of females to answer questionnaires.

A second data set allows the exploration of hypotheses about the relative influence of parents and peers on the readiness of pupils to participate politically. This data set contains all 347 pupils who answered in grades ten and 11 and whose friend and both parents filled in questionnaires at time one (1996). This data set enables us to compare the answers of adolescents with the answers given by their mothers, fathers and friends to the same questions.

The measures of political participation (dependent variables) are questions about political interest, about discussions with parents, peers and during class lessons, about information seeking in the mass media, about the readiness to participate in legal and illegal political protest actions, and about the readiness to vote in general elections. The formats of answers take the five-point Lickert scale from (1) 'never' or 'not at all' to (5) 'very often' or 'very strong'. The scale 'readiness to vote in general elections' is dichotomised in (0) 'non-voters' and (1) 'voters'. The scale 'information seeking in the mass media' is formed by four items: the reliabilities are satisfying (t1: alpha= .72; t2: alpha= .75; t3: alpha= .73). Each of the three protest scales is formed of three items and their reliabilities are also satisfying: legal protest (t1: alpha= .67; t2: alpha= .69; t3: alpha= .77), civil disobedience (t1: alpha= .67; t2: alpha= .71; t3: alpha= .69), and use of violence (t1: alpha= .80; t2: alpha= .82; t3: alpha= .77). The protest scales are adapted from 'Political Action'.[34] All the other participation scales, including the political interest scale, are single item scales. For all these measures of political participation the development over a three-year period of time is presented below.

The socialising contexts (independent variables) are captured by asking parents and friends the same questions about participation as the target adolescents. It is therefore possible to compare the answers of adolescents with the answers of their fathers, mothers and friends cross-sectionally as well as longitudinally. Other independent variables are the emotional relationship to parents and clique membership. In models predicting unconventional participation forms and the readiness to vote, the questions about political discussions with parents, peers and during class lessons and questions about political information seeking in the mass media as well as interest in politics, are used additionally as predicting variables.

CHANGES IN POLITICAL PARTICIPATION OF YOUNG PEOPLE: EMPIRICAL RESULTS

All the changes reported below are intra-individual changes because the same young people had been interviewed over a period of three years between their tenth and twelfth year of schooling. These intra-individual changes are presented on the group level by comparing the distribution of answers or the means at the different points in time. Changes are measured for political interest, for political discussions and information seeking, for readiness to participate in unconventional protest behaviour as well as for readiness to participate in general national elections.

Interest in Politics

At grade ten, in 1996, a majority of 52 per cent of the pupils were 'medium' interested. Almost one-third (30 per cent) were little or not at all interested. Only 18 per cent were strongly or very strongly interested. At grade twelve, in 1998, the little and not at all interested category decreased to 22 per cent, the highly interested group increased to 22 per cent, and the majority was still in the middle. As expected, this indicates an overall small but significant increase in political interest between roughly the age of 16 and the age of 18. The increase in political interest is significant for both sexes. However, as in other studies, in other countries and at other times, girls were significantly less interested than boys at all three points in time.

The reported gender differences were found by measuring political interest with a single question about interest in politics. Feminist researchers criticised this question as male-biased.[35] In the light of this criticism, the survey asked additionally for interest in different topics. The results show that girls are more interested than boys in topics like peace, ecology and problems of the Third World, whereas boys are more interested in governmental and international affairs than girls. This could mean that girls are not interested as much in the institutions of politics and in the everyday business of negotiation in government and parliament and that the single question measures mainly this sphere of front-page politics. But it does not mean that girls are generally disinterested. Where the well-being of people and environment is concerned, girls show even more interest than boys. One objection against this interpretation could be that the question eliciting interest in different topics measures attitudes rather than interest. However, the hypothesis is made here that girls are aware of fundamental problems of our society and that they show a specific political involvement which is different from the involvement of boys. Political scientists often seem to believe that the genuine involvement is that prevalent in boys and measured by the general single question about interest in politics.

FIGURE 1
INTRA-INDIVIDUAL CHANGES IN POLITICAL DISCUSSIONS AND INFORMATION
SEEKING OVER A PERIOD OF THREE YEARS (MEANS)

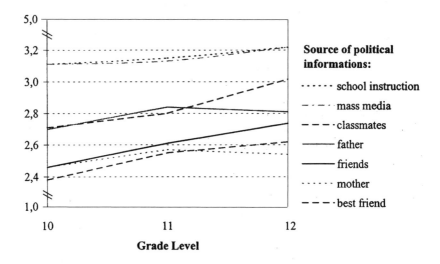

Discussions about Politics and Information Seeking

The survey asked the pupils to record on a five-point Lickert scale how often they talk with father, mother, best friend (same sex), friends and other pupils at school, how often they participate actively in political discussions during lessons, and how often they attend to news and political features in daily journals, on television and on the radio. The mean scores presented in Figure 1 show that participation during lessons at school and information seeking in the mass media were more important than discussions with persons outside school. In grades ten and 11 the most important discussion partners were fathers and other pupils at school. Two years later, in grade 12, the other pupils at school were more important than fathers as discussion partners, but fathers were still more important than the clique of friends, the best same sex friend and mothers. The importance of all sources of information and discussions was increasing between grade ten and 12 with the exceptions of fathers and mothers. The importance of fathers and mothers increased between grade ten and 11 and decreased between grade 11 and 12. It seems that the general involvement in politics was steadily increasing the older the adolescents were, but after grade 11 the importance of parents was no longer increasing.

The more adolescents were interested in politics the more they were seeking information in the mass media (t1: r = . 52, p < .001) and the more they were talking about politics with their best friend, with friends, with classmates and with parents (significant correlations between r = .27 and r = .46).

Readiness to Participate in Protest Behaviour

As in the study, 'Political Action',[36] the present analysis differentiated between legal and illegal protest behaviour. Illegal behaviour was again divided into civil disobedience and the readiness to use violence against things and persons.

Pupils were more ready for legal protest than for illegal protest. Only a minority of less than ten per cent was ready to endorse violence. The hypothesis adopted here was that the readiness to participate in legal protest and in civil disobedience would increase by age, like the interest in politics as part of the growing political identity. This was only partly the case. Between grades ten and 11 the readiness to participate in legal actions was growing in boys and girls, girls being more ready to participate than boys. But between grades 11 and 12 the readiness to participate legally was decreasing significantly for both sexes. In the case of civil disobedience, the increase and decrease were very similar, but on a lower level and without any gender differences. Both forms of participation are not only part of the growing political identity, but they are also influenced by circumstances. For young people, especially for girls, legal actions are more an option than actions of civil disobedience. In contrast, the use of violence was an option only for a small minority of adolescents. Girls were significantly less ready to participate in violence than boys, and the readiness to behave in such a way decreased significantly with age.

Voting Behaviour

Over a period of three years the pupils were asked the so-called Sunday question: 'If there were a general election next Sunday and you had already the right to vote, which party would you vote for?' For the current purpose the answers were dichotomised into voters and non-voters. A large majority of pupils was ready to vote, with significantly more boys being ready to vote than girls at all three points in time. In grade ten, 74 per cent of boys and 63 per cent of girls answered that they would participate in the general election. In grade 12, the percentage of voters increased to 86 per cent of boys and to 72 per cent of girls. Participation in general elections at the national level is the most accepted form of democratic involvement and participation. The more adolescents were interested in politics the greater was the probability that they were ready to vote (r = .26, p< .001).

THE INFLUENCE OF PARENTS AND PEERS ON POLITICAL PARTICIPATION OF YOUNG PEOPLE

As mentioned in the section on methods, the study collected information on socialising contexts under two headings. Firstly, we asked the young people about their relationships with parents and peers. Secondly, we put the same questions to parents and friends. In this way we were able to compare the answers of four persons to the same question and measure the agreement between parents and their children on the one hand and the young people and their friends on the other. Both sources of information are included in the regression models which form the basis of the interpretation presented below.

Cross-Sectional Analysis

In a first step, we analyse the predictors of four indicators of the readiness to participate politically. The results for 1996 are presented in Table 1. In the four models we controlled for it evaluates three context variables, that is,

TABLE 1

POLITICAL PARTICIPATION OF YOUNG PEOPLE: THE INFLUENCE OF PEERS, PARENTS, SCHOOL, THE MEDIA, POLITICAL ORIENTATION AND GENDER. A MULTIPLE REGRESSION ANALYSIS (1996) (BETA-WEIGHTS)

	Readiness to vote	Readiness for legal protest	Readiness for civil disobedience	Readiness to use violence
Variables of peer context				
Communication	−.15*	.19**	.19**	.16*
Clique membership	n.s.	n.s.	n.s.	.16**
Readiness of friend	.15**	.17**	.15**	.26***
Variables of parent context				
Communication	.12*	n.s.	n.s.	n.s.
Importance of parents	n.s.	n.s.	−.14*	−.20***
Readiness of mother	.14*	.17**	n.s.	−
Readiness of father	n.s.	n.s.	n.s.	−
Additional interest and information seeking				
Political interest	.29***	n.s.	n.s.	n.s.
School lessons	n.s.	.11+	n.s.	n.s.
Mass media	n.s.	n.s.	n.s.	n.s.
Control variables				
Left-right-orientation	n.s.	−.21***	−.12*	n.s.
Gender (0=male, 1=female)	n.s.	.15**	n.s.	−.14*
R	.42***	.56***	.37***	.43***
R^2	.17	.32	.14	.19
Adj. R^2	.14	.29	.10	.16

Notes: * p < .05, ** p < .01, *** p < .001 + p < .10, n.s. = not significant

'parent and peer context', 'political discussion and information', 'political interest' and one political attitude variable 'left-right orientation'.[37]

The young people's readiness to participate in conventional politics by voting in general elections was best predicted by their interest in politics (see Table 1, column 1). School lessons and obtaining information from the mass media did not impact on the readiness to vote. Voting appears to be influenced, however, by the parent context. The more young people talked with their mothers and fathers about politics, the higher was their willingness to vote. Where mothers themselves were inclined to vote, the readiness of their children to vote increased significantly. There was no similar effect of fathers' readiness to vote on their children. This suggests that mothers have a greater influence than fathers on the interest of their children to participate in politics.

The peer context also mattered. The readiness of friends to vote had a positive effect on young people's own readiness to do so. Friends agreed significantly in their attitudes towards voting. Interestingly enough and in contrast to the findings on the influence of parents, communication with peers about politics had a negative impact. The more young people talked with friends about politics, the less inclined they were to vote. Yet, clique membership did not influence voting orientation. On the face of it, girls were less interested in voting than boys. In the detailed analysis, however, this gender effect disappeared when we controlled for political interest, that is, the greater readiness of boys to vote was due to their greater interest in politics. Left-wing or right-wing orientations had no effect on the readiness of young people to vote.

Unconventional forms of participation are more strongly influenced by peers than parents. Communication with peers about politics and the readiness of friends to endorse unconventional forms of political participation increased the willingness of young people to do the same. This impact was evident for all three kinds of unconventional participation listed in Table 1 (columns 2–4): legal protest, civil disobedience and the use of violence. With regard to the use of violence, agreement with friends is greater than for other forms of political action. Clique membership only had a positive impact on the willingness to use violence. This suggests that violent political behaviour is a clique phenomenon.

Parents have comparatively little influence on unconventional forms of political participation. Only the readiness of mothers to engage in legal political protests has a significant effect. It is worth noting that the two illegal forms of political participation, civil disobedience and the use of violence, were related to a disturbed emotional relationship with parents. The less important parents were in the lives of their children, the greater was the readiness of these children to engage in illegal political behaviour.

Young people's interest in politics, what they had learned in school or information gleaned from the mass media had no significant effect on unconventional forms of political participation. Legal protests were the only form of political participation to be influenced by school lessons, although this influence was small (significant on the ten per cent level). Young people with left-wing political orientations were more inclined than others to participate in legal protests and in acts of civil disobedience. The study did not find a link between political orientation towards the left or the right and the use of violence. Gender, however, did matter. Girls were more inclined to participate in legal actions than boys who were more drawn towards assertive political behaviour, including violence.

Longitudinal Analysis

The findings of the cross-sectional analysis presented in Table 1 and discussed above may be considered a plausible but not proven interpretation of the causal effects of young people's social context on political participation. To firm up the evidence, we undertook a longitudinal analysis of political participation and the variables influencing it. Key results for 1996 and 1997 are summarised in Figures 2 and 3 and outlined below.

To strengthen causal explanation, we are using longitudinal regression models in which the dependent variable measured at 'time two' (here 1997) is predicted by variables measured at 'time one' (here 1996). The causal interpretation is only correct for persons who changed their minds in the interim. Therefore, a necessary condition for the causal interpretation is the inclusion of the attitude to be predicted, that is, the dependent variable measured at 'time two' as predictor at 'time one' in the model.[38] This is the approach adopted here.

Figure 2 shows that the readiness of young people to vote in 1997 was predicted in 1996 by a readiness of fathers and friends to vote. The cross-sectional analysis presented in Table 1 had revealed for 1996 that fathers' readiness to vote had no effect on the voting inclination of their children. It appears that children who did not change their minds about voting between 1996 and 1997 were influenced little by their fathers but tended to be influenced more by their mothers. The children who did change their minds, however, appeared to be influenced more strongly by their fathers than their mothers. The impact of friends on the willingness to vote was already apparent in the cross-sectional analysis for 1996. It was also relevant for 1997 and the change of political participation recorded in the longitudinal analysis. Thus, the results outlined in Figure 2 sustain the causal interpretation that young people who changed their minds between 1996 and 1997 with regard to their willingness to voting in general elections were influenced by their fathers and their friends.

FIGURE 2

PREDICTING POLITICAL PARTICIPATION: VOTING.
THE INFLUENCE OF PEERS, PARENTS, MEDIA AND GENDER ON YOUNG PEOPLE
BETWEEN 1996 AND 1997 (MULTIPLE, REGRESSIONS; BETA-WEIGHTS ON
ARROWS)

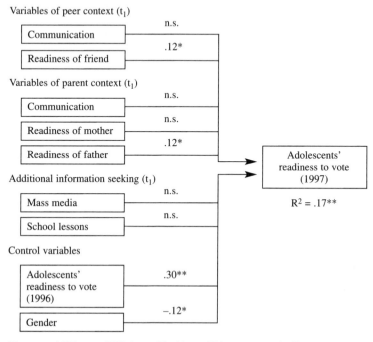

Notes: t_1 = 1996; t_2 = 1997, * p < .05, ** p < .001, n.s. = not significant.

The interest of young people in legal protest actions followed a similar pattern (see Figure 3). Fathers' readiness in 1996 to engage in legal protest predicted the same behaviour of those children who had changed their minds by 1997. Young people who were more inclined to favour legal protest actions in 1997 than they had done in 1996 were influenced by the readiness of their fathers to engage in such action in 1996. The results presented in Figure 3 again support the casual interpretation of the influence of fathers on the political participation of young people.

CONCLUSION

Using data from a longitudinal study conducted between 1996 and 1998, we set out to answer two sets of questions concerning the political socialisation

FIGURE 3

PREDICTING POLITICAL PARTICIPATION: LEGAL PROTEST.
THE INFLUENCE OF PEERS, PARENTS, MEDIA AND GENDER ON YOUNG PEOPLE
BETWEEN 1996 AND 1997 (MULTIPLE, REGRESSIONS; BETA-WEIGHTS ON
ARROWS).

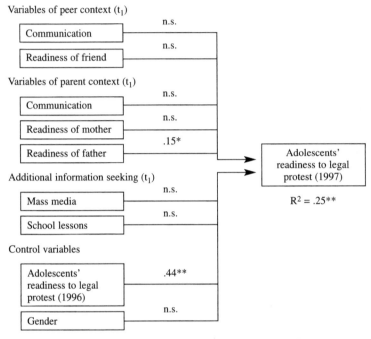

Notes: t_1 = 1996; t_2 = 1997. * p < .001, ** p < .05, n.s. = not significant.

of young people attending grammar schools (*Gymnasium*) in east Germany. The first set of questions focused on the intra-individual development of political participation; the second set explored the influence of two social contexts: parents and peers. Indicators of political participation were interest in politics, political discussions, information seeking about politics as well as conventional (voting) and unconventional (legal protest, civil disobedience, violence) forms of political behaviour.

The literature on political participation has consistently linked interest in politics with levels of education. Thus, as the best educated of their age group, young people attending a grammar school (*Gymnasium*) should show a particularly high interest in politics. In the new Länder, this also appears to be the case, but at a lower level than in the old Länder, the majority showing only a medium interest. As with their endorsement of democracy in the Federal Republic of Germany, the young people appear to hold back with their involvement.[39] However, as pupils get older, their interest in politics, search for information, the importance of political discussion and their readiness to vote in elections tended to increase.

Interest in politics has been shown to be lower among girls than among boys. Our study also arrived at this result. Yet, responding to feminist critique, we also explored gender differences in the interest for specific topics.[40] Here we found that young men were more interested in political institutions and the front-page reports about national and international political events while young women's interest in politics concentrated on peace, the environment and problems of the Third World.[41] The interest of young women in these policy fields reflected their positive attitudes towards the issues involved without necessarily translating into all forms of political participation. In fact, young women were more inclined than young men towards legal protests and this is related to their specific political interests. This link between forms of participation and interest in certain issues suggest that more research is needed into the gender differences of political socialisation.

Between the ages of 16 and 18, the political interests of young people, discussions about politics, information seeking and the readiness to vote all increased. Our study set out to explore whether a similar increase is evident with respect to two forms of unconventional participation, that is, legal protest and acts of civil disobedience. Our data did not confirm such a development. While the inclination to engage in unconventional forms of political participation increased between the ages of 16 and 17, it decreased between the ages of 17 and 18. It appears that unconventional political participation depends on the developing political identity of a young person as well as on specific political circumstances. In our study, we were unable to explain why the inclination towards unconventional participation decreased and supposed that political events interrupted the path to greater unconventional political involvement.

In Western democracies, a 'participatory revolution' during the 1970s boosted protest politics and unconventional political participation; in the new Länder it commenced with the *Wende*. Despite this diversification of taking part in politics, voting remains the dominant form of political participation. A clear majority of the grammar school students in our study and of young people in the new Länder generally is willing to vote in elections. By contrast, only a minority of grammar school students is inclined to use violence as a means of illegal and unconventional political protest. Young men are more prone to favour assertive behaviour than young women, while for both genders the willingness to use violence for political means decreased with age. The data in our study do not support the concern that increasing numbers of young east Germans condone and use violence as a form of political participation.

Parents and Peers

In order to determine the social contexts impacting on political participation, we presented, in a first step, a cross-sectional multiple regression analysis. Again using regression models, we examined in a second step how the readiness to vote and the inclination towards unconventional political participation in 1997 was predicted by variables measured in 1996. We found, as outlined in Table 1, the influence of peers on political participation to be greater than that of parents, and the influence of mothers to be greater than that of fathers. However, the longitudinal analysis cast some doubt on the dominant role of peers and of mothers in the political socialisation of young people and showed that fathers influenced young people who changed their minds between 1996 and 1997 (see Figures 2 and 3). The results of the longitudinal analysis do not imply that mothers and peers do not impact on the political participation of young people. We found that in all three years of our study, 1996, 1997 and 1998, there was more agreement between mothers and their children about political issues and forms of participation than between fathers and their children. Possibly the influence of mothers pre-dated the onset of our study in 1996; it is even possible that some young people influenced their mothers. The correlation between the political attitudes of mothers and their children may be interpreted as mutual influence. In addition, the results presented in Table 1 suggest that young people tend to have friends who share their political orientations. Friendships or membership in a clique can have a positive or a negative effect on the inclination to participate in politics. The more young people discussed politics, the less they were interested in conventional participation, that is, voting (see Table 1, column 1). The reverse was true for unconventional forms of political participation. Cliques and friendships generated a 'reinforcing climate' for the use of violence, but less so for other unconventional forms of political behaviour.

To sum up, our study provided evidence that peers have more influence than parents on young people's political participation, although it seems more accurate to conclude that peers create a 'reinforcing climate' rather than exercise a specific influence. Our study also found evidence for the closer link between mothers and their children with regard to political participation than between fathers and their children. However, for those young people who changed their minds, fathers come to be more influential than mothers in their political socialisation.

NOTES

1. H. Meulemann, *Werte und Wertewandel. Zur Identität einer geteilten und wiedervereinten Nation* (Weinheim, München: Juventa, 1996), p.313.
2. H. Oswald, 'Political Socialisation in the New States of Germany', in M. Yates and J. Youniss (eds.), *The Making of Citizens in a New Democracy: A Study of Youth in Former East Germany* (Cambridge: Cambridge University Press, forthcoming). See also P. Förster, 'Systemwechsel und politischer Mentalitätswandel', in H. Oswald (ed.), *Sozialisation und Entwicklung in den neuen Bundesländern – Ergebnisse empirischer Längsschnittforschung*. (Beiheft 2 der *Zeitschrift für Soziologie der Erziehung und Sozialisation*, 1998).
3. Meulemann, *Werte und Wertewandel*, p.318.
4. M. Kaase, 'Politische Einstellungen der Jugend', in M. Markefka and R. Nave-Herz (eds.), *Handbuch der Jugend- und Familienforschung*, vol. II (Neuwied: Luchterhand, 1989).
5. U. Hoffmann-Lange (ed.), *Jugend und Demokratie in Deutschland* (Opladen: Leske and Budrich, 1995).
6. O.W. Gabriel and J.W. van Deth, 'Political Interest', in J.W. van Deth and E. Scarbrough (eds.), *The Impact of Values* (New York: Oxford University Press, 1995).
7. U. Starke, 'Young People – Lifestyle, Expectations and Value Orientations since the Wende', in E. Kolinsky (ed.), *Between Hope and Fear – Everyday Life in Post-Unification Germany* (Keele: Keele University Press, 1995), p.170.
8. Oswald, 'Political Socialisation in the New States of Germany'.
9. J.W. van Deth, 'Interest in Politics', in M.K. Jennings and J.W. van Deth (eds.), *Continuities in Political Action* (Berlin and New York: Walter de Gruyter, 1990), p.275.
10. P.E. Converse, 'Attitudes and Nonattitudes', in R. Tufte (ed.), *The Quantitative Analysis of Social Problems* (Reading, MA: Addison-Wesley, 1970).
11. Kaase, 'Politische Einstellungen der Jugend', pp.608–9.
12. R.J. Dalton, *Citizen Politics in Western Democracies. Public Opinion and Political Parties in the United States, Great Britain, West Germany and France* (London: Chatham House, 1998), p.23.
13. Kaase, 'Politische Einstellungen der Jugend', p.610. Also J.W. van Deth, 'Interest in Politics', in M.K. Jennings and J.W. van Deth (eds.), *Continuities in Political Action* (Berlin, New York: Walter de Gruyter, 1990), pp.301, 305.
14. H. Schneider, 'Politische Partizipation – Zwischen Krise und Wandel', in Hoffmann-Lange (ed.), *Jugend und Demokratie in Deutschland*, pp.280–81. Also van Deth, 'Interest in Politics', pp.302, 305.
15. Kaase, 'Politische Einstellungen der Jugend', p.612.
16. W. Meltzer, *Jugend und Politik in Deutschland. Gesellschaftliche Einstellungen, Zukunftsorientierung und Rechtsextremismus-Potential Jugendlicher in Ost- und Westdeutschland* (Opladen: Leske and Budrich, 1992).
17. P. Lazarsfeld and R. Merton, 'Mass Communication, Popular Taste, and Organized Social Action', in B. Lyman (ed.), *The Communication of Ideas* (New York: Harper, 1948).
18. W. Schulz, 'Vielseher im dualen Rundfunksystem. Sekundäranalyse zur Langzeitstudie Massenkommunikation', in *Media Perspektiven* (1997). Also H.-D. Klingemann and K. Voltmer, 'Massenmedien als Brücke zur Welt der Politik', in M. Kaase and W. Schulz (eds.), *Massenkommunikation – Theorien, Methoden, Befunde* (Opladen: Westdeutscher Verlag, 1989).
19. P. Kuhn, 'Mediennutzung und politische Sozialisation' (unpublished Ph.D. thesis, University of Potsdam, 1998).
20. M.K. Jennings and R.G. Niemi, *The Political Character of Adolescence* (Princeton, NJ: Princeton University Press, 1974). Also A.C. Acock and V.L. Bengtson, 'Socialisation and Attribution Processes: Actual versus Perceived Similarity among Parents and Youth', *Journal of Marriage and the Family*, 42 (1980); S.H. Barnes and M. Kaase (eds.), *Political Action. Mass Participation in Five Western Democracies* (Beverley Hills, CA: Sage, 1979); R.J. Dalton, 'The Pathway of Parental Sozialisation', *Political Quarterly*, 10 (1982).
21. H. Oswald and I. Völker, 'Gymnasiasten – Religiöse Partizipation und politische Orientierung unter dem Einfluß der Eltern', in H.-G. Wehling (ed.), *Jugend zwischen*

Auflehnung und Anpassung (Stuttgart: Kohlhammer, 1973). Also Jennings and Niemi, *The Political Character of Adolescence*.

22. Jennings and Niemi, *The Political Character of Adolescence*, p.164. Also Acock and Bengtson, 'Socialisation and Attribution Processes', p.509; A.C. Acock, D. Barker and V.L. Bengtson, 'Mothers' Employment and Parent–Youth Similarity', *Journal of Marriage and the Family*, 44 (1982), p.448.

23. Oswald, 'Political Socialisation in the New States of Germany'.

24. H. Oswald, 'East German Adolescents' Attitudes towards the West German Democracy', in P. Daly (ed.), *Images of Germany* (New York: Peter Lang, in press).

25. M. Kaase, 'Partizipatorische Revolution – Ende der Parteien?', in J. Raschke (ed.), *Bürger und Parteien* (Opladen: Westdeutscher Verlag, 1982).

26. Barnes and Kaase (eds.), *Political Action*.

27. Jennings and van Deth (eds.), *Continuities in Political Action*.

28. M. Kaase, 'Mass Participation', in Jennings and van Deth (eds.), *Continuities in Political Action*, p.27.

29. Ibid., p.37.

30. C. Dickmeis, 'Die Entwicklung von gesellschaftlichen Werthaltungen und ihre Beziehungen zu politischen Einstellungen und Handlungsbereitschaften bei Jugendlichen in Ost- und Westberlin', in H. Oswald (ed.), *Sozialisation und Entwicklung in den neuen Bundesländern – Ergebnisse empirischer Längsschnittforschung* ('Beiheft' no 2 of *Zeitschrift für Soziologie der Erziehung und Sozialisation*, 1998), p.167.

31. Kaase, 'Mass Participation', p.40.

32. Ibid., p.41.

33. The study was financed by a grant from the *Deutsche Forschungsgemeinschaft* (DFG).

34. Barnes and Kaase (eds.), *Political Action*. Also Jennings and van Deth (eds.), *Continuities in Political Action*.

35. C. Kulke, 'Geschlechterverhältnis und politischer Aufbruch von Frauen: Wandlungsprozesse zwischen Herausforderungen und Verhinderungen', in B. Claussen and R. Geissler (eds.), *Die Politisierung des Menschen – Instanzen der politischen Sozialisation – Ein Handbuch* (Opladen: Leske and Budrich, 1996). Also J. Jacobi, 'Sind Mädchen unpolitischer als Jungen?', in J. Heitmeyer and J. Jacobi (eds.), *Politische Sozialisation und Individualisierung – Perspektiven und Chancen politischer Bildung* (Weinheim and München: Juventa, 1991).

36. Barnes and Kaase (eds.), *Political Action*.

37. Measured on a ten-point scale from 1=left to 10=right. Generally, young people with a left-wing orientation show a greater readiness to participate in politics than those with a right-wing orientation, and we designed our model in such a way as to exclude the common variance of the attitude variable with the context variables.

38. Usually, an attitude measured at 'time one' is a good predictor of the same attitude measured at 'time two'. If one does not control for the attitude at 'time one' to be predicted at 'time two', then the effect of another predicting variable is a mixture of the cross-sectional effect (for those which did not change) as well as of the longitudinal effect (for those which did change) and only the longitudinal effect (the so-called cross-leg effect) is open for a causal interpretation.

39. See Oswald, 'East German Adolescents' Attitudes'.

40. Detailed discussion in Kulke, 'Geschlechterverhältnis und politischer Aufbruch von Frauen'; Jacobi, 'Sind Mädchen unpolitischer als Jungen?'

41. See Meltzer, *Jugend und Politik in Deutschland*, for similar results.

Social Transformation Studies and Human Rights Abuses in East Germany after 1945

ANTHONY GLEES

This paper offers a qualitative, and, in part, quantitative account of human rights violations undertaken by the ministry of state security of the German Democratic Republic. Arguing that this subject has not always received proper attention, consideration is given to the role that these violations played in the governance of the GDR, so as to define it as a state without genuine constitutional protection of civic rights. For the purposes of current social science research into German transformation today, and in order to evaluate competing methods for converting yesterday's injustices into tomorrow's stability and consensus, it concludes that in contrast to the Federal Republic, which was always a constitutional state, or (Rechtsstaat), *the GDR was at all times an* Unrechtsstaat.

How states interact with their subjects has rightly been seen as an indicator of the nature of governance in the state in question. In seeking to evaluate the nature of the GDR, it is therefore necessary to describe accurately the experience of those of its subjects who wished to avail themselves of their civic rights. We should not baulk at applying this yardstick since it was the one chosen by the GDR itself. The ruling Communists always claimed that in the GDR there was full, constitutionally assured liberty and democracy, and a wide array of codified human rights on which people could rely. What is more, this was a claim which was often allowed to go unchallenged. Whilst it might be said everyone 'knew' at the time that the GDR was a 'police state', this 'knowledge' led to little serious analysis: on the whole, the citizens of the GDR were thought to be subject to strict 'discipline' (the term is Charles Maier's) but not totalitarian repression.[1] Whilst the full panoply of democratic rights might be denied them, they were not, it seemed, victims of any sort of government-inspired terror.

To explore the implications of all this is to illuminate a number of issues as much political as historical. One precondition for the development of a truly civil society is that its citizens are able to come to a proper reckoning with their past. Whatever mechanisms eastern Germans employ (a subject in its own right, not covered here), it is vital that they be constructed upon

Anthony Glees, Brunel University.

an accurate assessment of who suffered, and how, when and why they suffered. A frank description of the truth of the experience of Communism by east Germans before 1989 thus serves a post-1990 social as well as political and legal function because it offers the victims of the Communist regime recognition whilst alerting non-victims to the nature of their experience. Those individuals detained by the GDR authorities were forced to agree never to mention their experiences in detention, an undertaking that only leaving the GDR, or the collapse of the state, could expunge.[2] Even where before 1989 they were able to flee to the west, it was often hard for them to gain a hearing. Both western and FRG parties and governments had their own reasons for not wishing to dwell on allegations of human rights abuses, especially before 1985. They wished to maintain formal relationships with the GDR, and not pander to extreme right-wing groups (who used what were seen as atrocity stories for their own purposes). In the 1980s two leading Social Democrats, Hans-Jochen Vogel and Horst Ehmke, demanded the closing of the unit at Salzgitter charged with registering Stasi abuses to help 'normalise' relations between the two German states.[3] Since 1990, however, there has been a growing concern to research the wrongs suffered by east Germans under Communism in a variety of ways, which include the establishment of a Bundestag Commission of Enquiry (*Enquêtekommission*).[4] There is also evidence of a consensus within Germany that unless this is done the process of social healing can hardly take place, whatever the policy model for addressing the past may be.[5]

For some observers, both the period of Soviet occupation and of the German Democratic Republic are examples of police states, even of totalitarian regimes, in which the human rights of citizens were violated in a variety of ways, ranging from the simple withholding of basic rights, to torture and even death. For others, serious human rights abuses were but an early, transient and relatively limited feature of GDR political development which was, it was suggested, moving inexorably towards what might be termed 'Scandinavianisation' or greater freedom. The events of 1989, they contend, indicate not the repressiveness of German Communism, but its capacity to provide civic education for its subjects, and its potential for change. To them, the peaceful transition to real democracy, achieved without bloodshed, thus represents an essential truth about the GDR.

There is currently confusion as to whether we can (or should) differentiate on politico-historical or theoretical grounds between human rights abuses during the apparently different repressive conditions existing during Soviet occupation (1945–49) and the life of the German Democratic Republic (1949–90) – itself often disaggregated into a Stalinist (1949–56), post-Stalinist (1956–71), and Honecker phase (1971–89), or, even whether the east German political experience should be seen as one single period of effective

Soviet occupation, as epitomised by some in the old Federal Republic by their use of the term 'SBZ' well into the 1950s, or *'sogenannte DDR'*, and by others who have described the GDR as simply a Soviet 'satellite'.

The worst excesses, in terms of numbers abused, and killed, occurred before 1950, and mainly during the Soviet occupation of the GDR. But, as current research shows, these abuses did *not* stop in 1949; they continued until the fall of the Wall. The number of people working for Erich Mielke's Stasi *increased* dramatically (rather than declined) so that by 1989 there were some 250,000 of them (about 90,000 officers and 173,000 agents or 'informal colleagues', known as *IM*s).[6] Significant numbers of people were imprisoned and systematically tortured by them throughout the 1980s. The rigging of votes and the administration of toxic hormones to young athletes without their knowledge are further examples of abuses committed by Germans on other Germans, continuing to 1989.[7]

Thus, a proper consideration of human rights abuses in eastern Germany must be an indicator of the nature of the polity that was the German Democratic Republic. If eastern Germans suffered significant government-inspired fear and repression after 1945, and after 1949, the nature of the GDR must be interpreted accordingly. Even if it is contended (ignorantly) that repression ceased in 1949, its residual impact inflicted on the eastern Germans a bitter element of continuity between the period from 1945 to 1949, and what followed. Yet, as we shall see, since human rights abuses were a consistent feature of the total eastern German experience, and not confined merely to the first post-war period, the hitherto still somewhat hazy periodisation of GDR political development may have to be amended.[8]

Before turning to the actual evidence of human rights abuses, it is important to consider the methodological/historiographical problematic. One outcome of the collapse of Communism in eastern Germany and German transformation has been to make possible the re-evaluation of academic accounts of the Soviet-occupied zone of Germany, and then of the GDR, and of the Communist record on human rights abuses from 1945 to 1989: post-1990 accounts of the GDR have prompted a re-interpretation of pre-1989 accounts.[9] Very little research into the GDR was undertaken before 1978.[10] This chapter thus begins with a look at some of the more influential UK, US and German studies. It is not intended to be a comprehensive list although there is no reason to think that it is an unfair one.

There are good reasons for doing so. These accounts had an impact not just on the way the GDR was perceived at the time, but also subsequently. Furthermore, avoidable errors may be identified to which social scientists should be alerted. It is not unhelpful to show that mistakes were made, and facts missed, or that in the case of human rights abuses and the central role played by the Stasi, nor is it disingenuous to expect academics to have known about evidence before the collapse of the GDR made it readily available. Whilst there are no grounds for believing that any of the academic accounts served sinister purposes, there is evidence that scholars were sometimes willing to advance interpretations without making it plain that they could have been based on partial sources. Some researchers may have offered over-favourable interpretations of the GDR out of genuine admiration for the efforts and tribulations of the eastern German people. But it is also true that those analysts who set most store by objectivity and empirical observation (and sought to travel to the GDR to see for themselves what was going on there) were paradoxically those most at risk from manipulation. They could only ever see what the regime wished them to see. What is more, by associating themselves with the GDR authorities (in order to gain access to the state) they also put themselves at risk in other ways.[11] Finally, the significance of both the Stasi and human rights violations in the GDR *was* understood and reported by journalists and, most importantly, Amnesty International after 1962.[12]

PRE-1990 EVALUATIONS OF THE GDR: ECONOMIC AND POLITICAL

As has been suggested, the perception of the GDR, even after its collapse in 1989/90, was conditioned by the economic and political studies of it that were compiled before that time. A considerable number of them were to some extent inaccurate. This was to have a direct political consequence: gaps in our understanding of the GDR, particularly, perhaps, its economic condition before 1990, were one reason why German transformation policies after 1990 were so difficult to construct – and seemed frequently misjudged. As the Bundesbank chief, Hans Tietmeyer, wrote in 1998: 'We in the West were largely unaware of the internal state of the GDR economy up to that point. The studies published by research institutes and other bodies were not very instructive'.[13]

It is not hard to see what he was driving at. The leading west German GDR scholar Hermann Weber wrote in 1988 that: 'the GDR has existed for forty years, much longer than the fourteen years of Weimar, or the twelve of the Third Reich. This proves that the GDR, like the FRG, is one of the historically most stable states in recent Germany history'.[14]

One year earlier, in 1987, Ian Jeffries declared in a well-regarded book on the eastern German economy that 'the GDR is a world-ranking industrial country with the highest standard of living in the Socialist bloc … the relative success of the GDR economy makes radical reform less urgent'.[15] Whilst by no means uncritical, even at this very late stage Jeffries was unable to predict the imminent economic collapse of the GDR. In this, however, he was doing no more than simply echoing the academic wisdom of the time; indeed, his readiness to illuminate some economic problems implied some unease with the situation, but there was no indication of the impending catastrophe.[16]

Many, if not most, studies of the GDR produced since the 1960s had in fact stressed what was regarded as its impressive economic strength, and more than one spoke of an 'economic miracle' which it was claimed had occurred in the GDR during the late 1950s and 1960s.[17] David Childs, for example, one of the most celebrated British observers of GDR affairs, writing in 1966, approvingly quoted a 'Times Report' stating that the GDR economic miracle was 'more miraculous' than the FRG one. 'It is little known', Childs continued, 'that the GDR is about the ninth most powerful industrial state in the world, and about the fifth most powerful in Europe.' He conceded that up to 1966 expansion was not as strong as it had been in the 1950s but argued that was at least 'partly due to temporary factors such as the crisis of 1961' (by which he meant the building of the Berlin Wall).[18] In his standard 1969 textbook, David Childs declared that the GDR's economic achievements 'are, in certain respects, remarkable ... producing per capita in 1965 more steel than Italy, more electricity than West Germany, and more cement, TVs, refrigerators, and washing machines than Britain'.[19] Childs concluded:

> the GDR still has great problems, not least of which is to convince both world opinion and a good many of its own citizens that it is a legitimate state which is here to stay ... But who can doubt it is any less of a state than so many other internationally recognized states ... Who can doubt that short of a nuclear war it is likely to last? *It is a state which could rapidly become as viable politically as it is becoming viable economically.*[20]

It is important to emphasise that, as a 1983 Stasi report on Professor Childs shows, he was, in the eyes of the GDR regime, *by no means* seen as a friend of eastern Germany. Quite the reverse: he was described as the author of works 'aimed against the GDR'.[21]

Hanns Werner Schwarze, writing in 1973, declared:

> Since the mid 1960s, the material living standards of the population of the GDR have been indisputably higher than those of all the other Communist bloc countries including the Soviet Union ... In the Communist bloc [the GDR] is often referred to as the 'West of the East'. And not only in the East, but also in the West is there talk of an 'East German Economic Miracle' that compares reasonably with the West German *Wirtschaftswunder*.[22]

John Hoover, writing at the end of the 1970s, confirmed these optimistic forecasts: 'the GDR [has] the chance to become *"a showcase of development, productivity and social justice"*'.[23] The shortage of consumer goods, he declared, had been overcome. East Berlin was:

> a brilliant new city of light and culture, designed with its open areas more for people than for motor vehicles ... much of the planned reconstruction [of the city] has been completed. In the heart of the city, gleaming stores, hotels and public buildings line the main thoroughfares ... shop windows offer attractive displays of tempting merchandise, and buyers respond. Eating places are numerous. Squares and streets throng with animated people who would be inconspicuous in San Francisco, London, Sydney or Toronto.

Hoover continues:

> one of the first impressions a visitor to the GDR receives is the quantity of food consumed ... Venison, wild boar and wild fowl appear commonly on menus ... Supermarkets and other food stores are amply stocked with worldwide varieties of produce, tropical as well as temperate ... Meat counters offer a full range of cuts of beef, lamb, pork and poultry while seafood sections are stocked with ocean fish, lobsters and shellfish. Restaurants are well patronised as most people can apparently afford to eat out ... There is no unemployment. Indeed, authorities try to cope with a chronic manpower shortage. Since 1949 planned goals have been regularly exceeded and an economic miracle wrought ... The GDR in all likelihood will continue to prosper and develop during the coming years.[24]

Charles S. Maier thus hits the mark with his conclusion that: 'By the late 1980s, many observers held [the GDR] to be a Communist "success story"'.[25] Yet barely one year later, Maier continues, 'its economic residue was perceived in terms of second-rate machines, crumbling housing, cardboard cars, and an atmosphere choked by industrial fumes and lignite dust'.

The GDR's economy was, therefore, evaluated as being far more healthy than it was in reality. Maier advances three perfectly plausible explanations for this rather dismal verdict on Western skills in interpreting the truth about the GDR. First, there was clearly some evidence which supported the notion that the GDR's economy was functioning remarkably well. Secondly, Maier suggests that there were detailed accounting reasons which confused Western analysts. Thirdly, and perhaps most disconcertingly, he points to a desire that many Western, in particular FRG, political and business leaders had in promoting closer ties with the GDR, which generated straightforward self-deception. 'The most disastrous consequences were concealed because Western policy-makers, intellectuals and businessmen decided that their interest lay in stabilizing the eastern blocs.'[26]

If this is the case for the economic reality of the GDR, it is equally true for portrayal of human rights abuses before 1990. Karl Wilhelm Fricke (himself a victim of the Stasi) and employed not by any (west) German university, was a notable exception.[27] Even an acknowledged expert like Martin McCauley, who mentions secret police chief Mielke's name on three or four occasions in his standard 1983 book on the GDR, ignored the critical role the secret police chief played in the intimidation of 17 million Germans. David Childs's 1971 study makes no mention of Mielke at all, and none of the Stasi, or any of the human rights abuses.[28] Writing in 1977, Jonathan Steele, a noted British journalist, stated that 'Ulbricht was not unlike Konrad Adenauer', and Ulbricht's former personal secretary was quoted (without comment) claiming that 'we have created a state which is clean and decent, where orderliness reigns and people are hard working', as was Stefan Heym's comment that 'all the GDR lacked was sparkle'.[29] Kurt Sontheimer and Wilhelm Bleek, authors of a standard text on the GDR, make absolutely no mention of repressive measures or those who enacted them.[30] Klaus von Beyme's 1984 book on the GDR makes no mention of Mielke, and only one quite indistinct one of the Stasi.[31] Weber's 1988 book contains only two one-line references to him.

A study by C. Bradley Scharf has no reference to Mielke, but does quote an Amnesty International Report of 1980 which points to the existence of some 3,000–7,000 political prisoners in the GDR.[32] He adds that in October 1979 some 1,500 political prisoners were released as part of a general amnesty. On the other hand, Scharf regarded the issue of opposition as a minority one: 'the vast majority of citizens' seem content, and regard 'a certain amount of self-aggrandisement and hypocrisy [as something that] characterizes virtually all the nations of the world'.

Even an interesting 1986 account about the opposition in the FRG by Roger Woods made no reference to the *MfS;* Mielke is referred to on only three instances, and always in the context of one particular speech made in October 1978.[33] A section called 'Defining Opposition' makes no mention of the existence of political prisoners, and lists opponents as consisting first of dissident intellectuals, then of 'GDR citizens who wish to leave the GDR', and, third, as members of the 'unofficial peace movement'.[34] He adds: 'there have been just *a handful* of dissident intellectuals in the Honecker era, and although it has been argued of the peace movement that 5,000 in the GDR are the equivalent to sixty times that number in the GDR … the fact remains that the movement involves thousands, not hundreds of thousands'.[35] There is no mention here of the penalty that active dissent might invite in the form of Stasi repression. A survey is quoted, based on a poll of '1,200 political prisoners released to the FRG in 1975 and 1976', yet it is not accompanied by any comment on the startling fact that there were 1,200 such prisoners in the first place. Woods concludes that 'despite its denials that radical critics are in any way a representative group [*sic*] in East German society, the severity of the official reaction is a clear sign the party takes its critics seriously'. But no explanation is given as to what 'severity' might mean even though a document reproduced in the text mentions (in a letter to President Reagan) that GDR citizens wishing to leave the GDR have been imprisoned for this.[36]

One of the very few British books which gave real weight to repression and the existence of political prisoners in eastern Germany prior to 1990 was Timothy Garton Ash's 1981 book on the GDR. Yet he, it seems, grossly underestimated the numbers involved. He suggested that there were 'at least' 3,000 political prisoners in the GDR, but fewer than 7,000, and he does not contradict a statement by Honecker, which he quotes, that by 1979 the practice of taking political prisoners had been discontinued.[37] Garton Ash notes 'this last comment is interesting because it confirms that *before the amnesty* there *had* been political prisoners. We can deduce that there are at least 3,000 political prisoners in East Germany'.[38]

In fact, of course, in seeking to evaluate the importance of the persecution of political prisoners by the Stasi much depends on the way in which the numbers are expressed. Garton Ash appears to say both that there were certainly no more than 7,000 political prisoners in the GDR and that the practice of taking them had stopped by 1979. Yet, as it explored below, whilst this figure may be correct for a *single* year, it is in itself inadvertently misleading because each year new prisoners were taken, as others were released. It is the *total* that matters when evaluating the regime. Obviously, the expulsion of dissidents was preferable to incarcerating them. But the nature of the regime did not change just because some, or even a majority, of dissidents had been expelled or sold as merchandise to the West. It was also, of course, quite wrong to believe the last political prisoner had been taken in 1979.

We should not forget that from 1963 until 1989, 33,755 political prisoners had come to the FRG, either as refugees, or as those whose freedom had been bought by the FRG government: scholars working in the 1970s could, perhaps, have dwelt at greater length on the significance of these cases.[39] To make this point is by no means to castigate the research of any individual scholar, and certainly not one who understood better than most. Yet the fact remains that the actual number of political prisoners in eastern Germany from 1945 to 1989, calculated in 1996, was 36 times greater than one of its most perceptive observers had allowed in 1981; from

1949 to 1989 the number of people sentenced for political 'crimes' was *at least* 200,000.[40]

It may in any case be argued that the *numbers* of those who were killed, died and abused is, in one sense, irrelevant. From the point of view of the victim, persecution by a government for political beliefs peacefully held, and lawfully communicated, is, in itself, a valid 'performance indicator' of the behaviour of that government quite irrespective of the numbers involved. Yet the vast numbers involved indicate the *extent* to which persecution was used to exert control, and to intimidate society as a whole. Furthermore, persecution has, and is intended to have, a long shelf-life.[41] It is sometimes suggested that the worst abuses of human rights took place under the Soviet occupation, and that this cannot be laid at the door of the eastern German Communists. Whilst it is certainly the case that the worst abuses chiefly in terms of numbers killed, and possibly in brutality of treatment, took place before 1953, and especially from 1945 to 1949, it was the GDR that was the 'beneficiary' of this legacy. Brutality thus served as a 'bottom-line' warning to dissidents throughout the period of Communist rule in Germany. Indeed, it seems unwise to differentiate between Soviet and German Communism when ascribing guilt for human rights abuses. Even if the most evil acts were committed or inspired by the Soviets, there can be little doubt that leading eastern German Communists played a core part in the persecution process both under Soviet occupation, and thereafter until the regime collapsed in 1989.[42] The damage done to individuals since 1945 persists to the present date.

Even in one, relatively small, secret police gaol, Berlin-Hohenschönhausen, no more than 20 minutes drive away from Unter den Linden, there were 900–3,000 deaths from 1945 until 1989. Water torture was used there regularly until 1960; prisoners were repeatedly confined, beaten and tortured in the gaol's sound and lightproof rubber cell until 1989. Skeletons which cannot be identified continue to be disinterred to this day from the grounds of this prison. They are, it should be added, without any doubt victims of the Communists for the simple reason that there was no prison on this site before 1945.

The human rights issue, we must assume, was deemed peripheral since most academic authors did not subject it to penetrating analysis. The readiness to use eastern German economic data uncritically to provide an economic judgement was matched by a desire to use eastern German political 'data' to provide a judgement on human and civic rights. Whilst authors did not go out of their way to extol the GDR constitution, they seemed extremely coy about showing that the respect for civic rights was an utter sham, about which they can never have been in doubt, even if the full extent to which this was so may not have been readily apparent.

In its official statements about itself, the regime presented itself as a
Rechtsstaat:

> the human rights aspired to by the working people for centuries have
> become reality in the GDR. These rights are not comparable with the
> customary basic rights of citizens in capitalist countries, for they are not
> only rights *vis-à-vis* the state, but rights to take part in shaping socialist
> society with the help of the state. The basic rights are guaranteed
> politically by the power of the working people, materially by socialist
> ownership, and juridically by the socialist legal system. The
> constitutional provisions on the basic rights are direct valid law ... The
> observance of the basic rights of all citizens is a social necessity.[43]

> Every citizen has the right to state his opinion freely and publicly.
> Free expression of opinion in word, writing and pictures forms part of
> the liberty of citizens, consciously to give shape to their own social
> life. It serves to impart new insights into the objective laws of
> development of nature and society, publicly present views on
> questions of political, economic and cultural life, conduct a public
> exchange of ideas and help all citizens to form a scientifically-based
> opinion on all current events and to take a partisan stand for the
> peaceful development of mankind. In this spirit the freedom of the
> press, radio and television is also guaranteed...They are political
> institutions. It corresponds to the humanist character of the socialist
> social system of the GDR that the right of the free expression of
> opinion may not be misused for purposes of militarist and revanchist
> propaganda, war mongering and proclamations of religious, racial and
> national hatred.[44]

> The GDR is not merely a lawful state, it is the only lawful German
> state ... in the GDR the important lessons of the past have been
> learned.[45] ... The development of the GDR stands in harmony with the
> democratic principles of the law of peoples (*Völkerrecht*); its policies
> correspond to those of the UN Charter. It is different with the FRG ...
> there the same forces hold power who supported the Hitler regime.[46]
> ... The population has in every area not merely comprehensive rights
> of co-determination, but the right to play an active part in leading the
> state and the economy.[47]

'Are the citizens of the GDR allowed to state their opinions openly and
freely?' the authors of this work ask. 'Yes', they reply,

> the right of free expression for all citizens is anchored in article 9 of
> the Constitution of the GDR ... it is unthinkable that in the GDR a

citizen who criticises the work of a government minister, who finds shortcomings in an institution or administration, would lose his position, or even be arrested. But more than this, citizens do not just have the right to state their opinion, they have the duty to do so. There is only one qualification: expressions of opinion, and meetings, must serve democracy and peace. Attacks on the democratic state are banned in article 6 of the Constitution.[48]

Are judges independent? Without any qualification the GDR holds to the principle of judicial independence.[49] ... Who is punished under law? Particularly severe is the way in which courts require agents to face their responsibilities: those who serve foreign, hostile secret organisations, or by spying or sabotage seek to disturb the process of building socialism in the GDR.[50]

It is revealing to see that the GDR authorities made such generous use of concepts like democracy, human rights and free speech. The GDR did not merely claim be a lawful state (indeed the only lawful German state) but a model state in terms of its upholding of the rule of democratically generated law. Even the harsher 1968 GDR constitution claimed to safeguard freedoms of speech, assembly, association, conscience, belief and the secrecy of post and telephone.[51] Thus the abuses of human rights perpetrated by the Stasi at the behest of the GDR leaders were not simply abuses *per se*, but also abuses within the framework of the legal description that the GDR used about itself.

This point is important for several reasons. As far as the GDR itself was concerned, its verbiage not only indicates that the regime was wholly cynical in its treatment of its dissident citizens, but that it would be comprehended as such by its subjects. They knew that 'spying, sabotage, and resisting the building of socialism' were not words with specific meanings, but catch-all indictments which gave terror a free rein. To have laws guaranteeing dissent, criticism and free emigration, and to persecute those who sought to make use of these laws, was plainly intended to make to their subjects a very basic point about the will and nature of the regime, and its total determination to exercise power. There are interesting distinctions and parallels here to be drawn with the Third Reich, which made not the least pretence at respecting human rights. Indeed, whereas the GDR produced more than one written constitution, the Third Reich produced none (the Weimar Constitution of 1919 was never abrogated). Yet in both states the regime's disregard for the rule of its own law served the same ends: to terrorise and intimidate the German subjects of those regimes.[52]

As a contemporary German author writes:

> Despite undeniable improvements, the investigation of suspects and
> the punishment of wrongdoers in the GDR was very emphatically
> different from in West Germany. Western standards were never
> achieved in the GDR, despite its membership of the UN and other
> international bodies (it was a signatory of the UN Charter, the UN
> Declaration on Human Rights of 10.12.48, the International
> Convention on Civil and Political Rights of 16.12.66, and the Helsinki
> Final Act of 1.8.75). The UN Human Rights Declaration prohibited
> the shooting of refugees which was also outlawed by the Helsinki
> Final Act. On 19 December 1966 the GDR signed an International
> Pact on Civil and Political Rights and Human Dignity.

The apparent 'double-speak' utilised by the GDR therefore increased the
terror that it was able to exert; less overtly frightening than Nazi thuggery,
it was probably equally intimidating. Curiously, it was the flouting of these
solemn commitments, recognised as being the law of the GDR, that allowed
border guards, their officers and their commanders to be prosecuted. The
Bundesverfassungsgericht (BVG) determined that prosecutions could take
place only against those who had transgressed GDR law, rather than FRG
law, but used the abuses of human rights in the context of the above
agreements to permit prosecutions in the above cases on 4 November
1992.[53] In fact, applying the test of what would have been illegal under the
GDR makes virtually all human rights abuses actionable.

The truth, therefore, was that the reality of political life in the GDR was
very different from the way in which the regime presented itself to the world
– or the way in which most observers had presented it. The very political
rights that eastern Germans were meant to possess were withheld from
them. Demonstrating this fact led to their being terrorised and persecuted:
'Political prisoners were always regarded as on a par with the most serious
criminals.'[54] Yet with one or two notable exceptions, this was something
never properly analysed either in the Federal Republic or in the UK. The
bitterness that many eastern Germans must have felt and still feel about this
omission can easily be imagined.

NUMBERS OF GERMANS WHO DIED FOR POLITICAL REASONS
IN THE EASTERN PART OF GERMANY AFTER 1945

The latest evidence suggests that more than 200,000 eastern Germans died
either directly, or indirectly (through starvation and untreated TB), as a
result of Communist policy from 1945 to 1989, one per cent of the total
population of eastern Germany.[55] Of these, the vast majority, some 170,000,

perished during the first and most cruel wave of Sovietisation, which lasted until 1953. At least 90,000 people were executed by the Communists for being opponents of the regime, or died as a result of a policy of deliberate starvation, and inhuman treatment; 70,000 died in camps in Germany, and some 20,000 in Soviet gulags.

These, however, are the deaths that are known about. Experts believe that the numbers of those who were executed, and buried without trace, will cause these figures to be revised upwards. For example, some 20–25,000 boys and young men were arrested on suspicion of being members of the 'Werewolf' Nazi underground. Only 2,500 ever returned home.[56] Many of those who did not were shot by the NKVD in 1945 and 1946. Most of them had been members of the Hitler Youth (membership was compulsory after 1939). The Russian authorities accepted, after 1990, that there was no evidence to substantiate the charges made against them, and they were officially 'rehabilitated'.

NUMBERS KILLED WHILST TRYING TO FLEE FROM THE GDR[57]

It is now the case that the numbers of people killed whilst seeking to flee the GDR is four times as high as originally thought: the Salzgitter office reported in August 1989 that 197 people had been killed. In August 1994 it revised this figure upward to a total of 807. Of these, 368 were killed at the border between the FRG and GDR, 244 at the Berlin wall, 121 at the Baltic frontier, 35 at the eastern borders of the GDR. Twenty-six border guards were shot whilst attempting to flee. More than 40 of those killed were children or youths; 30 victims were women. The age of those shot ranges from one to 86 years old. The last border death occurred (through drowning) on 23 September 1989. Numerous individuals killed by mines have still not been identified. Only a number of these cases will be pursued by the German police since there cannot be an identifiable killer for those who drowned, or killed themselves, or had accidents whilst fleeing.

NUMBERS OF POLITICAL PRISONERS HELD IN THE SOVIET ZONE OF OCCUPATION AND THE GDR

Imprisonment and torture were considered totally acceptable ways of imposing Soviet *and* German Communist rule on the people of eastern Germany. Death in prison and executions were, however, increasingly eschewed as the GDR got older (though they were never totally ruled out). A recent study states that from 1945 to 1950 some 127,000 eastern German citizens were imprisoned for solely political reasons, of whom one-third died, and 700 were executed by Soviet tribunals. Moreover, at least 128,000 prisoners were taken to the Soviet Union for forced labour, of whom one-third died. Moreover, the Soviet Union accused some 30,000 POWs of war crimes and punished them.[58] A further 127,000–200,000 were detained without trials by the Soviets; 128,000 were deported to the USSR. In all, 40,000 civilians were sentenced by the Soviets during the period of occupation by them. All in all, some 200,000 civilians were sentenced by the GDR authorities for political offences, of whom several thousand died.

From 1945 until 1950 122,671 people were interned at Sachsenhausen and Buchenwald.[59] Buchenwald was given only 89 days of rest before being reopened by the Soviets, Sachsenhausen scarcely longer.[60] In Sachsenhausen every second inmate died. In Jamlitz, used for one and a half years from September 1945 until June 1947, 5,000 died. Some 20,000–30,000 were deported to the USSR. Some of these were certainly Nazis, of whom some were undoubtedly Nazi war criminals (though this should not excuse either their deaths in custody or their imprisonment without trial). In one case, 50 per cent of a prison block at Buchenwald appeared to be ex-members of the SS or the Gestapo. But 50 per cent of them were not.[61] Whilst Germany's Western occupiers interned former Nazis prior to trial (and, in the case of the Americans, even used Dachau concentration camp for a time to house them), the Soviets and the German Communists quite plainly used internment as a weapon against those who were not Communists. Overall, the Stasi used 17 gaols for political prisoners.

Falco Werkentin writes: 'Estimates made today of some 200,000 to 250,000 people imprisoned in the years *1949–89* are realistic.'[62] He adds

> The GDR always refused to give figures of its political prisoners; as early as 1950 the ministry of justice forbade the use of the term "political prisoners". Yet the government itself wished to know how many political prisoners there were. In the 1950s "confessional justice-terror" (*bekennender Justizterror*) was the hallmark; the press reported political trials and there were show trials. Some 30,000 to 35,000 were imprisoned after the 1953 revolt. By May 1953 some 67,000 people were in gaol of whom 40–50 per cent were political.

Early in 1953 the regime began to fear dissent, Werkentin suggests, and a promise was made to review all sentences. On Stalin's death in 1953, 23,800 prisoners were released early by the Germans, and a further 5,000 by the Soviets. Yet the 1953 rising reversed the policy – and the numbers increased again. A further 1,500 were sentenced as a result of the revolt. By the end of 1953 there were 12,500 political prisoners in the GDR, by 1955, 15,000.[63] In 1960, 17,692 people were sentenced for political crimes (treason, speaking ill of the regime, passport offences); in 1961, 18,297. In June 1955 five people were accused of supplying RIAS with news. Ulbricht personally demanded a death sentence for one of them, Joachim Wiebach, 29 years old, who was beheaded at Dresden on 14 September 1955. On 20 April 1960 a border guard called Smolka, who had fled the GDR, was kidnapped and taken back to the GDR, where he was tried and, on 26 April 1960, sentenced to death.[64]

NUMBERS ARRESTED FOR TRYING TO FLEE THE GDR

The high number of people arrested in the final years of the GDR's life may be explained in terms of those who sought to flee to the Federal Republic. Despite the fact that article 10 of the 1949 constitution declared that every citizen had the right to leave the GDR, thousands were imprisoned every year for doing just this. As it was from 1949 to 1961 some 2.5 million left the GDR. After 1958, '*Republikflucht*' was re-defined as a crime against the laws regulating passports. Paragraph 213 of the 1979 legal code stipulated a maximum eight-year sentence for breaking the laws on crossing the frontier.[65]

From 1958 to 1966, 63,949 people were arrested for trying to flee the GDR. From 1964 to 1970, 20,820 people were punished with gaol sentences for this offence. In the Honecker years, 1971–89, 64,091 people were arrested for *Republikflucht* – on average 3,000 each year until 1987 (in this year 5,696 were arrested). In 1988 the number was 9,169. There are no figures for 1989. The number of people gaoled during the period 1979–89 totalled 23,368. In 1988 2,337 were gaoled; in 1989 2,569.[66]

THE TREATMENT OF POLITICAL PRISONERS IN THE EASTERN PART OF GERMANY

Gross brutality, and death, were features of German Communism right up to its end in 1989. There may be a temptation, both in Germany and outside, to blame the Soviets for human rights violations. Notwithstanding the qualification made above, however, German Communism cannot be exonerated from complicity in this dismal story. German Communists certainly played a core role in the Soviet purges, and even after 1949 the SED was always concerned to show that it was 'watchful' towards the class enemy.[67] After 1970 the situation improved, but in no way were human rights respected. The Kurt Schumacher Circle has published a 'check-list' of the major features of imprisonment during the period 1945–89: 'Criteria of political imprisonment of the NKVD and SED from 1948 until 1989.'[68] The subsequent Politburo member Hermann Matern was responsible for providing a 'code' of methods to be used to undermine the will to resist the Communists. This code appears to have been widely followed since virtually all of those who have given testimony, or provided written accounts of their persecution, have quite independently described the same treatment. The code included the complete humiliation of the prisoner by the denial of all human and civil rights; continuous hunger as a means of influencing both the physical and psychological condition of the prisoner; almost complete isolation from the outside world; denial of means to attend to personal hygiene; and forced labour.

It is instructive to note not just the uniformity of the methods of abuse that were employed, not merely the consistency of their application throughout the life of the GDR, but how closely they reflect the account given of them in Arthur Koestler's *Darkness At Noon*.[69] It becomes chillingly clear that we are dealing here with a pattern of abuse which was common throughout the Communist world, and subtly different in some, but not all, ways from that practised by the Nazis. The wholesale liquidation of political opponents was, it is suggested, held to be impossible given Germany's status under overall Four Power control. Apart from deportation to the Soviet Union, the only policy alternative, given the large numbers of people considered either actual or potential members of the opposition to Communism, was lengthy imprisonment.

In investigative custody, prisoners had a can in which to relieve themselves, a jug of water and one or two stools. Up to five prisoners were placed in a cell; cell windows were fixed to prevent fresh air entering; lights were never switched off; no change of clothing was provided; there were no washing facilities; the heads of male inmates were shaved bare; women were not given combs; there were no nail clippers, no toilet paper, no sanitary towels; infestation by fleas and lice was widespread and not treated. Medical assistance was provided only in the gravest cases. Daily fare was a slice of bread, a teaspoon of sugar, half a litre of watery soup, a spoon of potato mash with shreds of sauerkraut. No contact with relatives was permitted.

During the Soviet occupation, detainees were interrogated by Russian secret police or army officers. With no knowledge of Soviet law, they were invariably accused of 'counter-revolutionary activity', on evidence provided by the SED. A denial was always dismissed as 'a lie'. Interrogations were conducted in Russian and translated only in part; there were no lawyers, no defence lawyers, no witnesses for the defence could be called, no notes could be made. Most interrogations lasted for six hours or more at night. During the day sleeping was not permitted. Beatings were carried out with fists, rubber truncheons and other hard objects; serious threats were consistently made, including threats to arrest family members. Confessions were gained usually only after treatment of this kind, and were often signed after detainees had spent many hours up to the knees in cold water. Detainees were held for months in solitary confinement.

The prison at Bautzen, which had formerly been a Nazi camp, soon became an accepted symbol of terror in Communist Germany; it was widely known what being sent there meant.[70] Detainees were kept either in barracks, or large rooms containing some 400 people, rooms containing 40, or single cells housing from four to six of them. Detainees were placed together with criminals and former Nazi war criminals. Prisoners were often beaten by the NKVD or the Volkspolizei. There was no toilet paper, or sanitary towels. Testimony from another prisoner taken in 1948 corroborates this picture.[71]

WITNESS EVIDENCE OF ABUSES UNDER SOVIET OCCUPATION AND DURING THE GDR[72]

For reasons of space, it is not possible to devote more than a few lines to the vast number of testimonies to death, torture and lesser human rights abuses that emerged after 1990.

The Period 1945–49

Two young Social Democrats, man and woman, committed opponents of fusion between the SPD and the SED, were given 25 years' gaol in 1947 at the request of the SED, were tortured, beaten and deprived of sleep; one was sent to Bautzen, the other to Sachsenhausen. They were released in 1956. A West Berlin reporter was kidnapped in 1950 by the Soviets, beaten repeatedly over seven months to extract a confession, then sentenced to 25 years at Workuta in the Polar region.[73] A woman whose officer husband had defected to the Moscow-run National Committee of Free Germany found herself in 1945 accused of complicity in the execution of a Communist by the Nazis. She was held in custody by the Soviets in Bautzen, Jamlitz, the *Speziallager Nr 1* at Muehlberg, the *Speziallager Nr. 2* at Buchenwald (where she remained until February 1950). Transferred to Waldheim, she was sentenced to death with 46 others by a GDR court and spent the period from October 1950 until March 1953 on death row. Her sentence was commuted to life in 1954, and allowed her to flee to the West in 1956. She never saw her husband, who had divorced her without her knowledge (and had since 1945 been a senior Communist official in Brandenburg and leading member of the People's Army), or her daughter again.[74]

The Period 1949–89

Conditions for political prisoners improved after 1949, and then again after 1968 when a new, milder legal code was promulgated. Paragraph 3 declared that 'Socialist lawfulness and regard for human dignity means that no one can be disadvantaged for his nationality, his race, his religious beliefs, or his membership of a class'.[75] A new law of 7 April 1977 said that in line with 'the humane nature of the socialist state, efforts to reeducate prisoners should be made'. In fact, this was nothing more than forced indoctrination. Prisoners who resisted were treated with gross brutality. Nor was there any general improvement in prison conditions. There was, however, a trend in the GDR as well as in other states to decrease the numbers of individuals given custodial sentences. Yet even so, in the GDR there were 180–200 prisoners per 100,000 inhabitants, whereas in the FRG there were 87 – two and a half times fewer.[76] Furthermore, the documented accounts of the most appalling abuses of political prisoners right up the fall of the Wall in 1989 reveal that the pattern of abuse established in eastern Germany by the NKVD and M-Apparats, and then taken over by the Stasi, was neither incidental nor peripheral, but a core means of governance and suppression. A recent collection of testimony shows that abuse inherent in the cases cited above persisted in *kind* if not in quantity until 1989.[77] A young student, arrested by the Stasi in 1961 for trying to persuade American servicemen in East Berlin to take him with them to the West was offered freedom in return for spying for them. When he refused, he was kept in solitary confinement for 203 days, contracted dysentery, was given no medical help, and suffered appallingly painful indignities. In 1974 a doctor was arrested with his wife and child whilst attempting to escape to the West. His wife was taken to another room with their child. He did not see her again for four-and-a-half years, but heard her scream as their child was taken from her. The child was placed in an orphanage in Erfurt, but Vogel, the lawyer, managed to free her after two months. A dentist, arrested on 5 October 1976 and taken to the investigation prison of the *MfS* at Schwerin, was confined to his cell for several weeks for refusing to sign a confession, then sentenced to four years and transferred to Cottbus. Here he refused to work, and from September 1977 until May 1978 was locked in the 'Tiger's cage' there, roughly two metres square, with opaque glass in the window, with no WC. The cell was not heated and during the day he was not permitted to lie on his bunk. Freed after almost two years, he fled to the West.

Many dissident women suffered severe abuse after 1973, especially in Hoheneck gaol. One arrested in Berlin at the end of the 1980s was transported on the 'Grotewohl express' to Leipzig. She states:

> It was catastrophic there, the cell was filthy, rats came out of toilets. We had to sit on stools from 0500 until 2000 each day. On 12 December 1988 we were ready to move on. We were handcuffed (six criminals, and eight political prisoners) and given two sandwiches and a packet of biscuits. Loaded onto the train, marked 'caution live

freight' we travelled for seventeen hours. The cell on the train was 1m by 1m and contained five prisoners.

A man, arrested on 15 November 1988, was kept with six others in a 4m by 4m cell; four had been arrested trying to flee, the fifth was guilty of driving offences, and the sixth had been convicted of assault. The toilet was in the cell, and had to be used in the presence of others. It was also used as a chair. Another man, arrested in 1989 and gaoled at Potsdam, was one of seven political prisoners on a wing with over 100 ordinary criminals. Another, taken on 25 October 1988, was held in Cottbus gaol. 'I was confronted by the worst guard there. He ordered punishment exercises, standing still during the free hour I twice saw how he beat up prisoners without reason.'

Josef Kneifel, the so-called 'Panzer detonator' who had blown up a tank monument to the Red Army in March 1980 (no one had been hurt in the explosion), was arrested with his wife. Refusing to work, and referring to himself as a 'prisoner of the Communists', he was repeatedly beaten. The punishments increased after February 1984 when he was sent to Bautzen I. His conduct did not change. On 2 January 1987 he was chained to a steel net, on his back, unable to move, to torture him into agreeing to be 're-educated'. He was kept on the net for four days, then removed as he was close to death. He was 'bought' free in the summer of 1987 following the intervention of many FRG institutions, and a personal visit by Land bishop Hempel to Honecker. Another Cottbus political prisoner recalled that on 6 January 1978 he and three others were ordered to remove ice. They refused and five men, led by the 'Red Terror' (a guard called Schulze, convicted after 1990), ordered a 'canonade': ten to 15 men began to beat the four prisoners into submission.

CONCLUSION

The sum total of this evidence is that the abuse of human rights by the Stasi was seen as a legitimate means of governance by the leaders of the GDR. In short, it was clearly an *Unrechtsstaat*. Whilst there may have been reasonable doubts about the extent of repression prior to 1989, there ought to have been no doubt at all that it was a core element of the polity. In the absence of any attempt by the GDR to make a break with *its* own past, Western attempts to differentiate between the various phases of Communist rule in eastern Germany underplayed an element of continuity that always lay at its heart: those who would not support Communism were to be persecuted and violated. The Stasi was not simply a Communist version of Western security and intelligence agencies; it was an instrument of political control far closer to the Gestapo than to MI5, or the Bundesverfassungsschutz. That is why the numbers working for it *increased* as the regime aged, why by 1989 it had almost a quarter of a million employees.

Even after 1990 not all British and American authors have given the abuses of human rights in eastern Germany and the role played by the Stasi sufficient attention. David Childs and Richard Popplewell provide a workmanlike general account of the history and organisation of the GDR intelligence service, but they do not seek to establish any thesis about its place, or that of its chief Erich Mielke, in the political development of the GDR.[78] Timothy Garton Ash's new book on his own Stasi file discusses the Stasi, but his emphasis rests on their impact on one well-connected young Englishman.[79] Furthermore, much of this account may be fictional. Sordid as their treatment of him was, it is quite wrong to forget that spying on people was but the first, and the mildest, of the Stasi's methods of dealing with its victims.

This point is also ignored by Mary Fulbrook, who writes in her 1995 study of the GDR, 'although Mielke officially presided over the MfS, he ultimately presided only in a very indirect manner ... the Stasi was neither "sword nor shield" nor a "state within a state" but the "nerve system and brain centre" of the GDR'.[80] The Stasi 'gathered information, sorted it, sent messages ... and acted of its own accord'. Bautzen, one of the cruellest camps, *is* mentioned, but as a place, and not a gaol, and the GDR is contrasted favourably with the Third Reich. She explains that a reason for the justified disgust of the Third Reich was the fact that 'it was a brutal dictatorship [in which] the first concentration camps were opened as early as March 1933 for those who did not conform', but concludes that 'imposed under conditions of defeat and military occupation ... the SED never achieved the degree of popular support enjoyed by Hitler' and that 'even the most cursory comparison of the GDR with the Third Reich will tend to reveal a far greater number of differences than similarities which it would be inappropriate to begin to explore in any detail'. 'Inappropriate'? One might wonder why.

It is perfectly true that in her 1992 essay on the 'Two Germanies', Fulbrook had stated that there had been repression and that the Stasi had 'used terror'.[81] It had, after 1989, become apparent that the Stasi had files on two-thirds of all eastern German adults. Yet the taking of political prisoners was not described by her and she offered no insights into how this terror was exercised, or its extent (apart from the statement that it was 'less in scale' than that of the Gestapo), and she rejected any description of the GDR as a 'totalitarian dictatorship'. The 'reality', she had insisted, was 'more complex' because of the changes in the nature of the GDR and in the 'balance between coercion and consent', striking a transcendental note by arguing that repression could be 'ideologically justified [by the regime]' in that the 'essentially humanitarian ideology of Marxism' had been capable of being 'perverted to heighten repression'.

Fulbrook's verdict on the Stasi is echoed, in passing, by Richard Evans. He concludes that

> There were some who argued [after 1990] that the [failure to convict Communist leaders] was a disgraceful state of affairs ... But the crimes of the two systems Nazism and Stalinism were very different in nature and in scale ... Murderous though the GDR was, its victims can be numbered only in *hundreds*, not in millions.[82]

The rhetorical certainty of this final phrase is not merely inaccurate but hurtful, and a touch misleading on two counts. First of all, if what counts is the experience of the victim and the principle of persecution, the numbers involved may not be the primary issue. Second, however, if numbers *do* count, then 'thousands' is surely a more fitting way of recognising the extent of the problem.

Anne McIlvoy goes further still, rejecting any focus on Stasi crimes: 'The Stasi has been unanimously declared the scapegoat for the evils of the East German system ... there are as many victims of the country's bureaucracy as there are of the Stasi's whims.'[83] Whilst it is not entirely clear what 'declared the scapegoat' means (it could mean that everyone thinks the Stasi has been made the scapegoat, that is to say *wrongly* made to take the blame for the 'evils' of the GDR, or that everyone has decided, wrongly, that the Stasi is responsible for these evils), nor indeed that 'whims' is a proper term for its work, to equate those who suffered from bureaucrats with those who were persecuted and imprisoned is misleading. Not surprisingly, under the circumstances, she concludes:

> To dissect the workings of the state security system, name the informers and look in horror at its methods and aims will not help Germany to come to terms with this chapter of its past ... overexposure and overpromotion of this topic will result in people drowning in a sea of ghastly detail rather than gaining any useful perspective on the Stasi and its legacy.

Charles Maier, too, seems wary about this topic. It is true that he writes of 'Stasi stains: the old regime on trial' in respect of the legal proceedings against some of its leading figures, Mielke and Wolf in particular (the former was sentenced for his part in a 1931 murder, not for any action taken by the Stasi; the latter received an even more derisory sentence). He adds: 'United Germany was just one of many states that have had to confront the dilemma of coming to terms with the human rights abuses of earlier regimes ... The GDR, after all, had been a German regime, but not just a German enterprise'.[84] Yet he then concludes 'the GDR had been German, first of all, less in any similarity to the Third Reich than to the earlier central European *Polizeystaat* whose bureaucrats had maintained that they must discipline their subjects for their own collective good'.

Not only can it quite plausibly be claimed that the similarities between the GDR and the Third Reich before 1938 (this date is important) were stronger than Maier, and others, seem prepared to allow, but by locating the GDR's record of terror in the realm of pre-1914 bureaucracies he misses the modernity of the Stasi's repression (a theme established by Ralf Dahrendorf in 1965). Even if it is right to argue that the aim of the Stasi was 'discipline' (which seems quite unjustified), and not extermination, the means it employed, which ranged from actual and psychological torture to drugging and bugging, led to very many deaths, and always suffering to the individuals concerned. Discipline must never be confused with assault or abuse. Similarly, the objection that most citizens may not have been directly affected by Stasi terror is as irrelevant as a comment on the nature of the GDR as it would be in the case of Nazi Germany.

This does not, of course, mean that the Nazi regime and Communist regime in the GDR were 'the same'. However, whatever view one may take of the two most difficult aspects of these abuses (the differences in numbers involved, and the notion that abuses in the period 1933 to 1945 were chiefly applied to victims regarded as ethnically or racially 'other', whereas those that took place after 1945 in eastern Germany were directed at those regarded as politically 'other'), it is *into* German political development and experience that these abuses need to be fitted. Germans were amongst the perpetrators but also amongst the victims of these abuses, which were motivated by the political desires of governing elites. Some of these victims had plainly dedicated themselves to the eventual overthrow of Communism. Many others, particularly before 1961, were ordinary Germans, who might well have lived peacefully within a Communist system (much as they had lived quietly through the Third Reich) but were deemed 'bourgeois', and thus enemies of the new state.

The Stasi *was* the 'sword' and 'shield' of German Communism, and terrifying because of this. The social damage it did to Germans was immense, and lasting, yet the mechanisms so far employed to address their pasts, and build new futures, have still not been satisfactorily refined, and are frequently contradictory: silence, judicial retribution, or 'truth and reconciliation' are alternatives with differing effects. What is clear, however, is that in describing the GDR's political culture, social scientists lacked caution. They should have given greater weight to the testimony of those who alleged human rights violations whether or not to do so went against the mood of the time, or 'better relations' with the GDR. These abuses would have been a more convincing measure of change in the GDR than almost any other Communist public policy, and more enlightening than the economic plans and social goals trumpeted at the time, and passed on to Western ears and eyes before 1990.

NOTES

Special thanks are due to David Rose; to Bernhard Wilhelm, Margret Bechler, Harald Strunz, Manfred Kittlaus, Hermann Kreutzer, Guenther Toepfer, Rainer Lippmann, Joerg Drieselmann, Mike Froehnel, Heinz Geruell, E Hellwig-Wilson, and Cornelius Creutzfeldt in the Federal Republic of Germany; and to Eva Kolinsky, Chris Flockton and the members of the 'Social Transformation Workshop', and Willie Paterson in the United Kingdom.

1. C.S. Maier, *Dissolution: The Crisis of Communism and the End of East Germany* (Princeton, NJ: Princeton University Press, 1997), p.328.
2. K.-D. Muller, '"Jeder kriminelle Morder is mir lieber ..." Haftbedingungen fur politische Häftlinge in der SBZ und der DDR und ihre Veranderungen von 1945–1989', in *'Die Vergangenheit lässt uns nicht los...' Haftbedingungen politischer Gefangener in der SBZ/DDR und deren gesundheitliche Folgen*, Erweiterte Berichte der gleichnamigen Fachtagung am 25.4.1997 in Hamburg für Ärzte, Psychologen, Gutachter, Juristen der Sozialgerichtsbarkeit und Mitarbeiter der Landesversorgunsamter, published no date (1997) by the Gedenkstätte für die Opfer politischer Gewalt Moritzplatz Magdeburg, Der Landesbeauftragte für die Unterlagen des Staatssicherheitsdienstes der ehemaligen DDR des Landes Berlin and others. With a forward by Hans-Joachim Hacker, p.10.
3. C. Hoffmann, 'Aufklärung und Ahndung totalitären Unrechts: Die Zentralen Stellen in Ludwigsburg und Salzgitter', *Aus Politik und Zeitgeschichte*, B4 (1993).
4. See Materialien der Enquête-Kommission, *Aufarbeitung von Geschichte und Folgen der SED Diktatur in Deutschland*, 30 vols. (Baden-Baden: Nomos, 1995; pb edn in 18 vols. Frankfurt am Main: Suhrkamp Verlag, 1995).
5. This analysis prompts consideration of the best practice of dealing with human rights abuses ('silence' on the matter, truth and reconciliation, or justice and retribution paradigms). For two recent, and important, studies which address this matter, see: N. Frei, *Vergangenheitspolitik. Die Anfänge der Bundesrepublik und die NS-Vergangenheit* (Munich: Beck, 1997, 2nd rev. edn); J. Herf, *Divided Memory. The Nazi Past in the Two Germanies* (Cambridge, MA, and London: Harvard University Press, 1997). Under federal German law, judicial proceedings against human rights abusers can be pursued only if the crimes of which they are accused were crimes under GDR law. Whilst this excludes several categories of what would in Western eyes be considered unacceptable political crimes, the fact is that to do so would, in effect, be a justification of the plea of 'superior orders' which the Nuremberg Tribunal quite specifically ruled was no justification. Furthermore, the GDR itself signed several international treaties, including the UN Charter in 1973, the International Pact on Civil and Political Rights in 1966, and the Helsinki Final Act of 1975, as well as the two follow-up articles in 1983 and 1986. (The Federal Court (Bundesgerichtshof) found, on 4 November 1992, that the use of guns at the Wall was illegal because it was 'a most grave offence against human rights'.) It thus seems plausible to argue that the crimes of the GDR regime were contraventions of GDR law in the wider sense of their international treaty obligations. There may therefore be opportunities for prosecution which the German courts currently refuse to consider. German courts have only until 31 December 1999 (extended in 1997, the previous cut-off date) to file cases against those GDR secret police officers, and their helpers, alleged to have been responsible for human rights abuses of their victims,

including causing their deaths under orders, or through wilful neglect, or torture and wrongful imprisonment. The reason is that these are all crimes which will fall under the 'statute of limitations' German law imposes. Only actual murder cases lie outside the scope of the statute. For the arguments in favour of an *amnesty*, see G. Shaw, 'Zeit für den Schlussstrich', *German Life and Letters,* Vol.50, No.1 (Jan. 1997).

6. A recent computation is given in L. Colitt, *Spymaster: The Exciting True Story of Markus Wolf – The Real-Life Carla* (London: Robson Books, 1996), p.64. By 1989 there were 100,000 officers and 150,000 informal agents, twice the 1973 total. Its budget was 30bn Marks throughout the 1980s. See also D. Childs and R. Popplewell, *The Stasi: The East German Intelligence and Security Service* (London: Macmillan, 1996), p.112.

7. See A. Glees and D. Rose, *The Observer,* 10 Aug. 1997.

8. For the problem of the periodisation of the GDR, see H. Weber, *Die DDR 1945–1986* (Munich: Oldenbourg, 1988). Weber notes (pp.116–17) that whilst Western scholars found it easy to differentiate between different phases of Communism (not always accurately, as it turns out with the benefit of hindsight), GDR writers liked to stress the continuities in the political life of their country.

9. On the subject of the re-evaluation of the GDR, see K.W. Fricke, 'Politische Strafjustiz im SED-Staat', and Rudolf Wassermann, 'Zur Aufarbeitung des SED-Unrechts', both in *Aus Politik und Zeitgeschichte* B4 (1993). Also P. Eisenmann and G. Hirscher (eds.), *Bilanz der zweiten deutschen Diktatur* (Munich: von Hase and Koehler, 1993); M. Fulbrook, *Anatomy of a Dictatorship. Inside the GDR* (Oxford: Oxford University Press, 1995); B. Faulenbach, M. Meckel und H. Weber (eds.), *Die Partei hatte immer recht. Aufarbeitung von Geschichte und Folgen der SED Diktatur* (Essen: Klartext, 1994); C. Hoffmann and E. Jesse, 'Die "doppelte Vergangenheitsbewältigung" in Deutschland 1945 und 1989. Unterschiede und Gemeinsamkeiten', in W. Weidenfeld (ed.), *Deutschland. Eine Nation-doppelte Geschichte* (Cologne: Wissenschaft und Politik, 1993); K.H. Jarausch, 'The Failure of East German Anti-Fascism: Some Ironies of History as Politics', *German Studies Review,* 14 (1991); E. Jesse, 'War die DDR totalitär?', *Aus Politik und Zeitgeschichte,* B4 (1994), and 'Vergangenheitsbewältigung nach totalitärer Herrschaft in Deutschland', *German Studies Review Special Issue* (1994); N. Naimark, *The Russians in Germany: A History of the Soviet Zone of Occupation* (Cambridge, MA: Harvard University Press, 1995); and A. McIlvoy, *The Saddled Cow: East Germany's Life and Legacy* (London: Faber and Faber, 1992).

10. Weber, *Die DDR,* p.105.

11. Thanks are due to Willie Paterson for this insight.

12. Amnesty International UK Country Reports after 1975, and publications after 1962, held at Westminster Reference Library.

13. H. Tietmeyer, 'Recollections of the German Treaty Negotiations of 1990', in S.F. Frowen and R. Pringle (eds.), *Inside the Bundesbank* (London: Macmillan, 1998), p.81. Thanks are due to Stephen Frowen for this information.

14. Weber, *Die DDR,* p.105 (trans. A. Glees).

15. I. Jeffries and M. Melzer, *The East German Economy* (London: Croom Helm, 1987), p.1

16. Jeffries and Melzer, *The East German Economy,* p.2. Jeffries wrote: 'the tendency of consumers to compare their living standards not with their poorer socialist neighbours, but with the West ... makes demonstrating the superiority of socialism and party legitimacy uphill tasks', yet he concluded: 'the relative success of the GDR economy makes radical reform less urgent'.

17. See, for example, L. Hornsby (ed.), *Profile of East Germany* (London: Harrap, 1966); A.M. Hanhardt, *The German Democratic Republic* (Baltimore, MD: The Johns Hopkins Press, 1968); J.P. Hoover, *East Germany* (London, Sydney and New York: Sterling Publishing, 1977).

18. Childs in Hornsby, *Profile,* pp.18 and 22–5.

19. D. Childs, *East Germany* (London: Benn, 1969), pp.136 ff.

20. Ibid., p.274 (emphasis not original).

21. MfS ZMA XX 20585 Bd. 6–8 1981–83, 6 Dec. 1983. Marked 'Streng Geheim', Childs's name was included on a list of 'politically negative persons' who were 'operationally relevant' contacts of the GDR Secret Service. The list also included Ian Wallace and John

Sandford, both noted GDR commentators at the time.

22. H.W. Schwarze, *The GDR Today: Life in the Other Germany* (London: Oswald Wolff, 1973), p.16.
23. Quotations from Hoover, *East Germany*, pp.5, 15, 17, 48 (emphasis not original).
24. Hoover, *East Germany,* pp.57–62.
25. Maier, *Dissolution*, pp.xi and 82 ff.
26. Ibid., p.94.
27. See K.W. Fricke, *Opposition und Widerstand in der DDR. Ein Politischer Report* (Cologne: Verlag Wissenschaft und Politik, 1984). H. Weber, *Die DDR,* praises Fricke, and testifies to the uniqueness of his work in all studies of the GDR (p.159). Even so, Weber accords only one paragraph in his entire book to the activities of the MfS, and only ten pages to the general subject of 'opposition and persecution' in which there is only one vague reference taken from Fricke to the effect that there had been 4,000 political prisoners in the GDR.
28. This is the second edition of his standard work on the FRG.
29. J. Steele, *Socialism with a German Face: The State that Came in From the Cold* (London: Jonathan Cape, 1977), pp.4, 5, 12, 75.
30. K. Sontheimer and W. Bleek, *The Government and Politics of East Germany* (London: Hutchinson, 1975).
31. K. von Beyme (ed.), *Policymaking in the GDR* (Aldershot: Gower, 1984): 'There is the watch regiment of the Ministry of State Security (more than 5,000 men) whose task it is to protect government buildings and institutions', p.174.
32. C.B. Scharf, *Politics and Change in East Germany: An Evaluation of Socialist Democracy* (Boulder, CO: Westview and London: Pinter, 1984), p.167.
33. R. Woods, *Opposition in the GDR Under Honecker 1971–85. An Introduction and Documentation* (London: Macmillan, 1986).
34. Woods, *Opposition*, pp.17–23 (emphasis not original).
35. Ibid., p.42.
36. Letter to President Reagan dated 23 Jan. 1984.
37. T. Garton Ash, *'Und Willst Du Nicht Mein Bruder Sein'* (Reinbek: Rowohlt, 1981), p.177. Garton Ash, who mentions Bautzen as an object of terror amongst GDR citizens, writes (my translation): 'publicly the GDR did not own up to having political prisoners. During an interview with the British publisher Robert Maxwell in February 1981 Erich Honecker was confronted with the latest Amnesty International report which said that there were from 3,000–7,000 political prisoners. Honecker said that this was a lie and that the difference of 4,000 in the estimate showed how seriously such people approached these matters. He added "since the amnesty of 1979 there is not one single political prisoner in this land".'
38. Garton Ash, *'Und Willst Du...'*, p.178 (emphasis not original).
39. L.A. Rehlinger, *Freikauf. Die Geschäfte der DDR mit politisch Verfolgten 1963–1989* (Berlin: Ullstein, 1991).
40. Die Gedenkstätte für die Opfer politischer Gewalt et al., *Die Vergangenheit* (1996), p.15.
41. Compare R. Bessel, 'Police of a New Type. Police and Society in East Germany after 1945', *German History*, Vol.10, No.3 (1992). He writes: 'having to live a lie ... may have induced people [in east Germany] all the more to repress their own politically dangerous feelings and identify with the Socialist order which [the police] outwardly represented'.
42. See Herf, *Divided Memory*, in particular his account of the persecution of the so-called 'Cosmopolitan opposition' in the GDR after 1949.
43. *Introducing the GDR* (Dresden: Verlag Zeit im Bild, 1971, 2nd edn.), pp.37–76; 'Social and State Order', p.57.
44. Ibid., p.64.
45. Ibid., p.11.
46. Ibid., p.13.
47 Ibid., p.20.
48. Ibid., p.21.
49. Ibid., p.44.
50. Ibid., p. 45.
51. See n.77.

52. This point was point made in 1981 by Garton Ash, *'Und Willst Du...'*, p.23. He speaks of 'kalkulierte Abschreckungsmittel'. He points out that *Neues Deutschland* published the text of the 1975 Helsinki Final Act' which spoke of the aim of 'free movement and contact' in the continent. See, too, M. Klopfer and G. Michael, *Das Stasi-Unterlagen Gesetz und die Pressefreiheit: Verfassungsfragen des Gesetzes über die Unterlagen des Staatssicherheitsdienstes der ehemaligen DDR.* Schriften zum öffentlichen Recht 0582-0200 Bd 630 (Berlin: Duncker und Humblot, 1993).

53. Die Gedenkstätte für die Opfer, *Die Vergangenheit*, p.13.

54. Ibid., pp.12, 13.

55. Ibid., pp.13, 15, 24. Information from Manfred Kittlaus, Head of ZERV, Berlin Police, Ministerialdirektor a. D. Hermann Kreutzer, Dr Bernhard Wilhelm, Berlin, May 1997.

56. See B. Priess, *Unschuldig in den Todeslagern des NKWD* (Calw: Benno Priess Eigenverlag, 1995, 4th edn); B. Priess, *Erschossen im Morgengrauen: "Werwolf"-Schicksale mitteldeutscher Jugend* (Calw: Benno Priess Eigenverlag, 1997). Published with the support of the Federal Ministry of the Interior. Priess was himself wrongly convicted of being a *'Werwolf'* and suffered corrrespondingly.

57. Written information from Hermann Kreutzer, Berlin 28 Feb. 1998 (Kurt-Schumacher-Kreis document: prepared for the Federal Government, published at the Angeburger Allee 41, 14055 Berlin).

58. Die Gedenkstätte für die Opfer, *Die Vergangenheit*, pp.13–17.

59. See, for example, D. Rose and A. Glees, *The Observer*, 10 Aug. 1997 and 4 July 1944. Also G. Finn and K.W. Fricke, *Politischer Strafvollzug in der DDR* (Cologne: Wissenschaft und Politik, 1981); G. Finn, *Sachsenhausen 1936–1950: Geschichte eines Lagers* (Berlin and Bonn: Westkreuz Verlag, 1988, 2nd edn).

60. It was surely unacceptable to use these, and other, Nazi concentration camps as concentration camps.

61. Interview with Hermann Kreutzer, 11 June 1996, Berlin.

62. F. Werkentin, 'Zur Dimension politischer Inhaftierungen 1949–89', in Die Gedenkstätte für die Opfer politischer Gewalt (ed.), *Die Vergangenheit*, p.143 (emphasis not original), see pp.129–43 for a breakdown of these figures.

63. Wekentin raises the question as to whether economic crimes should be considered political. He argues that they should because political opponents were often accused of such crimes.

64. Fricke, *Opposition*. In the 40 years of the GDR, Fricke states, some 150,000 to 200,000 fell victim to 'political justice', the majority before 1961.

65. F. Werkentin, 'Zur Dimenion politischer Inhaftierungen', pp.136–7.

66. Die Gedenkstätte für die Opfer, *Die Vergangenheit* (1996) p.16 reports the following figures:

Period	No. of political prisoners per year	Proportion of political prisoners in prison population as a whole
1950–55	11,000–14,000	1/3
1956–64	6,000–7,000	1/5
1965–69	7,500	1/3
1970–74	5,800	1/4
1975–79	4,200	1/4
1980–84	4,500	1/5
1985–88	3,800	1/6

See also p.59. The numbers for a particular set of years will obviously be a combination of those imprisoned in previous years, and those newly imprisoned, p.15, n.15.

67. See n.58. Information from Hermann Kreutzer 28 Feb. 1998. Documentation published by the Kurt-Schumacher-Kreis, Berlin.

68. See n.58.

69. Arthur Koestler, *Darkness at Noon,* trans. Daphne Hardy (London: Macmillan, 1941).

70. Information from Hermann Kreutzer, himself imprisoned in Bautzen 11 June 1996, interviewed in Berlin. Kreutzer alleges that at least 170,000 individuals were arrested by the

'M-Apparats', German Communist agents of the Russians from 1945 to 1947, of whom he, a Social Democrat from Thuringia, was but one. Some 60–70,000 died of starvation and typhoid. Kreutzer claims that many of those who were arrested were considered to constitute a political or potential political opposition to Communism, as he was himself.

71. See Die Gedenkstätte für die Opfer, *Die Vergangenheit*, pp.153–9, detailing the testimony of Albert Wesemeyer arrested in 1948 for Social Democratic activity (making contact with Schumacher, for example) in Erfurt. He had been in prison for four years during the Third Reich. See also D. Rieke (ed.), *Sozialdemokraten als Opfer im Kampf gegen die rote Diktatur: Arbeitsmaterialien zur politischen Bildung* (Bonn: Friedrich Ebert Foundation, 1994). He states (p.6) that from 1948–50 some 200,000 Social Democrats were persecuted, or forced to flee; 5,000 were imprisoned, of whom 400 died.
72. Thanks are due to the British Council, *The Observer*, and more recently BBC TV Current Affairs, for funding research on these accounts in Germany from 1994 to 1998. Interviews were conducted with Dr Bernhard Wilhelm, Ministerialdirektor i. R. Hermann Kreutzer, Heinz Gerull, Mike Froehnel, Frau Dr R. Camphausen, E.O. Hellwig-Wilson, Joerg Drieselmann, Rainer Lippmann, Harald Strunz, Guenter Toepfer MdA, Polizeidirektor Manfred Kittlaus (head of ZERV), Margret Bechler (Wedel). Also Klaus Eichner and Hans Voelkner, formerly of the MfS.
73. See S. Binski (ed.), *Zwischen Waldheim und Workuta: Erlebnisse politischer Häftlinge 1945–1965*, with an introduction by K.W. Fricke (Berlin and Westkreuz Druckerei, 1994, 2nd edn).
74. See also M. Bechler, *Warten auf Antwort: ein deutsches Schicksal* (Frankfurt/M and Berlin: Ullstein, 1993, 18th edn).
75. Ibid., p.19.
76. Ibid., pp.20, 61–3. Childs and Popplewell, *The Stasi*, note (p.96): 'The 1968 GDR constitution was not as liberal as that of 1949 but it had the usual clauses safeguarding freedoms of speech, assembly and association (arts 27, 28, 29) and freedom of conscience and belief was upheld in art 20 whilst the secrecy of post and telephone was "guaranteed" under art 31.'
77. See Die Gedenkstätte für die Opfer politischer Gewalt, *Die Vergangenheit*.
78. Childs and Popplewell, *The Stasi*.
79. T. Garton Ash, *The File: A Personal History* (London: HarperCollins, 1997).
80. Fulbrook, *Anatomy*, pp.47, 53, 196, 285–6.
81. M. Fulbrook, *The Two Germanies: Problems of Interpretation* (Atlantic Highlands, NJ: Humanities Press International, 1992), pp.37, 38, 39, 42.
82. R.J. Evans, *Rituals of Retribution. Capital Punishment in Germany 1600–1987* (Oxford: OUP, 1996), p.868 (emphasis not original).
83. McIlvoy, *The Saddled Cow*, p.107.
84. Maier, *Dissolution*, pp.311, 319, 322, 323, 328.

Multiculturalism in the Making? Non-Germans and Civil Society in the New Länder

EVA KOLINSKY

One of the legacies of GDR state socialism arises from its exclusion of non-Germans from civil society. The paper examines the treatment of contract workers before and after the collapse of the GDR and argues that non-acceptance of 'foreigners' persisted once the new Länder were required to accommodate their share of asylum seekers. While west German society had undergone an – albeit reluctant and incomplete – shift towards multiculturalism, the presence of non-Germans in their society did not feature in eastern Germans' agenda for unification and the transformation that was to follow. A decade on, the number of non-Germans in the new Länder remains very low, their non-acceptance widespread and acts of xenophobic violence a regular and growing occurrence.

The unification of Germany initiated a period of system transformation which was to recast the east in line with the western model. With the hindsight of nearly a decade it is evident that expectations of a smooth transfer were unrealistic in most policy domains as east Germans proved less keen to give up established ways of doing things for allegedly more effective and modern replacements. *Ausländerpolitik*, the treatment of non-Germans in civil society, was no exception; indeed it constituted a special challenge.

In principle, system transfer elevated west German practices to the status of a model, but *Ausländerpolitik* was a flawed model. Since the mid-1950s, when the first batch of labour recruits arrived from Italy to work in the German economy, policy had always hovered uneasily between an acceptance of non-Germans as social citizens and efforts to limit their numbers or restrict their rights of participation in civil society. Successive governments offered financial incentives to boost re-migration but also revised legislation to consolidate rights of residency. Until the mid-1960s, foreigners faced expulsion if they became unemployed or homeless; since then, those who had qualified for residency rights also gained rights to

Eva Kolinsky, Keele University.

benefit, although practice differed between German Länder. In the 1990s, the legislation was revised further to offer long-term residents the unrestricted right to remain in Germany and also allow children born in Germany to non-German parents to choose German citizenship on reaching the age of 18. By the time unification dismantled the last remnants of the German–German border in 1990, west Germany had a non-German population of about eight million, admitted nearly 200,000 asylum seekers per year and as a society showed signs of multicultural development, not least in its big cities, where about one in four inhabitants were non-Germans by nationality and culture.[1]

Despite this emergent diversity, Germany has refused to define an immigration policy, regarding itself instead as a non-immigration country – *kein Einwanderungsland*. An immigration policy would dismantle the system of investigating the case of each individual newcomer after his or her arrival in Germany, and entail instead an entitlement to citizenship and equal participation in civil society for a specified number of people. A debate on reviewing German citizenship policy and on strategies of social inclusion for non-German newcomers and their second and third generation offspring is, however, currently under way.

The German Democratic Republic had undergone no such development. Non-Germans, if they were admitted at all, were segregated from civil society; contacts between Germans and foreigners were forbidden and subject to Stasi surveillance. Diplomats, foreign students and others with non-German passports and access to foreign currency could travel without restrictions and purchase luxury consumer goods which were not available for *Ostmark*. These privileges bred resentment in a population who had grown tired of the persistent shortages it had to endure and who accused the foreigners in their midst of causing or at least exacerbating them:

They had little contact with GDR citizens. People in the GDR were only surprised that more and more foreigners seemed to be there. Nobody bothered to ask why, nobody discussed it. But when people in the GDR saw how the Vietnamese would spend all their money on goods to take home with them into their war-torn homeland, then they felt sure they knew what was going on and complained 'They are buying us dry!'.[2]

Contract workers or *Vertragsarbeiter*, the GDR equivalent of the *Gastarbeiter*, were even more rigidly segregated from the general population and deprived of civil liberties. The duration of their stay – a maximum of five years – their employment and pay were all agreed at governmental level. Passports were withheld by the GDR authorities, leaving contract workers without rights of mobility or travel. Wages were lower than those for eastern Germans and up to 15 per cent paid directly to the sending government. Should that country be in debt to the GDR, the pay of individual workers was docked. Sending countries were as interested as the GDR in excluding contract workers from German civil society and many stipulated that half the wages earned should be paid only after a worker returned home.[3] In addition, contract workers were excluded from everyday life in many different ways. Communication was virtually impossible without a command of the German language or an opportunity to learn it. Moreover, contract workers were accommodated in hostels which were guarded and locked at night. Rental charges, which were five times higher per square metre than those levied from Germans for a regular flat, added to exclusion through material hardship.[4] Even at the workplace, contract workers were often victimised. Without a trade union or other agency to speak on their behalf, they had little chance of receiving fair treatment [5]

Historically, the exclusion of non-Germans from civil society constituted public policy and informed social conventions in Germany's authoritarian and pre-democratic eras. Formulating strategies of inclusion, acceptance and integration can, therefore, be regarded as a facet of democratic political culture and of a society in which all residents enjoy human and citizen rights regardless of background, religion, cultural orientation or ethnic origin. In eastern Germany, the challenge of including non-Germans into civil society had to be faced for the first time after the end of state socialism. The transformation from a homogeneously German to a multicultural society entails an emergence of pluralism and an acceptance of diversity in everyday life. The following discussion examines to what extent this transformation of east German civil society has taken shape. It will show that even after the collapse of state socialism allowed east Germans to set their own agenda, the treatment of non-Germans continued to bear the hallmark of exclusion and has been marred by hostilities. As the new Länder are committed to accommodating their share of asylum seekers, some immigration is evident, but at two per cent the proportion of non-Germans in the population remains as small as it was in 1939.[6] Outbursts of xenophobia and a right-extremist protest milieu make the transition to a multicultural east Germany as remote as ever.

FAR FROM EQUAL: THE TREATMENT OF NON-GERMANS IN THE GDR

Officially, the GDR subscribed to internationalism and claimed to welcome non-Germans without reservations: 'Our country, and this has been generally proven and recognised, is without hostility towards foreigners, a country which practices solidarity with other peoples.' 'Hostility against foreigners? … In this country there is no hostility against foreigners, only solidarity.'[7] In reality, 'foreigners' were treated as if they had no place in GDR civil society and did not exist. The statistical yearbooks made no mention of them and accounts published after the end of the GDR with the explicit purpose of showing things as they really were perpetuated the silence.[8]

Numbers were small. In December 1989, 190,000 non-Germans lived in the GDR, 43,000 (23 per cent) of them held long-term or permanent, and the remaining 147,000 temporary, residency rights.[9] Of the temporary residents, nearly 120,000 were contract workers with severely curtailed civil rights. Contract workers were brought in from the mid-1960s to alleviate manpower shortages. Recruitment had intensified in the mid-1980s when the GDR tried to boost output by introducing a third shift in key industries. It was stepped up further in 1989 when Erich Honecker sought to compensate for the mass exodus of nearly 350,000 eastern Germans to the west and its disruptive effect on the GDR economy.[10] In 1990 alone, 60,000 workers were contracted in from North Vietnam and 90,000 signed for with Mozambique, although Honecker's government fell before its deal could be implemented. For the people in the GDR, the unparalleled influx of foreign workers in the late 1980s came as 500,000 had filed applications to become 'over-settlers' and move legally to the west and also at a time when many east Germans had an acute sense of economic stagnation as they experienced daily the failings of a planned economy in their working environment and their private lives.

In signing labour recruitment contracts, the GDR had initially favoured eastern European brother countries but shifted to Africa, East Asia and Cuba when popular movements towards democracy made the citizens of Poland or Hungary suspect as potential trouble-makers. To this day, non-German residents in the new Länder are less likely than in the old to originate from a European Union member state or from Turkey. Of the 222,100 non-Germans living in eastern Germany in November 1997, some 50 per cent originated from an African or East Asian country.[11] At a much lower level than in the old Länder, city populations developed a greater cultural mix than those in rural areas.

Leipzig and East Berlin continue to share the distinction they held in the GDR era of accommodating the most sizeable non-German populations. In 1990, Leipzig had a non-German population of 2.5 per cent; by December 1997, this had nearly doubled to 4.6 per cent.[12] East Berlin witnessed an even faster growth of its non-German population, which more than trebled to over 72,000 or 5.6 per cent in 1997.[13]

TABLE 1

CONTRACT LABOUR (*VERTRAGSARBEITER*) IN THE GDR (31 DECEMBER 1989)

Country of origin	Year of original contract	Overall numbers	As % of foreigners
Poland	1966	51,743	27.1
Hungary	1967	13,424	7.0
Algeria*	1974	n/a	–
Cuba	1978	7,999	4.2
Mozambique	1979	15,483	8.1
Vietnam	1980	60,067	31.4
Angola	1984	1,358	0.7
China*	1986	n/a	
USSR	n/a	14,885	7.8
Bulgaria		4,939	2.6
CSSR		3,218	1.7
Romania		1,162	0.6
Yugoslavia		2,055	1.1
EC countries		1,406	0.7
Austria		988	0.5
USA		108	0.1
Total		178,835**	100.0

Notes:
* These governments ordered their contract workers to return home as soon as the state socialism in the GDR began to crumble.
** The overall total is somewhat lower than the figure of 190,000 cited in other sources since some contract workers had already left before December 1989.

Source: Statistisches Jahrbuch der Bundesrepublik Deutschland 1992.

AUSLÄNDERPOLITIK DURING THE *WENDE*

In the regions which were to become the new Länder, the end of state socialism wrought devastation for foreigners, who found themselves in a social and legal no-man's land. In anticipation of market principles, eastern German firms no longer felt bound to keep their foreign workforce. Nothing was done to stop dismissals. In addition, socialist enterprises increased their charges for hostel accommodation from 30 to around 270 *Ostmark* per month in early spring 1990 and imposed a three-week deadline before evicting occupants. Other firms closed their hostels to cut costs.[14] Suddenly homeless and unemployed, former contract workers in the GDR fell through the post-socialist net. Without access to housing, without benefit entitlement and without networks of support in their German host society, they were forced to squat in derelict houses, sleep rough or return home.[15] Within months, two out of three foreign workers had been dismissed. At the end of 1991, the number of foreign workers on fixed contracts had plummeted to 6,670 compared to around 100,000 in December 1989.[16]

The governing coalition under Hans Modrow was preoccupied with preserving the GDR against the tide of unification and did nothing to protect foreigners or honour the labour agreements of its predecessor. The Round Table, the multi-party forum which emerged as an eastern German voice between December 1989 and the elections in March 1990, was unexpectedly confronted with an *Ausländerproblem*: unemployed and homeless foreigners needing assistance. National and regional Round Tables established special working groups on *Ausländerfragen*. These working groups recommended the appointment of designated advisers, *Ausländerbeauftragte*, to ensure that foreigners received assistance between their dismissal and their departure. Although concerned with alleviating hardship, the Round Table continued the socialist tradition of viewing *Ausländerpolitik* as a tier of foreign policy. The declaration issued when it concluded its business said nothing about social integration or the place of non-Germans in German civil society but adopted the loftier rhetoric of the socialist past:

> The rule of law and democracy are preconditions and results of respecting human rights and the dignity of the individual. In the context of a world community of peoples and of creating a European House, the relationship of the national and international in the GDR acquires a new dimension. The national policy towards foreigners leads to an extension and revision of traditional domestic policy. GDR foreign policy should, therefore, be guided by the principles of a just and ecologically sound economic world order as well as the principle of solidarity with economically weak countries.[17]

The elections in March 1990 moved eastern Germany closer to the west. A plebiscite for unification, the elections resulted in a CDU-led coalition government, the political collapse of the citizens' movements which had dominated the Round Table and the relegation of the PDS into opposition. The new government introduced regulations which clarified the legal situation of foreign nationals in the GDR and offered a limited number of choices. Modelled on the FRG programme of financial inducements to encourage former *Gastarbeiter* to leave, the pre-unification government in the GDR offered compensation for breach of contract through dismissal. Those who agreed to return home received a DM 3,000 returnees' allowance and 70 per cent of their previous wages until the day of departure. Those who would not or could not return to their country of origin could apply for temporary residency permits up to the duration of their original contract. Former contract workers were not, however, entitled to draw unemployment benefit or attend retraining programmes. As temporary residents, they were barred from regular employment and could only apply for permits as street traders.[18]

Although these regulations spelt out the rights and obligations of foreign nationals more openly than had ever been attempted in the GDR, their ultimate purpose was negative: to rid east Germany of the remaining former contract workers and other temporary non-German residents. Both eastern German post-socialist governments, that under Modrow and that under de Maizière, perpetuated the established practice of non-acceptance and non-integration of foreigners into German society. The dismissals and expulsions during the *Wende* suggest that xenophobia informed public policy even when the SED no longer dominated and former dissidents defined the agenda. The unspoken consensus in the GDR between government and public that 'foreigners' did not belong to German civil society remained in force.

MIXED MESSAGES OF TRANSFORMATION

Taking up the Round Table recommendations, advisory centres for foreign nationals were created after the elections in March 1990 in East Berlin and several other east German cities. Originally set up to oversee their departure, the brief soon changed to alleviating hardship. Given the GDR history of separating 'foreigners' from mainstream society, these agencies broke new ground by focusing on the needs of non-Germans during their residency in Germany. They were a new departure after half a century of '*Ausländer-Raus*' *Politik* in the east.

By way of an example, I should like to look at the situation in Leipzig. The *Wende* found the city with 12,000 non-German inhabitants. As an industrial base with chemical and lignite production, Leipzig had received contract workers; as a major university town and home of the Herder Institute which specialised in language tuition for foreign students, Leipzig also had a relatively large population of foreign students, researchers and university personnel. The city was the first to appoint a Special Adviser for Foreigners in April 1990. Defined as part of the general administration, the adviser could be involved in all decisions likely to impact on the situation of foreigners in the city.[19] Since 1992, *Ausländerbeautragte* have become a compulsory facet of local government elsewhere in the new Länder but are affiliated to social services or housing and therefore more restricted in their activities.[20]

The task and the obstacles were new. On the one hand, advice was targeted at foreign nationals, who could now turn to a special agency for help. On the other hand, advice was targeted at Germans who felt they had a problem with 'foreigners' in their neighbourhood or at work.[21] Demand for advice came from both quarters. In Leipzig, at least 3,000 contract workers had been dismissed, among them 400 Vietnamese who did not wish to return home. At the insistence of the Special Adviser, the city provided a property and entered into individual rental agreements with each of the 250 occupants. Although the accommodation was so overcrowded that it became in effect a hostel, the individualised rental agreements were a first step towards securing housing and social integration. By March 1994, the number of occupants had fallen to 150, since many left Leipzig or Germany. At that time, one-third of the residents were children.

Among the local population, reactions to the new neighbours were mainly negative. The house was damaged several times, its inhabitants intimidated. The office of the Special Adviser tried to reassure both sides and dispel misunderstandings through information and public relations efforts. Most were designed to provide information about foreign nationals and their cultures to overcome hostility. Matters had just begun to calm down, families had begun to feel settled, children began to attend nurseries and schools in the area, when the city cancelled the rental agreements of all occupants just two weeks before the deadline by which former contract workers had to provide evidence of housing and employment in order to extend their stay by two years. This *Bleiberecht* – right to remain – had been agreed in May 1993 between the interior ministers of the Länder and the federal government in order to alleviate undue hardship and avoid expulsions.[22] In Leipzig, public resentment appeared to win the day. In Joseph Zettler Strasse, where the former contract workers had lived for over three years, one of the residents put it bluntly: 'I do not care one way or the other whether these Vietnamese will be allowed to stay in Germany. But they have to disappear from our road.'[23]

The city promised to find a new home 'for everyone who works honestly'.[24] In fact, most of the 1,200 former contract workers who remained in Leipzig in 1994 were either already homeless or were being made homeless by the stroke of a pen and thus deprived of the chance to benefit from the *Bleiberecht* they might otherwise have enjoyed. After unification, former contract workers were explicitly excluded from the right to apply for political asylum because they had entered Germany with the agreement of their governments and not as refugees. Since then, restrictions for Vietnamese nationals in particular have been eased, given that they would be exposed to maltreatment in their home country after their protracted and unauthorised stay in Germany. Generally speaking, the non-acceptance of former contract workers during the *Wende* and after unification perpetuated the negative treatment of foreigners in the GDR. The *Ausländerbeauftragte*, however, constituted a significant departure from the practice of administering non-German residents as pawns of foreign policy whose acceptance into German society and integration as fellow citizens (*Mitbürger*) was actively discouraged.[25]

POST-UNIFICATION DEVELOPMENTS

Unification propelled the new Länder and their inhabitants into a world where migration had become a social reality and where national or cultural homogeneity in Germany at least was a thing of the past. When eastern Germans had challenged the restrictions imposed on their mobility and fought – successfully – for the right to travel, they wanted to replicate what they perceived as a west German lifestyle. For them, migration meant moving to the west[26] and did not extend to migration of other national or ethnic groups into their country. Yet, on the eve of unification in 1990, migration into west Germany stood at 1.2 million per year and 1.1 million of these newcomers had arrived as asylum seekers, resettlers or as family members of resident non-Germans with the intention to settle (see Table 2). Two years after unification, migration into Germany peaked at 1.5 million people. From 1993 onwards, restrictive legislation has curtailed the influx but it remains above the one million mark, although the share of asylum seekers, resettlers and family member among the newcomers has fallen from nearly 90 per cent to about 60 per cent of the total.

TABLE 2

MIGRATION INTO THE FEDERAL REPUBLIC, 1987–94 (IN 1,000)

Origin/type of migration	1987	1988	1989	1990	1991	1992	1993	1994	Total
EU countries	126	142	144	141	151	144	141	163	1,152
New Labour Migr.	5	7	8	14	157	266	222	181	860
Refugees ex-Yugoslavia	–	–	–	–	50	110	110	80	350
Asylum Seekers	57	103	121	193	256	438	323	127	1,618
(German) Resettlers	79	203	377	397	222	231	219	223	1,951
Others, inc. family	325	406	484	511	347	300	253	296	2,922
Overall	*592*	*861*	*1,134*	*1,256*	*1,183*	*1,489*	*1,268*	*1,070*	*8,853*

Source: Migration und Integration in Zahlen. Ein Handbuch, ed. Die Beautragte der Bundesregierung für Ausländerfragen (Bonn, 1997), p.216.

While Germans cheered for national unity, their country was no longer only for Germans. After unification, the simplistic solutions of GDR vintage no longer worked. The new policy agenda instituted residency rights for foreigners who had lived in the country for five years or more.[27] The new agenda also demanded the receipt and accommodation of asylum seekers from developing countries and trouble spots outside the European Union as well as of eastern Europeans who sought refuge after the collapse of Communist hegemony. The agenda of reception and integration also covered resettlers who arrived from eastern Europe with claims to German citizenship but little command of the German language or German culture.[28] Unification brought with it the obligation on the new Länder to accommodate newcomers. On the insistence of west German Länder administrations and under pressure from local authorities who claimed to have exhausted their facilities,[29] the unification treaty stipulated that the new Länder should share the burden by taking in 20 per cent of all asylum seekers and resettlers, a pro-rata allocation based on population figures. In the 1990s, one in three of the newcomers from other countries fell into these categories (see Table 2), among them about 300,000 asylum seekers.[30] Actual numbers accommodated in the east remained lower, since local authorities were slow to prepare reception facilities and asylum seekers themselves expected conditions to be worse than in the west and were reluctant to go there. In 1992, just 4,000 of a possible 120,000 asylum seekers were cared for in the new Länder.[31]

The insistence of the old Länder that the new should also take their share of non-German newcomers allowed little time to renounce the *Ausländer Raus* policy of the *Wende* and phase in the west German package of limitation and integration. First allocations of asylum seekers arrived in the new Länder in December 1990. In line with west German practice, newcomers were dispersed to local communities and suitable accommodation there. Policy makers, including *Ausländerbeauftragte*, responded with a sense of panic once asylum seekers began to arrive. Hasty provisions included tents and caravan camps. Contrary to west German practice, where asylum seekers were temporarily housed in public buildings such as school gyms or village halls, they were kept separate in the east at out-of-town, specially commissioned sites or in the hostels that had been vacated by contract workers. Even after the asylum law had been changed and numbers had begun to decline, east Germans continued to commission accommodation and sign new contracts with private entrepreneurs for thousands of places in caravans or barracks on out-of-town sites. As late as October 1993, one year after the new legislation had been passed and nearly half a year after it had been implemented, contracts worth over 1.4 million Deutschmarks were signed with private contractors in Saxony alone. Designed to run for a minimum of five years, these contracts were drawn up in such a way that they could not be cancelled nor the accommodation used for other purposes. By March 1994, every third place earmarked for asylum seekers in the new Länder remained empty at a monthly cost of DM 4,900 each. Plans provided for new out-of-town sites for asylum seekers to be developed until 1996.[32] An official from the Leipzig region summed up the problem as perceived by local policy makers in the east:

For Saxony, the accommodation of asylum seekers was something completely new and unexpected. Accommodation had to be found quickly. Resistance in the population who did not want to accept refugees in their neighbourhood, had to be taken into account. We were just glad that we had found somewhere, and that we had sites for several years to come.[33]

An Emnid survey found in 1992 that most Germans, east and west, objected to hostels for asylum seekers in their neighbourhood, and one in three expressed support for NIMBY (not in my back yard)-type action to keep foreigners out of their own area.[34]

Since unification permitted non-Germans to become residents in the new Länder, their demography has taken on a slightly more diverse and multicultural hue. With the move of east Germans to the west continuing, although much reduced since 1989, even a modest influx of non-Germans leaves its mark.[35] While Saxony and Saxony-Anhalt continue to register a net loss of population as more residents are leaving than newcomers arrive to settle there,[36] Brandenburg, Mecklenburg-Vorpommern and Thuringia have registered slight population increases since 1991.[37] Here, migration losses were lower and the influx of resettlers, foreign residents and asylum seekers contributed to a positive migration balance.

Generally speaking, non-Germans remain vastly underrepresented in the east. In 1997, just 3.2 per cent of Germany's non-German residents lived in the new Länder, although the region as a whole accounted for 20 per cent of the population. Even within this narrow margin, demographic differences are striking. In 1996, Thuringia had the lowest share of non-Germans in its population (0.9 per cent) while Saxony with two per cent and Brandenburg with 2.4 per cent took the lead.[38] However, Berlin, the Land which was created by merging the eastern and western parts of the city, highlights how strong the differences remain between the two parts of the formerly divided Germany. In 1996, nearly one in five West Berliners did not have German nationality: in traditional working class districts with cheaper housing and less affluent living environments such as Kreuzberg and Wedding, more than half the inhabitants were non-Germans.[39] In East Berlin, just one in 20 residents were non-Germans, although in two districts, Mitte and Lichtenberg, non-Germans amounted to nearly 15 per cent of the inhabitants. As mentioned earlier, after unification, the number of non-Germans in East Berlin more than trebled, reaching 72,234 in 1996.[40] The increase was particularly marked for (non-German) European Union nationals. The earliest data available on the nationality of non-German residents record the situation as of 31 December 1991. Then, 1,037 (non-German) European Union nationals lived in East Berlin; six years on, their number had risen to 11,672.[41] In the same period, the number of East Berliners with non-European nationalities more than doubled from 21,000 to over 55,000. Of the non-German population of East Berlin today, two out of three are non-Europeans. While Turks form the largest single national group in West Berlin, African and Asian nationalities dominate in the east. This demographic difference applies to the new Länder generally, where Turkish and other traditional *Gastarbeiter* nationalities which have been at the forefront of cultural diversification in west Germany hardly figure. The strong representation of African and Asian nationals may reflect the national origin of former GDR contract workers who managed to stay in Germany. More important, however, has been the uneven flow of migration into the old and the new Länder. While the old Länder today continue to receive family members from the original *Gastarbeiter* recruitment countries in addition to asylum seekers of other national backgrounds, non-German migration into the new Länder has resulted almost exclusively from asylum seekers and reflects their origins.

The social integration of non-German residents into civil society is greatly hampered by uncertainties of status and patterns of exclusion. One such uncertainty concerns residency rights. While most of the former *Gastarbeiter* have lived in Germany for ten years or more and now enjoy unrestricted residency rights, many asylum seekers and more recent newcomers do not. In 1996, some 25 per cent of non-Germans had been in the country for four years or less; even if their application for political asylum had been successful, their residency rights would still only be temporary.[42] Since virtually all non-Germans in the new Länder are post-unification arrivals, they are affected by the uncertainties of a temporary residency status. This status in turn excludes non-Germans from employment and unemployment benefit. Instead, temporary residents are dependent on state handouts which, since 1993, have increasingly been paid in kind rather than money.

Normalisation of status and life chances, one of the preconditions of social citizenship and equal opportunities of participation in civil society, remain elusive for non-Germans in the new Länder. Data published for Berlin show that in April 1996 close to 36 per cent of non-German East Berliners were in employment while 34 per cent depended on welfare payment or other state benefits. By contrast, just 16 per cent of non-German residents in West Berlin were welfare or state benefit recipients, while about ten per cent received unemployment benefit. In the east, 40 per cent earned less than half the average income at the time and thus lived below the poverty line, an additional 18 per cent had no income of their own and depended on family members for support.[43]

Since unification and the modest influx of non-Germans into the new

Länder, some traces of normalisation are discernible. School attendance is a
good example of normalisation. Labour recruitment populations tend to be
predominantly male and resident without their families. Settled populations
are more balanced in their gender structure and more likely to live in
families which include children. In the new Länder, the gender structure
remains unbalanced, with 70 per cent male and 30 per cent female residents.
Yet, the number of children born to non-Germans increased by 70 per cent
since unification.[44] Although it remains low, constituting less than two per
cent of the children born in the new Länder, its upward movement points to
a normalisation of lifestyles among non-Germans. School rolls tell a similar
story. In 1992, just 9,000 non-German children attended schools in the new
Länder compared with 788,000 in the old.[45] Again, the data for Berlin allow
a more detailed comparison.[46] In 1991, 0.75 per cent of pupils in East Berlin
were non-German nationals; by 1994, their share had risen to 2.6 per cent,
in 1996 to 2.9 per cent. In the same year, five per cent of the pupils starting
school for the first time in East Berlin did not have German nationality.
Bearing in mind that in West Berlin one in three six year olds and just over
22 per cent of all pupils are of non-German background, the hiatus between
west and east is undeniable. From a very low base, however, East Berlin and
– at an even slower pace – the new Länder generally have begun to offer
non-Germans 'normal' chances of social participation and are developing
traces of multiculturalism in civil society.

PRIVATE AGENDAS OF EXCLUSION

The unification treaty could require the new Länder to receive asylum
seekers, accommodate them and process their applications but could not
recast private agendas. These had been shaped in the GDR as active
endorsement of state policy or as acquiescence and a quiet retreat to a niche
society. Both converged in rejecting diversity, individualism and the
distinctive cultures of religious or ethnic minorities. GDR social policy had
the effect of eliminating difference from everyday life. Standardised
housing, low wages, a narrow range of standard issue goods and services
and other measures of prescribed equality aimed at producing a uniformity
of lifestyle as evidence of belonging and citizenship. In this 'monoculture
of ordinary people' there was no room for diversity of origin, religious
observance or cultural preferences and 'people were united by a dislike and
intolerance of everything and everybody that did not fit in'.[47]

The distrust of diversity targeted newcomers from outside Germany who
arrived in the new Länder after unification. In 1991, for example, ten per
cent of young east Germans disliked Turks, although at the time there were
virtually no Turks in east Germany. A sizeable minority (nine per cent) even

regarded west Europeans and Americans as inferior to Germans.[48] The undercurrent of distrust makes east Germans unwilling to support the arrival and settlement of non-Germans in their society. In 1994, 20 per cent rejected the presence of all 'foreigners', an additional 60 per cent doubted that integration could ever work, while just 20 per cent remained neutral or more accepting. While east Germans are more likely than west Germans to concur with immigration as a general principle, they tend to react more negatively to suggestions that non-Germans should live and work with or near them.[49] Nine out of ten doubt that asylum seekers have genuine reasons for remaining in Germany while nearly as many regard the government's legislation on asylum seekers as too lenient.[50] An east German member of the Bundestag voiced the misgivings of his compatriots: 'We really want to continue to offer asylum to people who suffer political persecution. But we could no longer tolerate that more than 90 per cent of asylum seekers had not suffered any political persecution and were misusing the right of asylum.'[51]

The unification of Germany did not install the democratic political culture in the east as it had developed in the west in the course of the post-war era. When east Germans opted for unification in the demonstrations of 1989 and the elections of March 1990, they opted for equal lifestyles with the west and took little interest in the structures and processes that underpin democracy. The social and economic realities that followed unification made large numbers of east Germans feel cheated in their expectations and helpless in the face of unfamiliar uncertainties such as unemployment and a competitive, market-based culture. These experiences gave the 1990 promises of how unification would transform the east the bitter aftertaste of deceit, with politicians, political parties and the democratic process generally thought to collude in condemning as negative everything that had existed in the GDR. As east Germans learned to express their opinions in public, many differed sharply from those prevalent in the west. Two years after unification, a survey into the east–west divide revealed that east Germans preferred a strong and active state: 89 per cent demanded more police to ensure public order and 84 per cent favoured protective custody for suspected trouble makers.[52] In west Germany, only supporters of the right-extremist Republican Party shared these views. Over 40 per cent of east Germans had no confidence that Germany's main political parties were competent to solve the problems of the day,[53] least of all curtail the influx of asylum seekers. Sixty-one per cent of east Germans expected violent clashes with asylum seekers in their neighbourhood.[54] In the GDR, they had taken politics to the street to force their views on the government; in post-communist Germany, confidence in the government seemed equally fragile and politics of the street an acceptable option.

This time, however, the presumed culprit was less remote than the GDR government had been, and direct action against 'foreigners' and asylum seekers seemed not only possible but called for. Although, as we had seen earlier, the actual number of non-Germans in the new Länder was small, they were vilified as unwelcome competitors for scarce employment and public funding and held responsible for a rise in crime and drug use since unification.[55] Assumptions about a link between non-Germans and criminality are even detectable in official publications. Thus, a graph presented by the city of Leipzig to celebrate a fall in the number of crimes and an increase from 22 per cent in 1994 to over 40 per cent in 1997 in the detection rate, shows a business-suited blond man with hat, suitcase and newspaper under his arm with a dark-haired and bearded pickpocket of clearly foreign appearance sneaking up from behind.[56]

The hidden assumption that 'foreigners' engage in crime is widespread in a political culture where confidence in democratic governance is low while non-acceptance of non-Germans remains virulent. This blend of xenophobia and a distrust in the ability of democratic authorities to make everyday life as secure and predictable as east Germans would like it to be, has turned law and order into a priority issue alongside unemployment[57] and made the use of violence against non-Germans acceptable. Although most east Germans have not themselves engaged in xenophobic violence, they condoned or even applauded it. In August 1991, at least 100 young east German neo-Nazis attacked a hostel for asylum seekers in Hoyerswerda, a small town in Saxony which had grown from 7,000 to 70,000 inhabitants in the 1950s but saw its steel industry grind to a halt after unification. The attack on the hostel lasted for three days while the local police stood by and the burghers watched from their windows.[58] Many held that the neo-Nazis dared to carry out what they all wished for and cheered when the police moved in to take the asylum seekers away. An observer from the old Länder spoke to the residents and caught their mood:

> Always the same points get mentioned, the same litany, monotonous and as if learnt by heart: the foreigners take our work. The foreigners live off our taxes. The foreigners are loud. The foreigners are dirty. The foreigners breastfeed their children in the street ... And then follows the ultimate trump card – and how often did I have to hear this here in Hoyerswerda!: 'You have no idea what it was like here with these foreigners! They even slaughtered a sheep in the meadow!' Regularly a triumphant look follows these remarks.[59]

In September 1992, a near-replica of Hoyerswerda took place in Rostock as several hundred young people attacked a hostel for asylum seekers for five days and set fire to it. As in Hoyerswerda, police stood by without interfering while the residents of nearby houses watched the spectacle and applauded the attackers. Again, the siege ended with the removal of the asylum seekers from the area. While the bystanders of Hoyerswerda and Rostock sided with the assailants, public policy could not subscribe to the private agenda of exclusion. The town of Hoyerswerda hosted a symposium on xenophobia in an attempt to distance itself from past events and promote tolerance. The city of Rostock rebuilt the former hostel and transformed it into a meeting place for Germans and non-Germans. A local official concluded: 'Thanks to the support provided by the city, the victims of the altercation have gained new self-confidence.'[60] In both cases, however, the xenophobic attacks achieved their short-term aim of closing the hostels and removing their occupants from German neighbourhoods.

Street gangs of neo-Nazi and skinhead youths, who advocate and practise violence against anything or anybody of foreign appearance, originated in the GDR as 'the alienation of a large section of east German youth from their state did not result in democratic awareness but in increased xenophobic and fundamentally violent orientations'.[61] Although unification removed the state against which this protest culture was pitched, it retained its anti-democratic stance and even gained momentum. The tacit complicity shown by ordinary citizens who would not themselves engage in physical assault is not confined to specific localities or age cohorts. In 1992, the Institute for Youth Research in Leipzig invited pupils between 14 and 15 years of age to put down their thoughts on the issue. It found little evidence of accepting non-Germans – Ausländer – as regular members of civil society.[62] Virtually all essays opened with the phrase 'I am of two minds about foreigners' and proceeded to enumerate reservations. Ten per cent of the young respondents found nothing wrong in using violence against foreigners, while 40 per cent believed that despite their reservations, integration should be attempted:

> I believe, first of all, that foreigners are human beings just like we are. It is not their fault that they are black or whatever. I personally have not yet met any foreigners. But I think everyone should at some point get to know foreigners in order to understand their problems and their culture and only then can he form a proper opinion.

Fifty per cent felt economically and socially threatened by 'foreigners' at a time of dislocation and transformation: 'In the new Länder in particular there are so many problems with the economy, we do not need additional problems here. My mother may lose her job. Just image if a foreigner should get this job!' This group articulated the sentiments that seemed to have been acted out in Hoyerswerda and Rostock. A hard core of ten per cent expressed their hostility more plainly: 'I can fully understand the attacks on the hostel, because a lot of anger has accumulated among the Nazis, skins and other people. When one sees that every third person you meet in the street is a foreigner, one really feels absolutely sick.' 'For the future, I wish for a country without foreigners.'[63]

MULTICULTURALISM IN THE MAKING?

Asylum seekers had barely set foot in the new Länder when violent attacks against them became a regular aspect of street life and people whose appearance seemed to mark them out could no longer feel safe. In Leipzig, for instance, the first six asylum seekers arrived in the city in December 1990 and were accommodated in a hostel for former contract workers. The Special Adviser had no knowledge of their arrival and was not consulted to assist with arrangements. During their first night in Leipzig, the hostel was attacked, most ground floor windows broken and doors damaged. Subsequently, the city installed a high wire fence and other security equipment to keep likely attackers at a distance and also to reassure residents that the 'foreigners' would not be a danger to them.[64]

In the old Länder, the number of violent offences with racist and xenophobic motives had already increased since the early 1980s, when neo-Nazi groups gave organised right-extremism a more aggressive and activist edge.[65] In the new Länder, the neo-Nazi youth culture had commenced as protest against the prescribed anti-fascism in the GDR. The multiple dislocations and uncertainties in the wake of unification boosted a sense of disaffection, in particular among blue-collar workers and young people at the lower end of the qualification hierarchy who saw their chances reduced of sharing in the new mobility of wages and opportunities. The most fertile ground for neo-Nazi views and actions have been the lower school types in the new Länder which were introduced after the abolition of the integrated Polytechnic High Schools of the GDR, and whose pupils have been selected from the lower ability range. In this environment, xenophobia is but a facet of youth culture.[66] Formal organisations and neo-Nazi groups which employ xenophobic violence in the old Länder have not played a significant part in the new.

These cultural and organisational differences make it more difficult to assess the scale of violence against non-Germans since official statistics only record an offence as xenophobic if the offender belongs to a neo-Nazi organisation or can be identified as a neo-Nazi.[67] Thus, many offences with a xenophobic motive disappear in the general crime statistics. Moreover, an attack involving several perpetrators is only mentioned once in the statistical accounts and many crimes go unreported altogether as victims are reluctant to notify the police. For a variety of reasons, therefore, the number

TABLE 3

RIGHT-EXTREMIST OFFENCES AND VIOLENCE AGAINST FOREIGNERS, 1989–96

Year	Total	Annual rate of change (%)	No. xenophobic assaults abs.	Xenophobic assaults (%)	Rate of change (%)
1989	255	+ 32.1	146	57	+ 42
1990	309	+ 21.2	152	49	+ 4
1991	1,492	+ 382.8	1,255	84	+ 726
1992	2,639	+ 76.9	2,277	86	+ 84
1993	2,232	– 15.4	1,067	72	– 29
1994	1,489	– 33.3	860	58	– 47
1995	837	– 43.8	540	66	– 37
1996	781	– 6.7	441	57	– 49

Source: Migration und Integration in Zahlen. Ein Handbuch (Berlin, 1997), p.167.

of offences committed against non-Germans can be assumed to be higher than indicated in published statistical accounts.

Despite their shortcomings, these accounts present a bleak picture (see Table 3). In 1991, the first year when the presence of asylum seekers could have an impact in the new Länder, 1,255 offences against non-Germans were recorded; one year later, their number had reached over 2,000, although Die Zeit arrived at a figure of over 6,000 xenophobic offences in addition to several hundred cases of arson.[68] Within right-extremist offences generally, those motivated by xenophobia shot up 700-fold after unification, constituting 84 per cent of all offences. Three out of four were committed in the new Länder, where assault, verbal abuse and physical violence directed against foreigners or individuals whose appearance suggested they might be foreigners became a daily occurrence. In 1991, seven in ten non-Germans living in the new Länder had already been subjected to abuse by Germans, four in ten were discriminated against or treated unfairly when shopping and one in five had endured physical assault.[69] In 1991, east Germans took the lead in xenophobic violence: as west Germans followed, the number of xenophobic offences doubled and the east–west imbalance shifted a little towards the west. Of the 17 deaths as a consequence of xenophobic violence, most occurred in west Germany, where the victims included settled non-Germans and former Gastarbeiter as well as asylum seekers. The detection rate of right-extremist crimes has always been low in the Federal Republic. In 1992, only 276 arrests were made, half of them in Saxony where a special unit had been created to combat extremism and arrest the perpetrators of violence.[70] In most Länder – new and old – between 70 and 90 per cent of all xenophobic offences which were reported remained unresolved.

TABLE 4

RIGHT-EXTREMIST AND XENOPHOBIC OFFENCES IN DETAIL, 1996–97

Type of offence	Right-extremist offences 1996	Directed at foreigners 1996	Right-extremist offences 1997	Directed at foreigners 1997
Murder	1	0	0	0
Attempted murder	12	11	13	8
Assault, bodily harm	507	307	677	406
Arson	33	27	37	25
Explosion	0	0	2	1
Breach of peace	71	27	61	22
Total	624	372	790	462

Source: *Verfassungschutzbericht 1997* (unpublished Report, Bundesamt für Verfassungsschutz, Cologne, 1998).

Since 1993, the number of offences officially associated with xenophobic motives has been significantly lower than the surge that followed unification, although the mid-1990s again saw an increase (see Table 3). About half the offences are committed in east Germany.[71] In line with earlier patterns of xenophobic violence, nearly nine out ten officially recorded offences were physical attacks on individuals (see Table 4). Close to a decade after unification and the arrival of non-German newcomers and residents, the number of xenophobic offences per inhabitant remains higher in the new Länder than anywhere else in the Federal Republic (see Table 5).

Between 1996 and 1997 it had risen in all east German regions except Thuringia. Although the number of xenophobic offences per inhabitant was lower in the old Länder than in the new, Hesse, the Saarland, Bavaria and Baden-Württemberg saw a steep increase. The continued and growing problem of xenophobic violence documented in Table 5 shows that none of the regions of Germany is free enough from such violence to provide a secure living environment for non-German residents, asylum seekers and other newcomers from different countries and cultures. Given that the east German regions, as shown earlier, accommodate fewer than four per cent of Germany's non-German residents, these residents face a particularly high risk of violence amounting to an extreme and visible form of non-acceptance. In the civil society of the new Länder, multiculturalism as tolerance of difference and right to social participation has yet to take root.

TABLE 5
RIGHT-EXTREMIST OFFENCES IN GERMANY BY LÄNDER AND POPULATION,
1996–97

Land	1996*	1997*	Change 1996–97 (%)
Brandenburg	2.81	3.79	+ 34
Mecklenburg-Vorpommern	2.20	3.74	+70
Saxony-Anhalt	1.55	2.43	+57
Berlin	1.07	1.91	+78
Saxony	1.67	1.90	+14
Thuringia	2.13	1.69	-21
Hamburg	1.76	1.05	-40
Schleswig-Holstein	2.07	0.87	-58
Lower Saxony	0.73	0.75	+3
Bremen	0.74	0.74	+/-0
North Rhine-Westphalia	0.55	0.66	+20
Baden-Württemberg	0.37	0.59	+59
Saarland	0.18	0.46	+155
Rheinland-Palatinate	0.27	0.45	+67
Bavaria	0.16	0.32	+100
Hesse	0.10	0.28	+180

Notes: * number of offences per 100,000 inhabitants. The *Verfassungsschutzbericht* does not report xenophobic offences by region but provides evidence that about 60 per cent of all right-extremist offences in 1996 and 1997 were directed against foreigners (ibid., p.74). Xenophobia is the single most important motive for right-extremist offences recorded in the report.

Source: Calculated from *Verfassungsschutzbericht 1997* (unpublished Report, Cologne 1998), p.77.

NOTES

1. An excellent account of migration and immigration in Germany (past and present) in D. Cohn Bendit and T. Schmid, *Heimat Babylon. Das Wagnis der multikulturellen Demokratie* (Hamburg: Hoffmann & Campe, 1992), esp. chs. 4 and 5. See also D. Horrocks and E. Kolinsky (eds.), *Turkish Culture in Germany Society Today* (Oxford and Providence, RI: Berghahn, 1996).
2. M. Schmidt, 'In der Fremde geduldet – zu Hause gefährdet', *Das Parlament*, Nos.2–3, 8/15 Jan. 1993, p.9.
3. H. Hermann, 'Ursachen und Entwicklung der Ausländerbeschäftigung', *Informationen zur Politischen Bildung no. 237: Ausländer* (Bonn: Bundeszentrale für politische Bildung, 1992), p.6.
4. For a detailed analysis see E. Kolinsky, 'Foreigners in the New Germany', *Keele German Research Papers*, No.1 (1995).
5. See N. Trong Cu, 'Situation der VietnamesInnen in der ehemaligen DDR – Erfahrungen und Überlegungen zur Ausländerproblematik', in *Ausländer im Vereinten Deutschland. Gesprächskreis Arbeit und Soziales Nr. 1* (Bonn: Friedrich Ebert Foundation, 1991), pp.86–7.
6. From *Germany. Geographical Handbook* Series vol.III *Economic Geography* (London: Naval Intelligence Division, 1944), p.106. Taking the regions which later become east Germany, Thuringia (0.5%) and Saxony (0.6%) had the lowest foreign population, Mecklenburg (2.5%) the highest, that is, agricultural labour. Overall, there were 186,000

non-Germans in the eastern regions in 1939.

7. Quoted by A. Berger, *Ausländerbeautragte* for the new Länder, from a letter in *Neues Deutschland* (Jan. 1990) and an interview with a local mayor, in 'Wir sind ein Volk?', in H. Boehncke and H. Wittich (eds.), *Buntes Deutschland. Ansichten zu einer multikulturellen Gesellschaft* (Reinbek: Rowohlt, 1991), p.128.

8. The ommission of data on foreigners is notable for instance in G. Winkler, *Sozialreport* (Berlin: Die Wirtschaft, 1990), and in E. Holder, *Im Trabi durch die Zeit. 40 Jahre Leben in der DDR* (Stuttgart: Metzler Poeschel, 1992).

9. I. Runge, 'Die Situation der Ausländer in der ehemaligen DDR', in M. Struck (ed.), *Ausländerrecht und Ausländerpolitik. Entwicklungen, Trends, Neuerungen* (Bonn: Friedrich Ebert Stiftung, 1990), p.54.

10. Data on the mass exodus in *Der Fischer Weltalmanach Sonderband DDR* (Frankfurt/Main: Fischer, 1990), p.135, and T. Garton Ash, *In Europe's Name. Germany and the Divided Continent* (London: Cape, 1993), p.659.

11. *Migration und Integration in Zahlen. Ein Handbuch* (Mitteilungen der Beauftragten der Bundesregierung für Ausländerfragen, Bonn, 1997), pp.91, 103.

12. That is, increased from around 10,000 to 18,600. Stadt Leipzig Amt für Wahlen und Statistik, *Statistischer Quartalsbericht* 1/1998, p.39.

13. 21,300 in 1990. *Statistisches Jahrbuch, Land Berlin*, 1991 (Berlin: Kulturbuch Verlag, 1991), p.53, and *Statistisches Jahrbuch, Land Berlin* 1997, pp.48 and 56.

14. East German firms moved as swiftly to close down child-care facilities. But here, local Round Tables stepped in to ensure that local authorities provided the care which firms had discontinued. In some cases, firm were persuaded to keep their child-care facilities open.

15. S. Gugutschkow, 'Situation der Ausländer in Leipzig: Jahrhundertelange Tradition der Weltoffenheit auch künftig pflegen', *Das Parlament*, Nos.2–3, 8/15 Jan. 1993, p.9.

16. Data from Bundesministerium für Arbeit und Sozialordnung, quoted in G. Gugel, *Ausländer, Aussiedler, Übersiedler* (Tübingen: Verein für Friedenspädagogik, 4th edn 1992), p.65.

17. Quoted from A. Berger, 'Wir sind ein Volk? Deutsche und Nichtdeutsche in den neuen Bundesländern', in Boenecke and Wittich, *Buntes Deutschland*, p.132.

18. Details in Kolinsky, 'Foreigners in the New Germany', pp.4 ff.

19. The only other city where the *Ausländerbeautrager* belongs to the general administration is Frankfurt. Here, Daniel Cohn Bendit created an the *Amt für Multikulturelle Angelegenheiten*, AMKA with similarly far-reaching influence across the whole spectrum of local politics.

20. Interview with Frau Ulrike Bran, an adviser in the Referat des Ausländerbeautragten, Stadt Leipzig, 2 March 1994.

21. S. Gugutschkow, 'Das Zusammenleben von Deutschen und Ausländern gestalten. Das Beispiel Leipzig', in *Ausländer im vereinten Deutschland* (Bonn: Friedrich Ebert Stiftung, 1991), pp.75–84. In Berlin, Anetta Kahane took on a similar role until unification merged the two parts of the city and also merged her office with that of her long-established western colleague, Barbara John.

22. Interview with Frau Heßke, Deputy Director of the Referat d. Ausländerbeauftragten der Stadt Leipzig, 28 Feb. 1994. See also *Leipziger Volkszeitung* 18 May 1993. In May 1993, a *Bleiberecht* was agreed between ministers of the interior of the new Länder and the federal government for all contract workers who had been resident in Germany before 13 June 1990.

23. *Leipziger Volkszeitung,* 18 May 1993.

24. Ibid., 21 Feb. 1994.

25. This is the term now used by the *Ausländerbeauftrager* in Leizpig for foreigners in the city.

26. By the end of 1989, nearly 4.4 million east Germans had left for the west. In the years 1990 to 1992, a further 800,000 east Germans went west. In Germany as a whole, the population grew by 0.9% to over 80 million; in the new Länder, it continued to fall and reached an all-time low point of 15 million inhabitants. See W. Hammes and H. Fleischer, 'Bevölkerungsentwicklung 1992', *Wirtschaft und Statistik*, 12 (1993), pp.895–6.

27. After five years foreigners may apply for permission to stay (*Aufenthaltsgenehmigung*); after eight years they may acquire an entitlement to stay (*Aufenthaltsberechtigung*).

28. Although Germans by passport, resettlers have not been accepted as compatriots in the east, are commonly referred to as 'Russians' and treated with hostility.

29. The mayor of Stuttgart and chairman of the German *Städtetag* claimed in 1990 that cities had to find accommodation for 1.5 million new citizens from the former GDR and from eastern Europe in addition to asylum seekers, and 'facilities to house these people are virtually exhausted'. In a similar vein, the mayor of Dortmund warned that allocating public buildings like sports centres, community centres or school halls as temporary shelter for newcomers could inflict lasting damage on the life of communities and create potentially explosive social resentments. See *Frankfurter Rundschau*, 1 Feb. 1990.

30. *Migration und Integration in Zahlen*, p.217.

31. *Das Parlament*, 43 Nos.2–3, 8/15 Jan. 1993, p.9.

32. *Leipziger Morgenpost*, 12/13 Feb. 1994. The paper quotes an official from the Ministry of the Interior in Saxony who projects the sense of urgency and even panic which seems to have dominated policy: 'We were already relieved that we did not have to put up tents to house them [the asylum seekers].' In Leipzig, one site for asylum seekers consisted of tents, another of some 400 caravans.

33. Quoted from *Leipziger Volkszeitung*, 27 Jan. 1994.

34. 'Umfrage zur Einstellung der Bundesbürger zu aktuellen Fragen der inneren Sicherheit' (Emnid), *Innere Sicherheit*, No.3, 7 June 1993, p.5.

35. For details of population movement see note 26.

36. The Land Saxony, for instance, registered 18,400 arrivals and nearly 41,000 departures of foreigners in 1990, a reduction of more than 22,000. In 1991, the number of foreigners decreased further by 2,600 with 9,800 new arrivals and 13,500 departures. See Freistaat Sachsen, *Statistisches Jahrbuch* 1992, p.59.

37. 'Bevölkerungsentwicklung 1992', *Wirtschaft und Statistik*, 12 (1993), p.894; also table, p.772.

38. 'Foreign Residents' Total Rises to 6,878,000', Press Release. Embassy of the Federal Republic of Germany, London, 19 May 1994. Also *Migration und Integration in Zahlen*, p.98.

39. *Statistisches Jahrbuch 1997*, p.54.

40. Data for 1990: *Statistisches Jahrbuch 1991*, p.53; for 1996: *Statistisches Jahrbuch 1997*, p.54.

41. *Statistisches Jahrbuch 1992*, p.55; *Statistisches Jahrbuch 1997*, p.53.

42. *Migration und Integration*, pp.85 and 91.

43. *Statistisches Jahrbuch 1997*, p.58.

44. See *Wirtschaft und Statistik*, 12 (1993), p.894 (Table 1).

45. 'Junge Ausländer an deutschen Schulen', *Arbeitsmappe Sozial- und Wirtschaftskunde* 512/190, May 1993 (Berlin: Schmidt Verlag, 1993).

46. The following is based on *Statistisches Jahrbuch*, 1992, p.148; *Statistisches Jahrbuch 1995*, p.154 and *Statistisches Jahrbuch 1997*, pp.123–4.

47. *Ideen und Handlungshilfen gegen Fremdenfeindlichkeit vor allem in den fünf neuen Bundesländern*, ed. Arbeitsstab der Beauftragten der Bundesregierung für die Integration der ausländischen Arbeitnehmer und ihrer Familienangehörigen (Bonn, July 1991), p.8.

48. G. Lederer *et al.*, 'Autoritarismus unter Jugendlichen der ehemaligen DDR', *Deutschland Archiv* 6 (1991), p.593.

49. W. Bergmann, 'Anti-Semitism and Xenophobia in the East German Länder', *German Politics*, Vol.3, No.2 (1994), pp.265–76.

50. Gugutschkow, 'Das Zusammenleben von Deutschen und Ausländern gestalten', p.78.

51. Taken from a comment by the MdB Manfred Kolbe, CDU on the changes in the asylum law and quoted in *Leipziger Volkszeitung*, 25 Jan. 1994.

52. 'Umfrage zur Einstellung der Bundesbürger zu aktuellen Fragen der inneren Sicherheit', *Innere Sicherheit*, No.3, 7 June 1993, pp.4–5.

53. W. Roth, 'Volksparteien in Crisis? The Electoral Successes of the Extreme Right in Context', *German Politics*, Vol.2, No.1 (1993).

54. *Innere Sicherheit*, No.3, 7 June 1993, p.4.

55. For an excellent discussion of xenobophia and its constituent views, see J. Bendix, 'Die Einstellungen zu Ausländern unter Rechtsgruppierungen in Europa', *Jahrbuch Deutsch als Fremdsprache* 19 (1993), pp.1–27.

56. Stadt Leipzig, Amt für Wahlen und Statistik, *Statistischer Quartalsbericht*, 4 (1997), p.23.
57. See the monthly listing of priority issues in *Politbarometer*; until 1995, listings were separate for the new and the old Länder and showed a higher concern about 'law and order' in the former. In June 1998, Unemployment, Asylum Seekers/Foreigners and Law and Order occupied the three top positions on the list of priority issues (*Politbarometer* 6, 1998 p.2).
58. A detailed analysis of xenophobic incidents in H. Willems, *Fremdenfeindliche Gewalt. Einstellungen, Täter, Konflikteskalation* (Opladen: Leske & Budrich, 1993), pp.97–210 and 223–31; also H.-G. Golz, 'Jugend und Gewalt in Ostdeutschland', *Deutschland Archiv* 5 (May 1993), pp.584–96.
59. R. Joedecke, 'Willkommen in Hoyerswerde', *Kursbuch* (March 1992), p.80.
60. Comment by a Rostock city official quoted in *Leipziger Volkszeitung*, 12/13 Feb. 1994.
61. W. Süß, 'Zur Wahrnehmung und Interpretation des Rechtsextremismus in der DDR durch das MfS', *Deutschland Archiv*, 4 (April 1993), p.389.
62. The invitation generated a sample of 100 essays. See W. Schubarth and D. Stenke, '"Ausländer"-Bilder bei ostdeutschen Schülerinnen und Schülern', *Deutschland Archiv*, 11 (Nov. 1992), pp.1247–54.
63. All quotes from Schubarth and Stenke, pp.1250–52.
64. Interview with Frau Heßke, Office of the Special Adviser in Leipzig, 28 Feb. 1994.
65. E. Kolinsky, 'A Future for Right Extremism in Germany?', in P. Hainsworth (ed.), *The Extreme Right in Europe and the USA* (London: Pinter, 1992). For an analysis of right-extremist offences, see E. Kolinsky, 'Terrorism in West Germany', in J. Lodge (ed.), *The Threat of Terrorism* (Brighton: Harvester, 1988).
66. Interview with Frau Heidi Wilsdorf, a grammar school teacher at the Thomas Gymnasium in Leipzig, 21 April 1993.
67. *Migration und Integration*, p.166.
68. *Die Zeit*, 26 Jan. 1996, p.1 reported the following data:

Year	Arson attacks	Other xenophobic offences
1992	596	6,336
1993	284	6,721

69. *Ideen und Handlungshilfen gegen Fremdenfeindlichkeit*, p.12.
70. *Die Zeit*, 2 July 1993.
71. The Verfassungschutzbericht for 1997 shows that the highest number of right-extremist offences (119) were committed in North-Rhine Westfalia followed in second to fifth place by the Länder Brandenburg, Saxony, Mecklenburg-Vorpommern, Saxony-Anhalt and Berlin. In these new Länder, right-extremist offences against foreigners had increased by at least one-third since 1996. Only in Thuringia, Hamburg and Schleswig Holstein had the number of right-extremist offences declined. *Verfassungschutzbericht* 1997 (unpublished Report, Cologne: Bundesamt für Verfassungschutz, 1998). I should like to thank the Bundesamt für Verfassungschutz for providing me with a copy of the report.

Notes on Contributors

Wendy Carlin is Senior Lecturer in Economics at University College London.

Mike Dennis is Professor of Modern European History at the University of Wolverhampton.

Chris Flockton is Professor of European Economic Studies at the University of Surrey.

Anthony Glees is Reader in Government at Brunel University.

Karl Koch is Professor of Modern Languages at South Bank University.

Eva Kolinsky is Professor of Modern German Studies at Keele University.

Rosalind Pritchard is Reader in Education at the University of Ulster, Coleraine.

Hans Oswald is Professor of Educational Sociology at the University of Potsdam.

Christine Schmid is a researcher at University of Potsdam.

Index

Books of Related Interest

The Kohl Chancellorship

Clay Clemens, *College of William and Mary, USA* and
William E Paterson, *University of Birmingham (Eds)*

More durable than any other contemporary democratic head of government
and all previous German chancellors since Bismarck, Helmut Kohl has
earned a place in history by helping to end his own nation's division and
shape new Europe. In this volume, six scholars and journalists assess his
leadership and legacy. They analyze the chancellor's goals and governing
style, including his part in promoting European integration, as well as
Kohl's domestic political role – *vis-à-vis* his own party, its main opponents
and the public – among fellow European leaders. Written on the eve of
Germany's 1998 elections, this volume provides insight into the country's
recent past and near future.

Contents: Introduction: Assessing the Kohl Legacy *Clay Clemens*. Helmut
Kohl, The 'Vision Thing' and Escaping the Semi-Sovereignty Trap *William
E Paterson*. Chancellor Kohl as Strategic Leader: The Case of Economic
and Monetary Union *Kenneth Dyson*. The Art of Power: The 'Kohl
System', Leadership and *Deutschlandpolitik Karl-Rudolf Korte*. Party
Management as a Leadership Resource: Kohl and the CDU/CSU
Clay Clemens. Political Leadership in Western Europe: Helmut Kohl in
Comparative Context *Alistair Cole*. Opposition in the Kohl Era: The SPD
and Left *Gerard Braunthal*.

176 pages   1998
0 7146 4890 6 cloth
0 7146 4441 2 paper
A special issue of the journal German Politics

FRANK CASS PUBLISHERS
Newbury House, 900 Eastern Avenue, Newbury Park, Ilford, Essex IG2 7HH
Tel: +44 (0)181 599 8866 Fax: +44 (0)181 599 0984 E-mail: info@frankcass.com
NORTH AMERICA
c/o ISBS, 5804 NE Hassalo Street, Portland, OR 97213 3644, USA
Tel: 800 944 6190 Fax: 503 280 8832 E-mail: cass@isbs.com
Website: www.frankcass.com

Superwahljahr

The German Elections in 1994

Geoffrey K Roberts, *University of Manchester (Ed)*

The elections in 1994 in Germany gave rise to the word 'Superwahljahr'
('super-election year'). In addition to the election of a new Bundestag in
October, there was a presidential election, elections to the European
Parliament and elections for seven Länder parliaments. This book provides
a set of analyses of those elections, with emphasis on the Bundestag
election. British and German contributors examine the effects of the
elections of 1994 on the party system and consider the ways in which party
organisation in the former German Democratic Republic affected electoral
behaviour there.

166 pages   1996
0 7146 4682 2 cloth
A special issue of the journal German Politics

FRANK CASS PUBLISHERS
Newbury House, 900 Eastern Avenue, Newbury Park, Ilford, Essex IG2 7HH
Tel: +44 (0)181 599 8866 Fax: +44 (0)181 599 0984 E-mail: info@frankcass.com
NORTH AMERICA
c/o ISBS, 5804 NE Hassalo Street, Portland, OR 97213 3644, USA
Tel: 800 944 6190 Fax: 503 280 8832 E-mail: cass@isbs.com
Website: www.frankcass.com